MW00423981

Get Your Hands Dirty

Get Your Hands Dirty

Essays on Christian Social Thought (and Action)

JORDAN J. BALLOR

FOREWORD BY
HUNTER BAKER

WIPF & STOCK · Eugene, Oregon

GET YOUR HANDS DIRTY
Essays on Christian Social Thought (and Action)

Wipf & Stock
An Imprint of Wipf and Stock Publishers
199 W. 8th Ave., Suite 3
Eugene, OR 97401

www.wipfandstock.com

ISBN 13: 978-1-62564-047-5

Manufactured in the U.S.A.

For Amy

Contents

Foreword

A Princeton-educated colleague returned from an event a short time before I sat down to write this foreword. He came to my office and said, "Your friend Jordan Ballor is a smart guy." Indeed, it is true. Jordan Ballor is a smart guy. He got my attention about a decade ago when he began commenting on a blog (*The Reform Club*) I was writing with some other folks who were and are professionals in the public policy space. I knew early on that he possessed creativity, analytical skill, and the ability to write clearly and accessibly. But there are more important things about Jordan than the fact that he is, as my colleague described him, "a smart guy."

In order to explain what I mean, it is helpful to reflect on a conversation that has a lot of currency in our culture today. As a professor, I am keenly interested in what young people are thinking about how to live. Accordingly, I listened to a podcast featuring three millennials discussing the quandary over whether to have children. I noted that the discussion seemed to have a cost/benefit quality to it. On the macro level, must we accept the idea of having more children in order to have economic growth? On a more personal basis, will having children commit individuals to choices and expenditures which will limit their own freedom and development?

In this book, Jordan Ballor seeks to address some of these questions that are highly relevant to everyone living today. Interestingly, Jordan answers our quandaries with an eye toward the holistic nature of the person. He encounters men and women as beings with a profoundly spiritual nature that is not divorced from their physical existence. Considering the human being in light of scripture and the teaching of various Christian thinkers, Jordan offers a strong endorsement of procreation as a natural act to follow God's creation.

There is another element here. Jordan has personally wrestled with the same questions as the millennials on the podcast. As a talented young person married to a woman with a career, he could have made choices to protect his personal autonomy and reduce his expenses. Instead, he is the father of two children and has juggled those responsibilities in combination with producing an impressive output at the Acton Institute and completing doctoral studies in historical theology. He recognizes that it is good to be fruitful. His reflections are aided by his self-disclosure on the subject of having children. We learn for example, that at the time of the births of his children, Jordan smiled so much that his "face actually hurt." As a writer and as a cultural analyst, Jordan partakes of that which he recommends. In this sense, he is a truly integrated person. His life is seamless, not compartmentalized. The reader can afford to invest trustworthiness in him as an author, secure in the knowledge that this is no hypocrite philosophizing about hard choices he is unwilling to make for himself.

In addition to the value Jordan Ballor brings to the table as a guide who can be trusted to be genuine and to essentially eat his own cooking, there is the matter of his gifts as a translator. One of the reasons so many Americans distrust the work of scholars is that the prose they produce is often turgid, convoluted, and based on some insider logic that is opaque to readers. Why would we invest so much to make their research possible when the payback seems so limited? Jordan is that special kind of academic, perhaps in part because he had to make a living prior to earning his academic credentials, who has the gift of writing clean, straightforward essays and articles. He knows how to write for an academic audience, but also how to write more broadly to educated lay people. As an added side benefit, his very natural way of communicating includes a number of references to pop culture past and present. How many readers of this book expect to learn a lesson about ethics which includes a discussion of a memorable episode of *Bonanza*? And yet, there it is driving the point home in a highly effective manner.

Finally, Jordan Ballor's work is part of the answer to a problem which has beset "the religious right" for many years now. Today's left offers an appealing package of social libertarianism combined with economic statism which promises security and equality. Conservative Christians, on the other hand, tend to be partisans of an ordered liberty that places the lion's share of responsibility for well-being on the individual, his or her family, and the local community (including the church). Given this contrast, it should not be difficult to see where the natural advantage lies.

The statist program insists that it can be achieved with no special sacrifice from anyone except top earners. The program of ordered liberty is one where each person must sacrifice in order to build better lives for themselves and their family by doing things such as staying in school, avoiding sex and child-bearing prior to marriage, avoiding dependency on drugs and alcohol, and maintaining employment. All of this means that the partisans of ordered liberty must be better than their opponents. Much better. Being better means, in part, eschewing the stance of grievance toward a culture gone wrong. *Get Your Hands Dirty* is a nice roadmap to a more positive and effective engagement with the broader society.

Someday, every knee will bow and every tongue will confess that Jesus Christ is Lord. But that will happen because all will be faced with the uncontestable majesty of love personified, not because we have mastered political techniques and have won an irreversible landslide which will allow us to impose a program. In the meantime, let us point to a more excellent way and to do so with a measure of joyfulness. Jordan Ballor points to the more excellent way in his work. And all along, the reader is able to perceive the joy which undergirds the enterprise.

Hunter Baker is the author of *The End of Secularism* and *Political Thought: A Students Guide*. He serves as the dean of instruction at Union University.

Acknowledgments

THIS BOOK IS FORMED around a collection of essays written over the last decade and published in a variety of publications. As such, it is a mosaic of sorts, disparate pieces refined and brought together into a new pattern of reflection on the significance of Christian social thought and action today. The flow of the book is, in this way, more like that of an ongoing conversation than a logical proof.

The earliest essays that comprise this book date from my first days ten years ago as an intern working in first public policy and later communications at the Acton Institute for the Study of Religion & Liberty. Over the course of this decade I have had occasion to write in numerous venues, particularly at the Acton Institute's blog, which launched in 2005 and to which I have had the honor to be a founding contributor. Many of the source essays have their origins as contributions to Acton Commentary, a weekly publication focused on the intersection of faith and the free society.

I am especially grateful to the all the staff at Acton who have contributed so much to my intellectual and spiritual development over these years. These include particularly Kevin Schmiesing, whose editorial eye saved me from many an embarrassing mistake, John Couretas, whose encouragement and guidance has helped shaped the way I think about the craft of writing, and Ray Nothstine, a colleague and friend from whom I have learned a great deal and with whom I have had the pleasure of collaborating. Dylan Pahman has been a faithful friend and co-laborer on this as well as many other writing projects. Sam Gregg and Stephen Grabill have provided timely advice, sage wisdom, and much-appreciated encouragement. Others who have generously shared their wit and inspiration include John Armstrong, Anthony Bradley, Joe Carter, Dave "Animal Husbandry" Cooper, Brett Elder, Mel Flikkema, Jim Healy, Ken

Marotte, Joan Miller, Holly Rowley, and Marc Vander Maas. Special thanks and recognition are due to the co-founders of the Acton Institute, Rev. Robert A. Sirico and Kris Mauren, who have provided such a fruitful and meaningful haven for agitators for a free and virtuous society for more than two decades.

My time at Acton has also given me the opportunity to write for a variety of publications, and I'm grateful for the opportunity both to have contributed many of these pieces originally and to repurpose them for this set of collected reflections. I acknowledge and thank especially the editors and staff of *The Banner*, *BreakPoint*, *Capital Commentary*, *The Christian Post*, *The City*, *Comment*, *The Detroit News*, *First Things*, *The Grand Rapids Press*, *Mere Comments*, *Renewing Minds*, and *Think Christian*. I have also had the benefit of conversations and dialog with a number of others, whose wisdom and generosity of spirit has benefited me greatly, including Matthew Lee Anderson, Vincent Bacote, Hunter Baker, Victor Claar, Andy Crouch, Ross Emmett, Greg Forster, Josh Herr, Will Hinton, Rob Joustra, Brad Littlejohn, Steven McMullen, David Michael Phelps, Ron Sider, Todd Steen, Joseph Sunde, Gideon Strauss, and Jason Zuidema.

None of my work would be meaningful or possible without the love and support of my family.

I desire this little book to be part of the recantation that I shall make.

Eastertide 2013

Introduction

"God's people please God even in the least and most trifling matters. For He will be working all things through you; He will milk the cow through you and perform the most servile duties through you, and all the greatest and least duties alike will be pleasing to Him."

—Martin Luther

This book arises from the conviction that the Christian faith has something important to say about what we do here during our time on earth. There has always been a certain *otherworldly* element in Christianity, and within certain limits this emphasis is praiseworthy, even essential. The fallen world is not the way it is supposed to be, and Christians look forward in hope to life eternal in the new heavens and the new earth, the like of which no eye has yet seen and no ear has yet heard (1 Cor 2:9). The great St. Augustine distinguished between the unregenerate city of man and "the heavenly city, or rather the part of it which sojourns on earth and lives by faith," which enjoys temporal peace "only because it must, until this mortal condition which necessitates it shall pass away." This age of the world is something of a long interlude in the great arc from creation to consummation. A fundamental identity of Christians in this world must be that of pilgrims, passers-by on the way to glory.

And yet a proper understanding of the implications of this eschatological reality empower and equip Christians for responsible action in this world rather than leading us away from it. If one extreme lies in Christians being too heavenly minded for any earthly good, then another extreme lies in neglecting or ignoring the spiritual significance of Christian hope rooted in eternity. The thesis that faith and works are intimately connected is not something novel or innovative. It is, rather, thoroughly biblical. But that is precisely why it is worth rehearsing, again and again. We tend to neglect those truths which do not suit us, and faithfulness to the biblical witness will simply not allow us to rest content in our error.

So first we need the right ideas. We need to experience the "renewing" of our minds so that we will no longer "conform to the pattern of this world" (Rom 12:2). But we also need the right motives, techniques, and wisdom to connect responsible Christian social thought and action. Good intentions are not enough, or as Etienne Gilson put it, "Piety is no substitute for technique."

This book is a call to get your hands dirty in this world, a calling which we are liberated to take up through the cleansing work that Jesus Christ accomplished on the cross. Our Lord warns us that the disciple is not greater than the teacher, so as Jesus got his hands dirty accomplishing his mission, how much more should we, his followers, expect to have to mix it up in the hurly burly of modern life. The biblical image of *dirt* is often used to describe human sinfulness, and it is from this dirtiness that Jesus' satisfaction washes us so that we "will be whiter than snow" (Ps 51:7). But the more basic image of dirt in the Bible comes from the material makeup of the human person created in God's image. In the opening passages of Scripture we see how God forms Adam, a name derived from the Hebrew word for *earth*, from the ground, the dirt itself. Eve, too, is borne out of the dust and dirt of the ground, as she is recognized by Adam as "bone of my bones / and flesh of my flesh" (Gen 2:23). The first job human beings are given in this world is what TV personality Mike Rowe would certainly call a "dirty job," as God "took the man and put him in the Garden of Eden to work it and take care of it" (Gen 2:15). God makes man out of dirt and then puts him in a place of responsibility over it and its fruitfulness.

This basic ambivalence toward the *earthiness* of human existence is what gives rise to the twin errors of spiritualism and materialism. Sometimes it can be difficult to see how our hard work, cursed by the consequences of the fall into sin, can be praised as worthwhile at all. It's true, as the nineteenth-century critic John Ruskin contended, that "there is rough work to be done, and rough men must do it." But where Ruskin saw such manual labor as dehumanizing, toil which "takes the life out of us," a view that also appreciates the basic goodness of work, even manual labor, serves as an important corrective. Ruskin is right to note that our work changes us. He is wrong to think that rough work must do so in a destructive way.

As Lester DeKoster and Gerard Berghoef write, "While the object of work is destined to perish, the soul formed by daily decision to do work carries over into eternity." The vision of work as "a maturing of the soul, liberates the believer from undue concern over the monotony of the assembly line, the threat of technology, or the reduction of the worker to but an easily replaceable cog in the industrial machine." It's true that "one worker may replace another on the assembly line, but what each worker carries away from meeting the challenge of doing the day's shift will ever be his own." This is a perspective that rightly embraces both the spiritual and the material realities of the human person. Let this message be an inspiration to us all to approach our daily work in the knowledge of its soul-shaping power and the awesome responsibility that God has laid upon each one of us to respond faithfully to his call. Let us, in the words of Dietrich Bonhoeffer, break through the impersonal "it" of work to the divine "You," God who is worshiped in our service to our neighbors.

There's some significance in the fact that God rests on the seventh day only after he has created humankind in his image on the sixth day. This represents the kind of responsibility that God entrusts us with, to work on his behalf in this world, to be, as Luther puts it, the hands of God to our neighbors. He rests, in a sense, so that our hands can become his hands.

This is what it means to follow Jesus Christ today. This is what it means to get your hands dirty.

Get your hands dirty!

1

The Human Person, Family, and Civil Society

"When a father goes ahead and washes diapers or performs some other mean task for his child . . . God, with all his angels and creatures, is smiling—not because that father is washing diapers, but because he is doing so in Christian faith."

—Martin Luther

Running is one of the worst things ever invented. It is such a bad thing that judged on its own demerits, running must be deemed to be a powerful argument against the existence of God (after all, some philosophers claim evil things as evidence there is no God). This must be why God deigned to add grace, so that we might "run and not grow weary."

I say this as someone who, in the words of bluesman Willie Dixon, was "built for comfort" and "not for speed." The problem of running, at its core, is that it is *hard*. It tires you out. It makes your lungs ache, your body sore, and drains away at your mental resolve with every stride. I'm speaking here of running for its own sake, since running only really becomes acceptable when done for some other good purpose, like tackling a running back or making a layup on a fast break. In these cases running is a necessary evil. Some of the best sports, in fact, are those like golf that don't require any running at all.

St. Francis of Assisi famously called his body "Brother Ass," a balky, troublesome thing that represented a drag, shall we say, on his spiritual development, an impediment and a constant temptation to slothfulness. There's a certain inertia that attaches to bodily life in this world, a tendency that makes us want to rest and be comfortable. Running is decidedly *un*comfortable.

And it is the difficulty of running that is perhaps what makes it such a good image of the Christian life. Although there aren't any accounts in the Bible about Jesus running, the Scriptures are replete with the imagery of running. Foremost, perhaps, might be the line from Isaiah quoted above about the blessings promised to those who look to the Lord for deliverance: "They will soar on wings like eagles; they will run and not grow weary, they will walk and not be faint." And then there's the Apostle Paul, looking back on his life after the revelatory encounter with Jesus on the road to Damascus, concluding that he has "finished the race" (2 Tim 4:7). In both cases the trouble associated with running is foremost: the weariness, the obstacles, and in Paul's case, especially, the extent to which, in Jesus' words, "how much he must suffer for my name" (Acts 9:16).

In this way running really is a form, albeit a mundane one, of suffering. It represents a sign of the Christian call to sanctification, of putting to death the desires of the flesh. Many Christians pledge to abstain from something during the Lenten season as a way of living out in some tangible way the "dying to self" that is part and parcel of the Christian life. In this sense running can be a kind of ascetic practice, designed to discipline our bodies and our souls and orient the path of our life toward eternal rest in Christ.

There's one other biblical image of running that relates closely to this idea, and it's that of Joseph fleeing from Potiphar's wife in Genesis: "She caught him by his cloak and said, 'Come to bed with me!' But he left his cloak in her hand and ran out of the house" (Gen 39:12). The Heidelberg Catechism, a sixteenth-century, Reformed confessional standard, describes the "dying-away of the old self" as being "genuinely sorry for sin," causing us to "more and more hate and run away" from sin.

Running is a terrible thing, unless it is sin that you are running away from. Let us run away from sin, as Joseph did, pray for the grace to persevere to the end of the race, as Paul did, and take comfort in God, who through the empowering presence of the Holy Spirit, "makes both us and you stand firm in Christ" (2 Cor 1:21).

THE HUMAN PERSON

It is typical in public discourse today to resort to claims of simple "right." This "rights talk" has gotten so out of hand that Mary Ann Glendon, a law professor and former US ambassador, has described the resulting "impoverishment" of our public dialog. "Discourse about rights has become the principal language that we use in public settings to discuss weighty questions of right and wrong, but time and time again it proves inadequate, or leads to a standoff of one right against another," she writes. But the difficulty is "not, however, as some contend, with the very notion of rights, or with our strong rights tradition. It is with a new version of rights discourse that has achieved dominance over the past thirty years."[1] This new version of rights talk is characterized, in part, by "hyperindividualism," which abstracts rights as they have been traditionally conceived in the context of social realities, institutions, and responsibilities. The new rights talk is the right of autonomous "I" that cannot be gainsaid.

One of the latest examples of this is the purported "right to die," or the exercise of a personal decision to end one's life free of legal barriers or any other impediments. This "right to die" movement gained prominence with the Terri Schiavo case and the release of the Academy Award-winning movie *Million Dollar Baby* in 2004. In the context of court cases involving the perceived right to suicide or euthanasia, public opinion has displayed a growing affinity for certain aspects of Libertarian political thought, which generally espouses a radical personal autonomy. The National Platform of the Libertarian Party adopted at the May 2004 Convention in Atlanta speaks of "the right to commit suicide" as an application of "the ultimate right of an individual to his or her own life."[2]

What's most disturbing for the cause of Christ, though, is the increasingly broad acceptance of these kinds of views within Christian circles. Dr. Robert Baird, professor of philosophy and ethics at Baylor University, argued in a lecture for the right for persons to choose physician-assisted suicide. "Do not we as moral agents have the right to paint the final stroke, or write the last sentence?" he wondered.[3] Lest one thinks

1. Mary Ann Glendon, *Rights Talk: The Impoverishment of Political Discourse* (New York: Free Press, 1991), x.

2. National Platform of the Libertarian Party, adopted in convention, May 2004, Atlanta, GA, art. 1.3.D. Available at: http://www.lewrockwell.com/orig7/platform.html.

3. Jim Ray, "Prof endorses assisted death," *Lariat*, September 30, 2005. Available at: http://www.baylor.edu/lariatarchives/news.php?action=story&story=36928.

this is merely the opinion of some ivory-tower academic, the Baylor student newspaper followed up Baird's speech with an editorial in favor of the right to die, calling it a "fundamental freedom."[4] And a 2003 Pew Forum survey found that 38 percent of evangelical Protestants favored a move to "give terminally ill patients the means to end their lives," with much greater support among other religious groups (58 percent of Roman Catholics surveyed answered favorably to this question).[5]

Both scholars and laypersons need to realize that the advocacy for a "right to die" represents a significant challenge, diametrically opposed to a biblically Christian view of the human person—both in life and death. A brief theological primer on these issues seems warranted. This idea of the absolute right over one's life is incompatible with a biblical worldview. The Heidelberg Catechism, a historic document of confessional Reformed Christianity, asks and answers such a question in its most famous section, "What is your only comfort, in life and in death? That I belong—body and soul, in life and in death—not to myself but to my faithful Savior, Jesus Christ . . . ."

So Christians, at least, do not own themselves in any absolute sense. When writing about sexual immorality, Paul asks, "Do you not know that your body is a temple of the Holy Spirit, who is in you, whom you have received from God? You are not your own; you were bought at a price. Therefore honor God with your body" (1 Cor 6:19–20). This biblical concept of our bodies belonging to Christ means that the Christian's attitude toward his or her life and body is radically different than a Libertarian view. The human body, as an integral part of the whole person, is a possession or property, but in a limited rather than an absolute sense.

An idea of property rights in this limited sense implies that we are stewards of our possessions and that we are answerable to God for how we use these gifts. This is what is portrayed the parable of the talents (Matt 25:14–30) and the contention that God "will give to each person according to what he has done" (Rom 2:6). The very fact that Paul talks about judgment of both Christians and non-Christians implies that non-believers too are accountable to God for their stewardship. While Christians are

4. "Right to die at own time a fundamental freedom," *Lariat*, October 4, 2005. Available at: http://www.baylor.edu/lariatarchives/news.php?action=story&story=36990.

5. Pew Forum on Religion & Public Life, "Religion and Politics: Contention and Consensus (Part III)," July 24, 2003. Available at: http://www.pewforum.org/PublicationPage.aspx?id=622.

specially linked to Christ as his Body, all of creation (including unbelievers) ultimately belongs to God and is accountable to him.

Paul writes elsewhere in the book of Romans that "none of us lives to himself alone and none of us dies to himself alone. If we live, we live to the Lord; and if we die, we die to the Lord. So, whether we live or die, we belong to the Lord" (Rom 14:7–8). Whatever rights we may purport to have about choosing the time and manner of our death with dignity, they pale in comparison to the responsibilities and duties we have to God and our neighbors.

The intimate link between the two great love commandments—to love God and our neighbor—means that in living "to the Lord," we also live to, for, and with others. The social nature of the human person means that a view of absolute individual freedom, such that gives rise to the "the ultimate right of an individual to his or her own life," is simply inadequate. It cannot account for the legitimate social and moral claims put upon us by our friends, family, and neighbors, or for the duties put upon us by God.

In one of the more remarkable moments in recent pop culture, the character Jack Shephard on the TV show *Lost* gives a speech to a group of survivors of a plane crash who find themselves alone on a seemingly deserted island. "Every man for himself is not gonna work," says Jack. "It's time to start organizing. We need to figure out how we're gonna *survive* here. Now I found water . . . fresh water up in the valley. I'll take a group in at first light. If you don't wanna come, then find another way to contribute! Last week most of us were strangers. But we're all here now, and God knows how long we're gonna be here. But if we can't, live together . . . we're gonna die alone."[6] No man is an island even when they are on an island.

In *The Walking Dead*, a show that follows a group of survivors as they attempt to navigate the world after the outbreak of a zombie apocalypse, there's a dynamic that illustrates deeply how the death of someone impoverishes us all. The group needs everyone's gifts to survive. When members of the group give up hope, or are otherwise lost, it makes everyone that much more vulnerable.

If we are not "to grieve like the rest of men, who have no hope" (1 Thess 4:13), then we are not to approach death in conformity to the wisdom of the world. Surely it was such worldly wisdom spoken to Job,

6. *Lost* episode 1.5, "White Rabbit," (2004). Quote available at: http://www.imdb.com/title/tt0636303/quotes?item=qt0450847.

afflicted "with painful sores from the soles of his feet to the top of his head," when his wife said, "Are you still holding on to your integrity? Curse God and die!" (Job 2:7,9). Job, of course, had many more reasons than simply his bodily suffering to give up hope and die; he had lost his entire family and all of his worldly possessions. Instead, Job displayed a spiritual wisdom that contradicts the hopelessness of the world: "Shall we accept good from God, and not trouble?"

Whether we are blessed, following our struggles and suffering, in this life (as Job was) or the next, we must recognize that our time on this earth, no matter how marred by sin and evil, is God's gracious gift. And the Christian hope of heaven infuses this time with eternal significance. Let us all hope and pray that when we are faced with our death, which "puts an end to our sinning and is our entrance into eternal life," as the Heidelberg Catechism puts it, we might, like Job, hold on to our integrity.

But given the realities of sin and human idolatry, this integrity can sometimes seem impossible to hold on to. Even if we don't actively pursue our own death by direct means, we often behave in ways that are dangerous and destructive. Sometimes this is an expression of immaturity. Other times this is a manifestation of a kind of spiritual despair. Feeling unconnected to God and our fellow human beings, utterly alone, we seek meaning in the vain things of this world.

Consider the case of Ripsi.

The vanities of this world are on fine display in the phenomenon known as "reality TV." One such show is the *Bad Girls Club*, which began airing on the Oxygen cable network in 2006. The premise of the show revolves around a group of young women of diverse backgrounds brought together to live in one house: "What happens when you put seven 'bad' girls in a house together—the type of girls who lie, cheat and flirt their way out of trouble and have serious trust issues with other women?"

It doesn't take long for fireworks to fly. Only four days and a couple episodes into the first season's experience, one of the bad girls named Ripsi flies off into an alcoholic rage. After a long stretch of binge drinking (inexplicably she drinks more alcohol to sober up), Ripsi explodes into an attack on two of her housemates, amidst a flurry of broken dishes. After that fateful night, Ripsi claims she had no memory of the events and is somewhat apologetic (although she brags about her privileged background with one of the girls she attacked), but the fallout is already decided: Ripsi has to leave the house.

As she's packing to leave, Ripsi shows great disdain for her possessions, giving away a $500 designer dress to one of her housemates. Too lazy to carry her bags, she simply kicks them down the stairs and lets them land where they may.

But in the midst of this *prima donna* behavior, Ripsi makes this tearful confession: "I just wanna be happy. I'm not happy. Nothing in the world makes me happy. I could shop until I drop. I could go out with my friends. But there's a void in there. I have been looking for something my whole life and I don't know what it is. I just know that I haven't found it yet."

In this intimate and heartfelt admission, we find the confirmation of the truth of Augustine's famous theological confession to God: "You stir us so that praising you may bring us joy, because you have made us and drawn us to yourself, and our heart is unquiet until it rests in you."[7] Unless our affections are properly oriented toward God, nothing will make us happy. Ripsi exemplifies the perennial experience of fallen humanity which seeks fulfillment and happiness in various created goods, whether in the social bonds of family and friends or in material possessions. Solomon documents his search for meaning in the book of Ecclesiastes and takes Ripsi's confession to its final conclusion: without God no one can be happy; everything is meaningless.

Ripsi's confession is an unwitting witness to the reality that pervades all of fallen humanity, for as Augustine rightly contends, "all are striving for the same goal, enjoyment."[8] But by nature we seek happiness through the ignorance and corruption of our will and so we are doomed to seek happiness in sinful ways. Augustine writes, "Sin gains entrance through these and similar good things when we turn to them with immoderate desire, since they are the lowest kind of goods and we thereby turn away from the better and higher: from you yourself, O Lord our God, and your truth and your law."[9]

Ripsi's confession has provided us with a contemporary testimony to the reality of fallen humanity and the self-destructive nature of sin. What Ripsi is looking for, perhaps even without her conscious knowledge of it, is what all of us are ultimately seeking: the unsurpassed happiness that comes with a relationship with God, made possible through the work of Jesus Christ. Ripsi, like all of us, is searching for her identity as

7. Augustine, *The Confessions* (New York: New City Press, 2005), 1.1.1, p. 14.

8. Augustine, *Confessions*, 10.21.31, p. 200.

9. Augustine, *Confessions*, 2.5.10, p. 38.

a person created in the image of God and bought for a price, so that in the words of the Heidelberg Catechism's most famous opening section, "I am not my own, but belong—body and soul, in life and in death—to my faithful Savior, Jesus Christ."

The Acton Institute where I work recently moved into a new building, and one of the perks is that there is a parking lot right next to the offices. The Grand River runs through downtown Grand Rapids, and at our old offices I would park on one side of the river and walk to our building on the other side. Then I would walk back at the end of the day. Often I would use that time to reflect on the day's events. One wintry day I was ruminating, as theologians sometimes do, on the parable of the Good Samaritan, which Jesus told in response to the question, "And who is my neighbor?" attempting to abstract some greater principle from the story.

I was pulled from my reverie by a slouching man wearing a hat, who approached me and asked for help. His watch battery was broken, and he needed $2.50 for a new one. Somewhat irritated by the interruption, and weary from a busy day of work, I was skeptical. His speech was mumbled and his explanation unconvincing. Part of me was concerned that he might use the money for some ill purpose. However, compassion for the needy soul also weighed heavily on me. I was faced with the dilemma of how to most effectively help him. This uncertainty only spurred my irritation. Noting my hesitation, he sought to assuage my conscience by despairingly pleading that he needed to fix his watch so he could get to work on time. Then he authoritatively said, "I know you must be a Christian."

It sounded like a challenge, and I felt my duty was clear. I instinctively replied, "Yes, sir, I am," and as I spoke, I reflexively handed him the change I had left over from my morning coffee. He hurried away, leaving me relieved that the encounter was over. It wasn't until after later reflection that relief was replaced with regret and guilt.

It struck me that I had been contemplating the parable of the Good Samaritan just as a destitute man confronted me on a snowy street. This didn't prevent me, however, from completely ignoring the model of compassion embodied in the parable. I perceived the person in need as a distracting annoyance. He was essentially a problem that required a solution as quickly and painlessly as possible so I could continue on my way. My solution was to heedlessly throw some money at the problem and hope it would go away.

What did the Good Samaritan do differently? Everything! He didn't treat his fellow man like a problem, but rather as a human being, engaging him as a person. The Good Samaritan didn't simply toss the robbery victim some money and proceed blithely on his way. Instead, he did the much more "uncomfortable" task of providing for the person's needs as if they were his own, as he "took him to an inn and took care of him" (Luke 10:34).

During my exchange with the man with the broken watch, there was a restaurant just a few paces away. If I had taken the parable to heart and learned from its example, I might have offered to take the man into the warmth of the restaurant and buy him dinner and a coffee. This way I would have provided him with food and fellowship instead of flinging him money that could be wasted. In this way, I would have engaged the man as a person rather than a problem, an opportunity rather than an annoyance. As it happened, our exchange ended without my even bothering to ask the man his name.

The difference in these two attitudes toward the poor is played out every day in the world on a much larger scale. Private charities and faith-based organizations, modeled on the example of the Good Samaritan, seek to actively engage the needy as whole persons—body and soul. Faith-based organizations, when unimpeded by government restrictions, are able to bind up both the individual's physical and spiritual wounds, to minister to the whole person.

Conversely, the welfare state tends to treat the poor as a problem, a set of faceless names on a list. The solution to such problems is often seen in purely economic terms, a case of the "haves" versus the "have-nots." This attitude is counter-productive in numerous ways, not the least of which is that it tends to create a cycle of dependency. When a person is in need of assistance, the right solution is not to give them material assistance without empowering them to begin to provide for themselves, all the while ignoring their spiritual needs.

The Good Samaritan is a model of effective compassion because he engages the fallen man as a person; he treats him as his "neighbor." This can at times be inconvenient, and it is rarely simple, but there is no other way to make compassion effective than to follow Christ's command to "go and do likewise." The reality of human sinfulness means that there will always be people who are in need. Indeed, we are all in need of something, whether our lack is primarily material, spiritual, or relational. So in this fallen world, there will always be people who need help. But the fact that they are people, created in God's image with authority, responsibility, and dignity, means that we must help and be helped in particular ways. As the Lutheran pastor and president of Lutheran World Relief John Nunes puts it, in helping we must always do that which "ennobles" people.[10]

Those who advocate for more government action in relieving the problem of poverty are often quick to condemn those who extol the virtues of market economies for focusing too much on material concerns. This charge of materialism is, in fact, a core and valid insight contained in most critiques of consumerism, a phenomenon in which people tend to equate their own value and meaning with the things they can buy or possess. But consumerism is just one manifestation of the problems with a materialistic mindset, and the commodification of compassion at work in the assumptions of many progressives is equally troubling.

We have seen this kind of commodification at work in debates about the federal budget, where campaigns like "What Would Jesus Cut?" decry proposals to lower government spending on social programs. As Jim Wallis puts it, "the moral test of any society is how it treats its poorest and most vulnerable citizens."[11] But on this view a particular level of government expenditures is equated with that moral test. This kind of logic is also at work with efforts like The ONE Campaign, which takes its name for the proposed amount that should be devoted by governments to foreign aid programs.

The problem with this perspective isn't just that it views material reality as important and instructive. The Lord himself spoke to the relationship between physical goods and spiritual orientation: "For where your treasure is, there your heart will be also" (Luke 12:34). The problem is, rather, that the material becomes the primary, even sole, focus when making moral judgments. In this way campaigns that commodify compassion judge morality purely in quantitative terms. If we spend more on social concerns, we are deemed to be more compassionate, more just.

But this kind of moral calculus fails precisely because it doesn't account for the qualitative differences in various kinds of responses. Other things matter, such as the *who* and *why* of charitable assistance. An EBT card issued by a government official shouldn't be judged to be the same as a "cup of cold water" given by a Christian in the name of Jesus Christ.

10. See Rev. John Nunes in the *Effective Stewardship DVD Curriculum* (Grand Rapids: Zondervan, 2009).

11. Jim Wallis, "What Would Jesus Cut?" *Huffington Post*, February 10, 2011. Available at: http://www.huffingtonpost.com/jim-wallis/what-would-jesus-cut_b_821555.html.

And just as the Good Samaritan didn't call on the local Roman officials to address the situation of his fallen neighbor, Christians are not called primarily to rely on governmental solutions to poverty, thereby shifting our own moral responsibilities to our neighbor to someone else.

The difference between the quantitative and the qualitative views of compassion are illustrated well in the case of "The Widow's Offering" (Luke 21:1–4). In this encounter, Jesus watches as wealthy people come to offer their gifts to the temple. He singles out a poor widow, however, for particular praise when she places two very small coins (essentially pennies) as an offering. "Truly I tell you," he said, "this poor widow has put in more than all the others. All these people gave their gifts out of their wealth; but she out of her poverty put in all she had to live on."

Jesus' words upset our merely material paradigms for evaluating compassion. On the quantitative level, they require us to look not simply at the amount of a donation, but also at the proportion of that donation. The two pennies the widow gave represented a larger portion of her property than the comparably vast sums given by the wealthy. But this deepening of our quantitative judgments leads us into the spiritual realm, where the quality of the gifts might also be recognized. The widow's offering isn't judged to be greater simply because it represents a proportionally greater material offering. No, this proportionally greater giving also is evidence of a different spiritual motivation. When she is said to give "out of her poverty," Jesus points to more than her material status. This woman lives by faith, knowing that human beings live on "more than bread alone" and out of her spiritual, as well as material, poverty she puts in "more than all the others."

We cannot truly measure compassion merely by looking at the level of government expenditures or the amount of money given, as easy and as tempting as that might be. These material concerns are important, but not all-important, factors in coming to grips with the complex realities of charitable activity. So just as we shouldn't define the meaning of life in terms of income or GDP, neither should we commodify compassion by ignoring the spiritual realities of charity. We must recognize in our brothers and sisters in need the image of God, which includes spiritual as well as material realities.

But what might a proper response to the recognition of the complexities of our neighborly responsibilities look like? In large part, it involves getting involved with those we desire to help. It means, sometimes, getting into the messiness of real relationships with other people.

Rudy Carrasco, who is a veteran of charitable work, describes the kind of charity that many Christians are comfortable with as a kind of "drive-by" charity.[12] Instead of getting into the complexity and messiness of personal relationships, we are too often content to throw money at the problem and send the poor on their way, just like I had done with the man who confronted me on my way from work. The German theologian Dietrich Bonhoeffer wrote in his classic *Life Together* that God has given us obligations to our neighbor as a kind of cross to bear: "the Bible can characterize the whole life of the Christian as carrying the cross. It is the community of the body of Christ that is here realized, the community of the cross in which one must experience the burden of the other. If one were not to experience this, it would not be a Christian community. One who refuses to bear that burden would deny the law of Christ."[13]

But if true Christian charity means getting into the trenches with others, getting down and dirty with them if need be, what might that look like?

I don't watch a lot of TV, but I do appreciate a good Western. One of my favorite shows is *Have Gun-Will Travel*. The lead character, Paladin, is like a one-man A-Team. He's smarter, stronger, and quicker on the draw than any bad guys. Another of my favorites is *Bonanza*. Ben Cartwright and his three sons admirably carve out a life of meaning and integrity on their Nevada ranch, the Ponderosa.

In a particularly memorable episode, one of Ben Cartwright's friends, Jedediah Milbank, is injured during a rough housing mud-wrestling match between Adam, Hoss, and Little Joe, Ben's sons. As reparation, Ben volunteers the three boys to take care of Milbank's business for him. It just so happens that there are three tasks, so each of the boys gets one.

Adam Cartwright gets the final task and it is to evict a family from a ranch for non-payment. It seems that Milbank had set up an arrangement for the family to pay for half of the ranch up front, and the rest in monthly installments. As it happens the family is a number of months behind, and Milbank is eager to foreclose.

The eldest Cartwright brother dutifully rides off to the ranch, and happens upon a pleasant but beleaguered clan. It seems that the family had tied up most of their capital in a prize bull that had been mauled by a bear before it could sire more than a few calves. All but a handful of those

12. See Rudy Carrasco in *Effective Stewardship*.

13. Dietrich Bonhoeffer, *Life Together and Prayerbook of the Bible* (Minneapolis: Fortress Press, 1996), 101.

calves were then drowned in spring floods. When the water pump broke so they could no longer irrigate their crops, the family was left without any source of revenue.

That's the situation when Adam arrives. The pieces of the pump need to be repaired, but one necessary part must be purchased new and costs $200, a huge sum of money. The family just doesn't have it. Instead of foreclosing on the home, Adam, who shares his father's strong moral code, decides to help out the down-and-out family. They aren't poor because of the lack of effort or work, but simply because of circumstances and poor decisions, such as tying up capital in the risky move to buy the stud bull.

So what does Adam do? He helps the father fix the pieces of the well that can be repaired and comes up with a plan to use the pump to double the land that can be irrigated. This will potentially double the family's crop, helping them to get their heads above water again. The family will need to sell the few remaining calves from the stud stock to pay for the expensive replacement part for the water pump. In the meantime, Adam loans the family the money to get current on their debt to Milbank, averting the disaster of eviction.

This is a great example of how compassion can work within the market system. Certainly Milbank fills the role of the archetypal greedy capitalist, but the Cartwrights themselves own a 1,000 acre ranch and are incredibly wealthy by the standards of the day. The difference between Milbank and the Cartwrights is in how they used their wealth and power. By the letter of the law and justice, Milbank had a right to foreclose. By contrast, it was compassion that motivated Adam.

The Heidelberg Catechism, a confessional symbol of Reformed Christianity, notes that one of the reasons we work is so that we can be good stewards of our wealth. The Catechism tells us that we are to "work faithfully" so that we "may share with those in need." That's exactly what Adam Cartwright was doing with his wealth. And he does it in such a way that it was oriented toward the family regaining their own financial independence. He loaned them part of the money, as a sort of nineteenth-century version of a micro-capital investment, but also made sure they had to invest what they had in their own future by selling the remaining calves.

There's an important lesson to be learned in all this. Christians in the United States are in an analogous situation with respect to the developing world as the Ponderosa and the Cartwrights were to that struggling family. We can choose to embody the "cowboy compassion" of the Cartwrights or the craven greed of Jedidiah Milbank. We can get our hands dirty by grubbing for money, or we can get them dirty by helping fix a broken well.

FAMILY AND MARRIAGE

At some point, sooner or later, all new parents experience that moment when they realize that this new little life is their unique responsibility. It can be a bit surreal. Holding your little one, it strikes you that a tremendous gift has been given to you, a gift that brings with it significant and life-altering responsibilities. I, who am a bit slow on the uptake sometimes, took some weeks to realize that I was not only able but also *allowed* to bundle up my tiny son in his car seat and take him out of the house to run errands.

For mothers like Mary, I imagine the realization hits home a bit sooner. What a morning it must have been the day after Jesus' birth! Were the new parents awoken after the excitement of the previous night with the squalling cry of the newborn babe? Did the wonder of the evening before seem like a dream? Or were they too excited to sleep at all, spending the night instead intently watching their son doze peacefully? Much like my wedding day, I remember smiling so much at the birth of my children that my face actually hurt.

There has been some significant and ongoing conversation about the meaning of marriage and family in today's society, as well as serious worry about economic and demographic trends. These topics are timely and important, but one of the perennial lessons we must take from the birth of Jesus Christ is that God is radically invested in this world. His care, to the point of sending his Son to be born, live, die, and rise again, provides us with a model for dealing with our own hopes and fears in a world so often full of despair and darkness.

One of the common concerns that drives prospective parents to put off having children is economic, specifically that they won't have the financial resources to support a growing family. This is a worry that's been around as long as there have been families. The complaint was prevalent in Martin Luther's time, and he called it "the greatest obstacle to marriage." Luther, in perhaps one of his less pastorally-sensitive moments, didn't give much thought to such worries, but instead denounced this objection as showing "lack of faith and doubt of God's goodness and truth." After all, he argued, marriage and family are ordinances of God's grace, and someone tempted to doubt that God provides for persons in this estate must instead realize "first, that his status and occupation are pleasing to God; second, that God will most certainly provide for him if only he does his job to the best of his ability."[14] It's an old adage, and yet a true one, that if you wait to have children until you can afford them, then you will never have any.

Having children is, in this way, fundamentally an act of faithful hope in the face of sometimes overwhelming fearfulness about the brokenness and corruption of this world. We don't need to look very far or very long to see stunning illustrations of human suffering and evil. It was right into the middle of this fallen and seemingly hopeless mess that the Christ child was born. Thus the classic carol, "O Little Town of Bethlehem" rings true: "The hopes and fears of all the years are met in thee tonight." Where evil leaves us speechless, God speaks the Word of hope and salvation.

In the same way that God sent his Son through the power of his Spirit to live, work, and die in the midst of the dust, dirt, mud, and muck of this world, we too are called to "be fruitful and multiply" (Gen 1:28) in patient expectation and hopefulness for God's purposes in this world. To the extent that we shirk this calling, unwilling to sully ourselves with the troubles and cares of parenthood, it shows a fundamental lack of faithfulness and hope, or as Luther puts it, is evidence of a people who "trust in God as long as they know that they do not need him, and that they are well supplied."

Arthur Brooks, the president of the American Enterprise Institute, put it this way in a lecture: "As you get past a certain level of prosperity, it will become not cost-effective to have children. If you don't have beliefs that transcend your life you won't have [children] anymore." Brooks describes instead a society, in which "people dedicate themselves to a higher purpose, most notably to God," and in which, therefore, "people will live on into the next generation. The future of a prosperous society depends on a lot of things, but the fundamental currency of the success of any society is people, is humans. When you stop having the humans, your life is limited and your prosperity is doomed."[15]

14. Martin Luther, "The Estate of Marriage," in *Luther's Works*, vol. 45 (Philadelphia: Fortress Press, 1962), 47.

15. Arthur Brooks, "An Evening with Arthur Brooks," Acton University, Grand Rapids, Michigan, June 13, 2012. Available at: http://www.youtube.com/watch?v=CLVOYWaSYxU.

Not everyone is called to have children themselves, of course. God has a plan for each individual, just as he has guidelines for how marriage and family are to be arranged. But as Christians within a larger society we are called collectively to promote the cause of life and human flourishing. For many that will mean having children in a committed, two-parent household. For others it will mean the struggles of single-parenthood. So too it will mean for many the adoption and integration of those who need parents into a loving home, a particularly powerful way of modeling God's love. For those who do not or will not have children themselves, it means offering support to those in their own families and communities that do bear and nurture children.

But key to all this is recognizing the critically important place that families and children play in the broader health of a society, and therefore the significance they have for God's work in this world. "From generation to generation and from century to century," Dutch theologian Herman Bavinck (1854–1921) wrote, "the struggle against sin must be continued, and the spiritual and moral nurture must begin afresh with each person."

Given the complex of relationships we are each born into, the family is the bulwark of civilization in this sense, and on that basis Bavinck expressed the hope that "from the family outward, blessing and prosperity will once again spread across all the nation."[16] This is a hope that we too ought to share in fear and trembling, as it echoes across the centuries from that little manger in Bethlehem.

The Italian greeting *Buon Natale* ("Good Nativity") captures this reality a bit better than the English, "Merry Christmas."

Christmas is a wonderfully appropriate time to reflect on the hope of this birth for our world. Bavinck writes evocatively that "the holy family is the example of the Christian home."[17] Very often the "culture of life" and the "culture of death" are juxtaposed, but let's look at a particular aspect of that juxtaposition. Life and death are in some sense not precisely coordinate; if by death we mean the point of departure from this world and (in the traditional Christian understanding) the separation of the soul and the body, then the time of birth and death are in some sense more precisely related.

It's no secret that the developed world in general, and more recently the United States in particular, faces some serious demographic

16. Herman Bavinck, *The Christian Family* (Grand Rapids: Christian's Library Press, 2012), 52, 84.

17. Bavinck, *The Christian Family*, 40.

challenges. Much of this has to do with the absence of a culture of life in general, and a culture of birth in particular. The causes are indeed complex, but in a profound way they are spiritual rather than merely economic or political.

A number of important trends were revealed by the latest American census data in 2010, but none more important than the dynamic between demographics, economics, and morality. Yet the connection between the birthrate and American debt has been overlooked, in part because the nearly 10 percent increase in U.S. population from 2000 to 2010 hides the underlying drop in birthrate to its lowest levels in nearly a century. The vast majority of the decline in birthrate over the last decade has occurred since 2008, and the fertility rate in America also dipped below replacement levels in 2009, to a low of 2.01 children per woman (the replacement rate is 2.1).

While the intergenerational effects of these declines will continue to ripple forward through time, the dearth of births America has undergone in the last three decades is having profound consequences today. Former Pennsylvania senator Rick Santorum blamed the current public debt crisis in America on an "abortion culture." Santorum's contentions on this issue ring true. Focusing especially on the solvency of Social Security, Santorum said that "the design would work a lot better if we had stable demographic trends."[18]

There are a host of reasons that the birthrate in America has declined over the last 40 years. Santorum points rightly to the legal and cultural shift inaugurated with the nationwide legalization of abortion in 1973. And in the past decade, we have seen the pursuit of a radical environmental agenda by fringe elements that have characterized human life as inherently destructive and harmful to the natural world. The broader cultural implications of this kind of misanthropy should not be underestimated, especially as it filters out into the mainstream.

But financial ecology plays an important role as well. The downturn in the birthrate over the last few years reflects the pessimism and perceived constraint of raising children in the midst of economic recession. Healthy and vibrant economies promote the flourishing of healthy and vibrant families. But the reverse is also true. The vitality of each social

18. Gabriella Schwarz, "Santorum blames 'abortion culture' for problems with Social Security," *CNN.com*, March 29, 2011. Available at: http://politicalticker.blogs.cnn.com/2011/03/29/santorum-blames-abortion-culture-for-problems-with-social-security/.

institution is linked with the welfare of others, and the microeconomic effects felt by families necessarily have macroeconomic implications.

Nowhere is this reality more apparent than in Europe, and the recent austerity measures and civil unrest across that continent should serve as a cautionary tale for what could be in store for America if our demographic trends continue. As Samuel Gregg, director of research at the Acton Institute, has written so cogently, however, demography is not destiny. "Demography is only one variable among many. Moreover individuals and nations *can* make choices, and choices *change* our future," he says. "Sometimes circumstances, such as the global economy's present problems, can provide the incentive and opportunity to break away from apparently unalterable paths."[19]

This recognition points to the way forward for America to reverse the birth dearth and break away from the fatal connection between the welfare state mentality and declining populations. America certainly has a more comfortable margin than many of the developed nations in Western Europe. This is in part because, more than any other such country, the United States has relied on large immigrant populations to offset decreases in births.

But even so, the public debt crisis, driven largely by the looming insolvency of numerous entitlement programs, is symptomatic of the nation's woes and should not be ignored. America needs a renewal of the moral ecology that places primary value on dignity and respect for human life. We need a moral culture that prizes having children, that celebrates parenthood as a legitimate and praiseworthy vocation.

Without this kind of renewal, which would result in the literal "revival," or coming to life again, of the nation, there is far worse in store for us than chronically unbalanced budgets. Jesus taught Christians to pray, "Forgive us our debts." If we do not renew and reform our culture along the lines suggested here, a renewal that must be led by Christians acting as agents of transformative grace, the debts for which we must pray forgiveness will be far weightier than those incurred by the federal government.

Many parents, reflecting on the troubles of their own lives or the corruption of the world around them, wonder how they might in good conscience bring another life into this world. From this perspective,

19. Samuel Gregg, "Europe's Choice: Populate or Perish," *Acton Commentary*, July 13, 2010. Available at: http://www.acton.org/pub/commentary/2010/07/13/europes-choice-populate-or-perish.

bearing and raising a child is an act of hope and defiance in the face of the abyss. In a world that largely embraces meaninglessness and despair, merely having kids can be profoundly counter-cultural.

A culture of birth is, in this way, the foundation to broader social flourishing. As Bavinck puts it, "In the family we get to know the secret of life, the secret, namely, that not selfishness but self-denial and self-sacrifice, dedication and love, constitute the rich content of human living." And as Luther observed so vividly, the act of changing a diaper is a profound act of service and, as such, a profound act of worship to God.

But parenting involves much more than merely taking care of a child's physical needs. I remember a time when I settled down with a number of friends and family for a night of entertainment to watch "Inside Man," a film which explores the twists and turns involved in a bank robbery.

At one point in the film a young black kid is playing a video game on a portable game unit. We get a closeup of the game, wherein Matthew (played by Amir Ali Said), is controlling a car full of gang members about to do a drive-by shooting. As the car approaches the target, instructions flash prominently on the game screen, "Kill 'dat [N-word]!!!" Matthew, good at following directions, manipulates a few buttons, thereby moving one of the gang members to shoot the mark in the head, pasting "cherry pie" all over the outside of the building.

There's an intriguing conversation between Matthew and one of the bank robbers at this point in the movie, but I want to pass along what happened in the real world later. After the film ended, I asked the other adults in the room if they knew what real-life video game Spike Lee was parodying. They answered negatively, and I said, "It's the one the kids are playing in the next room." Sure enough, some of the kids were huddled around a console playing *Grand Theft Auto: San Andreas*.

This game was originally released with an ESRB rating of "M" for "Mature," then was readjusted to "Adults Only," after a political brouhaha, and then re-released as "M." There is a great deal of violence in the game, and at least some of the children playing it in the house were well under even the "M" age rating (17 years and older). The parents had no real knowledge about the content or the themes of the game.

This situation is no doubt repeated innumerable times all over the country on a daily basis. The National Institute on Media and the Family issued a report card some time ago that challenged parents directly: "Simply put, parents need to step up to the plate and the experts need to conduct more and better research." All this finally reflects the truth of the matter that parents bear the primary and ultimate responsibility for the education and moral formation of their children. In this day and age, that education and formation is conducted within a world pervaded by use of technology. It's our calling and challenge as parents and family members to make sure that we use computers, video games, and other technologies prudently.

The dangers of technology are just one example of the temptations endemic to our modern society. A recent survey by the Pew Global Attitudes Project finds that "religion is less likely to be central to the lives of individuals in richer nations than poorer ones."[20]

Given the Bible's many warnings about the danger presented by wealth, specifically the temptation to no longer rely on God and his providential care, the connection between prosperity and irreligion probably shouldn't be surprising. But what might be more surprising is that "the United States, the wealthiest nation, was 'most notably' an exception, scoring higher in religiosity than those in Europe. The level of religiosity in the United States was found to be similar to less economically developed countries such as Mexico. Americans tend to be more religious than the publics of other affluent nations, the survey stated."

But what upsets the seeming iron law connecting affluence to irreligion?

The only answer can be the penetration of the gospel message into people's hearts and minds. The gospel is the only antidote to idolatry. An example of this message is clearly evident in a *Christianity Today* column by John Piper, "Gutsy Guilt."[21] Piper takes apart the myth of prosperous comfort that Satan propagates. Piper writes with regard to sexual sin, perhaps the most difficult class of sins to conquer, "The great tragedy is not masturbation or fornication or pornography. The tragedy is that Satan uses guilt from these failures to strip you of every radical dream you ever had or might have. In their place, he gives you a happy, safe, secure, American life of superficial pleasures, until you die in your lakeside rocking chair."

This recalls C. S. Lewis' astute observation, in his classic sermon "The Weight of Glory," that "Our Lord finds our desires not too strong, but too weak. We are half-hearted creatures, fooling about with drink

20. Nathan Black, "Survey: Wealthier Nations Less Religious," *Christian Post*, November 5, 2007. Available at: http://www.christianpost.com/news/survey-wealthier-nations-less-religious-29971/.

21. John Piper, "Gutsy Guilt," *Christianity Today*, October 2007. Available at: http://www.christianitytoday.com/ct/2007/october/38.72.html.

and sex and ambition when infinite joy is offered us, like an ignorant child who wants to go on making mud pies in a slum because he cannot imagine what is meant by the offer of a holiday at the sea." Turning our material sensibilities into fetishes, whether oriented toward alcohol, violence, sex, money, or the myriad other temptations on offer daily, is a betrayal of our dignity as human beings created in God's image. "We are far too easily pleased," concludes Lewis.[22]

Material prosperity can be an occasion not only to stop relying on God for the provision of earthly goods, but can also be an opiate that dulls our awareness of even greater grace, the gift of justification. "Therefore, God, out of his immeasurable love for us, provided his own Son to do both. Christ bears our punishment and performs our righteousness . . . . Justification conquers fornication," writes Piper. Here we hear echoes of Martin Luther: "Be a sinner and sin boldly, but believe and rejoice in Christ even more boldly, for he is victorious over sin, death, and the world."[23]

Only when rightly and appropriately valued does wealth occupy a morally praiseworthy place in the world, as a means of glorifying God through service to our neighbor. The family is the first place where this service to others is evidenced, as we come in to the world entirely dependent on our caregivers for our well-being. It is also the first place where this service is cultivated, as we learn to be good children and siblings, to share with others and to forgive when we are harmed.

For all these reasons the family occupies an absolutely central place in social flourishing. The reality of the family destroys the idolatry of both socialist collectivism and atomistic individualism. We are human beings, created in God's image, in relation to him as our Heavenly Father as well as to our earthly parents. Thus the two great love commandments are to "love God" and our "neighbor," or as Jesus also puts it, "A new command I give you: Love one another. As I have loved you, so you must love one another. By this everyone will know that you are my disciples, if you love one another" (John 13:34–35).

22. C. S. Lewis, "The Weight of Glory," in *The Weight of Glory and Other Addresses* (New York: Touchstone, 1996), 26.

23. Martin Luther, letter to Philip Melanchthon, Wartburg, August 1, 1521, in *Luther's Works*, vol. 48 (Philadelphia: Fortress Press, 1999), 282.

Given the changing dynamics of social institutions in response to fluid moral consensus, economic realities, and political agendas, it's needful to explore the implications for marriage as an order of divine grace. God created human beings in complementary sexual relationship so that through intercourse in the context of marriage we might "be fruitful and increase in number" (Gen 1:28). In this way the union of man and woman in marriage is oriented to the task of *procreation*. Even in that term we get a clue at the mystery of human beings, male and female, being created in God's image. There's a sense in which we are image-bearers of God when we procreate. As God created the world, we *procreate* and fulfill the cultural mandate.

There's much more to be said about human sexuality than this, but the recognition of the intimate linkage between marriage, procreation, and family is essential to understanding from an orthodox Christian and biblical perspective the implications of changing the legal definition of the institution of marriage.

What might the legal recognition of same-sex relationships as marriage mean? Thomas Aquinas has a rule of thumb that we might take as a good starting point. Thomas distinguishes between *legality* and *morality*. In short, not all immoral things are to be made illegal. As Thomas writes, "The purpose of human law is to lead men to virtue, not suddenly, but gradually. Wherefore it does not lay upon the multitude of imperfect men the burdens of those who are already virtuous, viz. that they should abstain from all evil." The pivotal factor in determining when to make law becomes whether the criminalization of an immoral behavior would result in more or less evil, i.e. whether by doing so the state would be stirring up more evil or restraining it. The danger is that the new laws, which would more closely codify into law the requirements of the moral order, might result in a situation in which "the precepts are despised, and those men, from contempt, break into evils worse still."[24]

From a historical and traditional Christian perspective, that same-sex relationships are immoral is beyond doubt and that they violate at least the commandment regarding adultery is undisputed. The scope of the seventh commandment is sexual purity, and it has been the traditional Protestant and Roman Catholic practice to interpret these commandments with both positive and negative aspects, not only not to defile marriage but also to protect and promote it.

24. Thomas Aquinas, *Summa Theologica* (New York: Benzinger Bros., 1947), II.1.96.ii.

As part of the second table, reformers like Calvin, Luther, and others would agree that the enforcement of the adultery commandment at least theoretically falls under the purview of the state. The question of "same-sex marriage" is not simply a *religious* issue as the first table is often construed, but a moral and civic one relating to the second table. With this in mind, we must at least consider the possibility that homosexual activity, and certainly the kind of homosexual relations characteristic of same-sex partnerships, theoretically fall under the purview of civil law.

Let's assume for the sake of this argument, as so much of American society already has, that this sort of legal prohibition does not meet Aquinas' prudential criterion: the government proscription of homosexual activity creates more evil (in the form of an intrusive government, among other things) than it restrains. Keeping in mind the distinction between legality and morality, this is a powerful argument against the criminalization of homosexual activity.

This recognition does not leave us with only one way forward, however. The government's refusal to proscribe homosexual activity is not identical to government recognition of same-sex partnerships as legal marriage. A situation in which homosexual activity is not criminalized would leave us without any laws whatsoever from the government on this point, rendering the government's judgment of this activity as moral or immoral ambiguous at best.

But for the government to actively recognize and therefore promote same-sex partnerships as marriage would be to explicitly sanction this activity as morally praiseworthy, just, and helpful for society. Homosexual activity, just like any sexual activity outside of the marriage covenant, is immoral, and therefore the government has no valid role in promoting or establishing such activity as normative. There is thus an important and critical difference between saying something is legally permissible and that it is morally permissible or even praiseworthy. And in the debate about changing the definition of social institutions that are so foundational for society, the burden of proof must be on those who would argue for a new or re-definition. It must be shown that the new social forms are not harmful. We should apply what's been known as the "precautionary principle"—that some innovation must be proven safe—to the innovation of new social forms. In this regard the state has no duty to be reality-neutral, as if any social construction or practice that might be imagined ought to be considered equally valid.

In this way, the Christian view of the government's role regarding legal recognition of same-sex partnerships can take two forms. First, the Christian might say that the government should prohibit and enforce this portion of the second table in pursuit of restraining evil. This, in fact, is one of the reasons given historical for laws against homosexuality, which in some cases have only relatively recently been revoked. Second, the Christian might make a prudential judgment and say that the government would create more evil by making and enforcing such laws, and should therefore should make no positive law on this point. But there is no third option for the Christian view of the state, that is, that it should actively promote, recognize, institutionalize, and protect an immoral set of social relations.

The reason that this third way is not a viable option for orthodox Christian views of the relationship between the state and the social order is that the biblical view of government has its orientation toward the good. The government has no standing to be neutral towards the truth, and from the Christian perspective the truth is that marriage is an institution that is pre-political. As Dietrich Bonhoeffer, the German pastor and theologian, put it, "marriage . . . is not established by government but is to be acknowledged by it."[25] Abraham Kuyper (1837–1920), the great Dutch politician, statesman, and theologian described the relationship between government and marriage, as well as the other spheres of society, thus: "Internally each sphere is ruled by another authority that descends directly from God, apart from the state. This authority is not conferred, but merely recognized by the state. And even in defining laws for the mutual relationships among these spheres the state may not adopt its own will or choice as the standard, but is bound by the decision of a higher will, as expressed in the nature and purpose of these spheres."[26]

On this account, marriage and family exist apart and distinct from government and the church, and so both of these latter institutions merely recognize, affirm, and ratify the prior relationship rather than creating it *de novo*. The state's recognition of same-sex partnerships as marriage would be an innovative legal creation, not the recognition of an actual

25. Dietrich Bonhoeffer, "Government and the Divine Orders in the World," in *Conspiracy and Imprisonment: 1940–1945*, vol. 16, *Dietrich Bonhoeffer Works* (Minneapolis: Fortress Press, 2006), 520.

26. Abraham Kuyper, "Sphere Sovereignty," in *Political Order and the Structure of Society*, ed. James W. Skillen and Rockne M. McCarthy (Atlanta: Scholars Press, 1991), 260–61.

prior social relation that is continuous with the created and preserved order of heterosexual marriage. The state certainly has no obligation, or even permission, to recognize, promote, or establish a set of social relations that violate the moral order, especially as articulated in the second table commandments.

Some Christians, however, disagree with that conclusion quite vehemently. Rob Bell, a best-selling author and former megachurch pastor, recently responded to a question about same-sex partnerships and marriage, and said, "I am for marriage. I am for fidelity. I am for love, whether it's a man and a woman, a woman and a woman, a man and a man. And I think the ship has sailed. This is the world we are living in and we need to affirm people wherever they are."[27]

That last sentiment in particular is of special note, as Bell's comments come within the context of his rebuke of what evangelicalism has come to mean in the American context. Before answering the question about same-sex marriage, Bell said, "The beautiful thing would be if 'Evangelical' came to mean buoyant, joyful, honest announcement about all of us receiving the grace of God and then together giving back to make the world the kind of place God always dreamed it could be. Let's reclaim it, all of us."

Even if Bell's depiction of evangelicalism is a caricature, his own reclamation project of the evangelical identity is a perverse inversion of the gospel, something he accuses conservative evangelicals of doing. Bell compares the ancient Roman *evangelion*, a "military announcement that they had conquered one more land and subjugated one more nation-state," a kind of "global military superpower propaganda," with twentieth-century North American evangelicals. "So when *evangelical* becomes associated with global military superpower and coercive military tactics, it's the exact opposite of the origins of the word," he said. The origins are found in the early Christians, who "co-opted it for their own purposes. And they said we have good news. Their good news is that the world is made better through coercive military violence like the Roman Empire. Our good news is that the world is made better through sacrificial love."

But Bell's assertion that the ground motive of evangelicalism really is "to affirm people wherever they are" is, by curious contrast, "the exact opposite of the origins" of Christianity and the gospel. God does not affirm people where he finds them, in sin and on the road to perdition.

27. Rob Bell, "What We Talk About When We Talk About God," Grace Cathedral, San Francisco, CA, March 17, 2013. Available at: http://www.gracecathedral.org/cathedral-life/worship/listen/detail.php?fid=182.

As Augustine, who coined something quite close to the meaningful phrase "love the sinner, hate the sin," put it, only a particular vision of love really wins:

> If any of you perchance wish to keep charity, brethren, above all things do not imagine it to be an abject and sluggish thing; nor that charity is to be preserved by a sort of gentleness, nay not gentleness, but tameness and listlessness. Not so is it preserved. Do not imagine that thou then lovest thy servant when thou dost not beat him, or that thou then lovest thy son when thou givest him not discipline, or that thou then lovest thy neighbor when thou dost not rebuke him: this is not charity, but mere feebleness. Let charity be fervent to correct, to amend: but if there be good manners, let them delight thee; if bad, let them be amended, let them be corrected. Love not in the man his error, but the man: for the man God made, the error the man himself made. Love that which God made, love not that which the man himself made. When thou lovest that, thou takest away this: when thou esteemest that, thou amendest this. But even if thou be severe at any time, let it be because of love, for correction.[28]

In fact, the gospel is all about God not affirming us where we are, but taking decisive action to amend our situation: "God demonstrates his own love for us in this: While we were still sinners, Christ died for us" (Rom 5:8). Love affirms what is good but amends what is bad. This calls for discernment.

On one level, Bell must understand this, since he isn't content to merely affirm evangelicals where they are. He wants to change them, and not all of what Bell is against is incorrect. But Bell's selective rebuke towards evangelicalism really does show the incoherence of the position that everything must be affirmed in the name of love, except that which is not all-affirming.

The vision of marriage and family as grounded in the reality of human sexuality and the procreative blessing requires moral advocacy for monogamy. In fact, there's an argument that the government does have a role to promote stable families and monogamous marriage. The government depends on that which it does not create: human beings cultivated to be responsible moral agents in public life. The faith-based initiative pioneered by President Bush is in part an attempt to come to grips with this reality, as it seeks not to discriminate against religious charities

28. Augustine, "Homily VII. 1 John IV. 4–12," in *Ten Homilies on The First Epistle of John* in vol. 7, *Nicene and Post-Nicene Fathers* (Edinburgh: T&T Clark, 1886), §11. Available at: http://www.ccel.org/ccel/schaff/npnf107.iv.x.html.

because of their religious convictions. But some charities are recognizing that there are difficulties involved in receiving government support.

A case in point is a sexual purity project called the Silver Ring Thing. Founded as a private charity in 1995, the Silver Ring Thing had been awarded more than $1 million in federal grants from 2003 until 2005, when an ACLU suit challenged the group's funding. The suspension of funding left a rather large hole in the group's budget. Indeed, in 2003 more than half of SRT's revenue came from government grants.

So it would be natural to see the settlement of a suit as a loss for the Silver Ring Thing. But such a perspective is short-sighted. It is becoming clearer every day that the promise of President Bush's Faith-Based Initiative, and now President Obama's Office of Faith-Based and Neighborhood Partnerships, is in danger of faltering, and that Silver Ring Thing was presented with the opportunity and the challenge to wean itself off of government support.

Funding from the government always comes with strings attached, in the form of red tape and regulations, and even the occasional bureaucratic meddling. Once a religious non-profit gets government funding, the tendency is to become dependent on that money. The danger is then in becoming beholden to the government's interests instead of the guiding mission of the organization.

Under the terms of the settlement, HHS suspended all current financial support for the Silver Ring Thing and would not grant any future federal dollars unless the group adequately separated religious and secular components of its programming. This could be done by following a newly-created set of "required safeguards" that make sure federal funds are not used for religious purposes. The high percentage of government funds that has made up the SRT's budget was surely a temptation for the group to acquiesce to the HHS regulations and attempt to rigorously separate the faith element out of the program. But this is a temptation that the Silver Ring Thing resisted.

Many charities like the Silver Ring Thing will have come to count on federal support for their programs, and they will be faced with the difficult options of giving up government money and severely downsizing their services (which presumably will violate the trust that they have established with those they help), continuing to depend on government money by secularizing their programs, or seeking private funding sources to cover the gap. The last of these three options may be the best, but it also raises significant difficulties if the charity leadership has not prepared for such a need.

The Silver Ring Thing has been known for integrating the gospel of Jesus Christ into its message of sexual purity, and for this it deserves praise. SRT hands out Bibles at its rallies, is explicitly guided by Scripture in its youth program, and states that its mission consists in "offering a personal relationship with Jesus Christ as the best way to live a sexually pure life." This is only natural, as the group is evangelistic; the message of abstinence and biblical purity is part and parcel of the Christian gospel.

As such, the premise of the Faith-Based Initiative itself is suspect, as it assumes a dichotomy between faith and works that is unnatural and poisonous to the Christian religion. The Great Commission given by Jesus to the Church is to proclaim the message of salvation to the world, and the humanitarian work that Christian groups do must always be oriented to that ultimate goal. Otherwise the organization risks losing its distinctive foundation.

Richard Baxter, a seventeenth-century Puritan divine once wrote, "Do as much good as you are able to men's bodies in order to the greater good of Souls. If nature be not supported, men are not capable of other good."[29] This is the basis for Christian relief and social work. The ultimate goal is the comprehensive salvation and reconciliation of the human person, body and soul.

Some from within the Church will no doubt complain and worry that the ACLU victories like this will only further secularize our country. This may be superficially true, but the Silver Ring Thing has taken the opportunity to resist a far more damaging form of secularization: the kind that separates Christian faith from works. The responsibility now rightly has fallen to concerned Christians to pool their considerable resources and fill SRT's funding gap.

The temporary setback of the loss of government funding became a long-term opportunity for the Silver Ring Thing to refocus on its central mission. By resisting the temptation of the government's "forbidden fruit" and meeting its funding goals through private religious endeavors, the Silver Ring Thing can be accountable to God rather than Caesar. And that's the way it should be.

29. Richard Baxter, "How to Do Good to Many," in *The Practical Works of Richard Baxter*, vol. 4 (London: George Virtue, 1838), 940.

COMMUNITY AND CIVIL SOCIETY

The Black Hills of Dakota in the 1870s may seem like an unlikely place for a dramatic narrative pursuing themes of justice, service, and community, but that's exactly what the audience gets in compelling fashion in HBO's recently concluded series *Deadwood*. When creator and executive producer David Milch first pitched the idea to HBO executives, the setting was in fact ancient Rome.

Speaking of Deadwood's setting, a mining camp, Milch says, "This was an environment, as was Rome in the time of Nero, where there was order but no law whatsoever." The character Merrick, who runs the camp's newspaper, the *Deadwood Pioneer*, observes in the first episode that the camp is officially and formally "outside law or statute."

Set against the mythic landscape of the American West, *Deadwood* plays out the timeless political and social themes that have confronted every formative culture: the conflict between tyranny and liberty; the call of the conscience in matters of justice; the very human longing for order in a wild and lawless land. *Deadwood*, like all Westerns, may be viewed as a commentary about the particular time in which it was produced—America in the 21st Century. (HBO's characteristic use of nudity and extensive profanity may make this series even more "contemporary" to some.) Ultimately, however, *Deadwood* poses a question that transcends history: Can a raw and bloody town in the grip of gold rush fever overcome its own violence, greed, and materialism? Can it shape a destiny and find meaning outside of the idols of brute force and sudden fortune?

It's through the character of Seth Bullock (played by Timothy Olyphant), a former lawman from Montana, that we are introduced to the show's *leitmotif* of law and order.

As with most of the main characters in *Deadwood*, Milch has based the players on real-life figures, although he has toyed with the historical facts where it suits the story. So while Wild Bill Hickok and Seth Bullock never met in real life, they become fast (albeit brief) friends on the show. Bullock, along with his partner Sol Star, leaves service as a lawman in Montana to seek his fortune as a purveyor of mining equipment and hardware in the fast-growing Deadwood camp.

But the life of law enforcement isn't so easy for Bullock to leave behind. As he works on building the frame for the new hardware store, Bullock has an illuminating exchange with Hickok, who himself is a former lawman. Wild Bill notes that soon there will be peace with the

Sioux, then "pretty quick you'll have laws here." Seth replies, "I'd settle for property rights," to which Bill asks astutely, "Would you?"

Indeed, it becomes clear that given his character, disposition, and temperament, Bullock cannot just "settle for property rights." A man driven by conscience, ideals, and an innate sense of justice, Bullock eventually, and grudgingly, assumes the role of sheriff in Deadwood. His natural sense of equity provides an element of needed stability in the camp. Bullock is a natural lawman. In a later conversation with Wyatt Earp, another former lawman of some repute, Bullock admits, "I took the badge off myself once, without losing my impulse to beat on certain types." The decisive shift for Bullock, moving him into service to the broader community as sheriff, comes in a conversation with General Crook, who seeks brief respite in the camp from fighting the Sioux.

Bullock complains to Crook that the town's sheriff, whose position had been created for political purposes and had assumed a largely ceremonial role, was corrupt and inept. To this Crook responds, "In a camp where the sheriff can be bought for bacon grease, a man, a former marshal, who understands the danger of his own temperament, he might consider serving his fellows . . . We all have bloody thoughts." Bullock's calling from General Crook is to put those retributive instincts to the greater good of the camp.

If Bullock's contribution to the Deadwood camp consists largely in the administration of justice, the vocations of other figures are much more diverse.

When he recognizes that she has the gift of caring for people, the camp's doctor calls on Calamity Jane, the friend of Wild Bill Hickok, to assist with an outbreak of smallpox. This gift, belied by her rough carriage and not-so-functional alcoholism, ends up being a constitutive reason why the camp is able to survive such a dangerous outbreak.

Alma Garrett, whose husband's untimely death leaves her in control of a bonanza gold strike, is determined to open a bank in Deadwood "for the good of the camp." Her second husband, a gold prospector named Ellsworth, calls Alma "a financial powerhouse," praising her for her "service to the camp, turning her mine into houses and the like getting built, businesses begun, some for people that will never know her name."

In a glimpse of the absurdity that sometimes marks life in Deadwood, barkeep Harry Manning runs against Bullock for sheriff in the camp's first elections, not because he wants to be sheriff, but because he wants to be first deputy, in case Deadwood ever creates a fire brigade. Tom Nuttall, who employs Manning, points out the flaw in his man's thinking.

"I should cut your salary 20 percent, based on time you're absent campaigning . . . . Your plans are idiotic. You're running for sheriff to be a fireman," says Nuttall. "Why not build a firewagon that you then rent out to the camp?" When Nuttall offers to loan Manning the money (in the form of the aforementioned salary deduction) and help him build the wagon, plans are agreed upon to pursue an entrepreneurial venture that will provide the camp with a critically important public service. In Deadwood, when people get together, social life becomes rationalized along economic lines, people seek ways in which to specialize their service, and the social life of the camp moves, sometimes in fits and starts, toward peace.

Given the nature of the "Wild" West, however, *Deadwood* wouldn't be complete unless there were some more nefarious elements at work. Cy Tolliver (Powers Boothe) runs a brothel called the Bella Union, and is a primary competitor of Al Swearengen (Ian McShane) who helped found the camp and runs the Gem Saloon (and whorehouse).

Tolliver is a masterful manipulator, who at every opportunity attempts to turn his leading pro Joanie Stubbs to his will. While simultaneously offering Joanie the chance to venture out on her own, he tries to entice her back to the Bella Union to continue running women. Cy tells the suicidal and depressed Joanie, "What brings a gun to the temple is lack of gainful occupation and of being useful to others. I don't see you trying to kill yourself here. All you do here is good for the girls and me too." When Joanie tells him that she "don't want to run women no more," Cy avers, "that's turning from your gift and your training." Joanie concludes with stunning clarity that when Tolliver propositions her in this way, "I feel it's like the devil talking."

The main story arc that spans the entire series of *Deadwood* is the conflict between tyranny and liberty, the former personified by the archetypal robber baron, George Hearst (Gerald McRaney). From afar Hearst exercises decisive influence on the development of the camp in the first two seasons, and in the final season, his personal presence brings even greater pressure to bear on the camp.

In a fit of frustration, Swearengen complains of Hearst to Bullock: "Running his holdings like a despot I grant has a [certain] logic. It's the way I run mine; it's the way I'd run my home if I had one. But there's no practical need for him to run the camp. That's out of scale. It's out of proportion and it's a warped, unnatural impulse." Swearengen recognizes the swollen lust for power, the *libido dominandi* in Hearst's designs.

But even Hearst's will to dominate the life of the camp has its own rationalization. Hearst fancies that he is doing his fellow man a service in his devotion to mining gold, to acquiring "the color." Speaking with Odell, the son of his cook affectionately named "Aunt" Lou, Hearst says, "Before the color, no white man, no man of any hue, moved to civilize or improve a place like this had reason to make the effort. The color brought commerce here, such order as has been attained . . . . Gold is your chance. Gold is every man's opportunity."

In a rare show of sensitivity, Hearst continues, "That is our species' hope, that uniformly agreeing on its value, we organize to seek the color . . . I hate these places, Odell, because the truth that I know, the promise I bring, the necessities I'm prepared to accept make me outcast." Time and again Hearst puts aside his instinct to react rashly to offense or effrontery, and each time Hearst forestalls out of the greater interest in pursuing the gold. There's a patina of other-directedness in Hearst's self-understanding. Indeed, Hearst's influence isn't entirely without its merits, but at bottom his explanation of his task seems more like self-rationalization to cover for a deep-seated greed than the righteous employment of a man divinely called. Aunt Lou, who is Hearst's cook describes him thusly: "George Hearst, he do love his nose in a hole more and ass in the air and back legs kickin' out little lumps of gold like a badger." The early Christian father Clement of Alexandria describes that same human condition with a bit more theological insight:

> But he who carries his riches in his soul, and instead of God's Spirit bears in his heart gold or land, and is always acquiring possessions without end, and is perpetually on the outlook for more, bending downwards and fettered in the toils of the world, being earth and destined to depart to earth,—whence can he be able to desire and to mind the kingdom of heaven,—a man who carries not a heart, but land or metal, who must perforce be found in the midst of the objects he has chosen? For where the mind of man is, there is also his treasure.[30]

When Bullock confronts Hearst over his disregard for the law and Alma Garrett resists his attempts to consolidate her claim into his holdings, Hearst encounters just these sorts of frustrations. Speaking to Cy

30. Clement of Alexandria, "Who Is The Rich Man That Shall Be Saved?" in *Ante-Nicene Fathers*, vol. 2 (Buffalo, NY: Christian Literature, 1885), §XVII.

Tolliver, whom he has placed into his service, Hearst confesses that "just this afternoon such displeasure brought me near to murdering the sheriff and raping Mrs. Ellsworth. I have learned through time, Mr. Tolliver, and as repeatedly seem to forget, that whatever temporary comfort relieving my displeasure brings me, my long term interests suffer."

But in order to efficiently realize the acquisition of the color, Hearst is unwilling to allow any threats to his dominance to exist. Hearst's obsession with what Charlie Utter, a friend of Wild Bill and Bullock, would call "amalgamation and capital," moves him to have murdered those who would oppose him, such as workers who would organize into labor unions. Knowing that even with their combined efforts they cannot oppose Hearst by force, the leading citizens of Deadwood, including Bullock and Swearengen, cast about for a strategy that will not conclude with Hearst taking "this place down like Gomorrah."

In a moving scene in which the camp's leadership palavers, they decide to publish in the newspaper a letter from Sheriff Bullock to the family of one of the murdered union organizers. Comparing the letter favorably to the beauty of the social conventions present in the Declaration of Independence, David Milch says that the letter testifies to basic human decency: "You respect the guy's humanity, you're kind to his family, you honor him in his passing."

Jack Langrishe, a flamboyant theater man and friend to Swearengen, affirms the wisdom of such an indirect, but unmistakable, course of rebuke to Hearst. In the aftermath when Swearengen expresses doubts about the prudence of publishing the letter, Langrishe wonders why Al might doubt the appropriateness of "proclaiming a law beyond law to a man who is beyond law himself, its publication invoking a decency whose scrutiny applies to him as to all his fellows."

Despite Al's ostensible projection of himself as a rugged individualist, the image is seen for its superficiality by Langrishe. Speaking of the Deadwood camp to Swearengen, Langrishe asserts, "A thing of this order you'd as soon not see ruined or in cinders." To this Swearengen agrees, "I will if I have to, avoiding it, if I could," unwilling to see the camp exist under the sway of Hearst's tyranny.

In *Deadwood* we have the birth of a community in the unlikeliest of places: a gold rush camp where everyone is there first and foremost to seek "the color." When economic order and social institutions arise organically, even in the face of great evil, Christians recognize God's providential work through the means of natural law, self-interest, and charity. The struggle between Swearengen and Hearst represents the conflict between the liberty arising from spontaneous, organic order and the tyranny of authoritarian domination and oppression.

As Augustine wrote, "In this universe even that which is called evil, well ordered, and kept in its place, sets the good in higher relief, so that good things are more pleasing and praiseworthy than evil ones." In *Deadwood* we see both the way in which evil can limit evil, and how God's preserving grace is manifest in works of both pure self-interest and authentic charity.

While the profuseness of obscene language will undoubtedly prevent some viewers from appreciating the show (numerous expletives have been deleted from the direct quotes in the foregoing), as with Milch's approach to dialogue, which prefers gritty realism to conventionally styled conversation, the violence and sexuality of *Deadwood* is far more likely to evoke pity and compassion, and ultimately a recognition of the personhood of the characters, rather than to titillate.

By many accounts the rise to prominence of institutions *other* than the church or the state, like those that figure so prominently in *Deadwood*, marks the transition from the medieval to the modern era. Even so, it is true that many Protestant reformers considered the right balance of the relations between church and state to be of first importance in the proper formation of Christian society. Protestant theologians like Heinrich Bullinger, Peter Martyr Vermigli, and Wolfgang Musculus considered the danger of papal tyranny so great that they were willing to grant powers to the civil magistrate that alarm our modern sensibilities. To this extent, a basic dialectic between the powers of church and state persisted well into the sixteenth century.

But as Max Weber's oft-maligned account of the rise of capitalism alerts us, this transition from the late medieval to the early modern period also saw the rise of systematic reflection on economic topics by many of these same theologians. On the Protestant side—the aspect heavily emphasized by Weber—there was a flourishing of ethical reflection on questions of usury and charity. And among the Roman Catholics, in particular the so-called "School of Salamanca," thinkers like Domingo de Soto, Martín de Azpilcueta, and Luis Molina put forward nuanced and intricate explorations of issues related to currency and exchange. Thus arose in relatively short order what might be called "the market" as a rival to the traditional medieval institutions of church and state.

The revolution of post-modernity has largely left us bereft of the church as an institutional social force, and thereby has the medieval dualism of church and state been replaced with today's dichotomy between market and state. To wit: The General Social Survey has been conducting polls on American confidence in social institutions since 1976. The results for 2008 show a remarkable deterioration in confidence in every institution except for that most conspicuous and defining feature of the government—the military. Nowhere has the decline in mediating institutions between the individual and the state been more evident than in the development of the global economic downturn. Just as there are now perceived to be only two real institutions of social significance (the market and the state), so also are there only two entities to blame (corporations or regulators) and two avenues of solution (deregulation or nationalization).

Advocates for government intervention abound nowadays. But apologists for the market economy do themselves and their cause no favors when they ignore the fact that there are limits to what the market can and ought to be asked to do. Indeed, much of what has been called "market failure" is actually the result of applying market-based solutions to problems for which profit considerations ought to be considered secondarily—if at all. Within a market framework people tend to maximize efficiency and increase material well-being. But the market is not the answer for everything. It cannot tell us, for instance, how to arrange our familial or spiritual lives. The failure of the market to deliver a particular socially desirable result does not reflect any inherent flaw in the market economy itself, but simply attests to its limitations. These kinds of limitations come into sharp relief in situations where a specific end is deemed desirable regardless of economic limitations.

Thus it increasingly appears from the sub-prime lending disaster that the market is not the best medium for dealing with the question of homeownership among those with bad credit, no credit, or who are for whatever other reasons unable to get mortgages from commercial lenders. There is a class of people who—by our current social standards—ought to be homeowners but who are not being serviced by the traditional lending market. Edmund Phelps, director of Columbia University's Center on Capitalism and Society, has said that, "Democrats and Republicans have been very keen to make home ownership almost a national purpose."[31] But President Bush's now infamous invocation of the "ownership society" was the political reflection of a latent cultural and social reality: homeownership is an American ideal. This ideal vision itself has significant flaws. The promotion of large-scale homeownership can have seriously deleterious social consequences, insofar as the poor and middle classes have disproportionate amounts of their net worth tied to their homes. This exposes them to relatively greater risk of impoverishment amidst fluctuating housing markets. Homes are expensive to maintain in terms of material costs, physical labor, and mental distress. As Phelps notes, "If you rent, that's it. You don't have to pay any interest to anybody. You don't have to pay any maintenance costs to anybody. You don't have to worry about whether the boiler is going to break down. While if you own your own home, you have a hundred aggravations."

Homeownership also decreases the ability of workers to easily move out of economically distressed areas to regions where jobs are available, thus reducing the mobility and fluidity of labor. So one assumption we must question is whether homeownership ought to be promoted beyond the standards set by the market. The market effectively sets its own limits by disqualifying those whose credit is judged too risky. Indeed, it is simply not the case that every individual or family needs to own a home, any more than it is the case that every person needs to go to college, have a driver's license, or own a flat-screen TV.

And yet without correcting our assumptions about the ideal of homeownership, there still is a group of people that by American standards ought to have the opportunity of homeownership and are not provided that opportunity in our society. The argument for the failure of the market to provide this opportunity usually proceeds along these lines: The poor are disproportionately affected by lending standards, so that mortgage rates are prohibitively high or even unavailable to those of lesser means. The poor, because their applications are deemed to be riskier, end up paying higher rates than the rich, if the poor are able to even get a mortgage loan in the first place. In a world where the government or corporations are the only options, the social demand for a solution to this failure of the market to do what we want it to do (provide poor people

31. Edmund Phelps, "Why home ownership is U.S. obsession," *APM Marketplace*, March 26, 2009. Available at: http://www.marketplace.org/topics/business/taking-stock/why-home-ownership-us-obsession.

with mortgages) necessarily results in a reaction from the government in any number of overt requirements or subtle incentives.

We are now seeing the fruits borne out of this perspective. If we return to the insight of an age in which the market and the government were not the only two options of resort, we might come up with an alternative framework for action. The magisterial reformers, particularly John Calvin, are often credited with innovating upon the medieval prohibitions on usury, or lending at the expectation of profit. It is true that Calvin represents a rather more permissive approach to usury, in the sense that he did not think that lending at profit was always and in every case immoral (this was the opinion of Calvin's Bernese contemporary, the reformer Wolfgang Musculus). But the more permissive and more restrictive perspectives on usury in the sixteenth century agreed, across confessional and political boundaries, that seeking profit from lending to the poor was condemnable. Calvin wrote that usurious lending to the poor violates a "common principle of justice," and Musculus decried it as "plainly inhuman to pursue a profit from the sweat and calamities of the poor."[32] When markets fail to achieve socially desirable results, the government is not simply the only, first, or even best, avenue of redress.

Traditionally the answer to market "failure" has not been governmental intervention but the non-profit charitable model. Where avaricious compulsion or well-intentioned coercion created the problems of the sub-prime market, the principle of charity represents the solution. In this framework the poor are viewed not as sources of profit but rather as objects of love. This does not mean that we ignore insights into human nature that we learn from economic or political analysis. Our charitable giving is made effective when we integrate what we know about people from every area of human knowledge. We know, for instance, that people tend to denigrate that which does not cost them. The "cheap grace" of some kinds of charity must be balanced with the "costliness" of personal investment. This is why charities like Habitat for Humanity emphasize the need for "sweat equity," which both ennobles the person as not only a passive recipient but also as an active and responsible moral agent. A non-profit charitable model does not mean that houses need to be given away for free.

Our current political emphasis is one that threatens to undermine the independence and effectiveness of faith-based non-profits and Christian ministries, a challenge we've examined in the case of the Silver Ring

32. See Jordan J. Ballor, *Covenant, Causality, and Law: A Study in the Theology of Wolfgang Musculus* (Göttingen: Vandenhoeck & Ruprecht, 2012), 155.

Thing. When the choice is between the profit-motive of the market and the welfare offered by the state, the resulting political logic pushes inexorably towards the marginalization of private charity. The dichotomy of market and state places us between the Scylla of seeking profit in all of our interactions and the Charybdis of coercive force and intrusive regulation. When both the state and market are properly limited, room is made for the vital institutions of social life to flourish and for a culture of charity to be truly nurtured.

Unfortunately, such civil associations and voluntary organizations that once formed a critical piece of American social life are on the verge of extinction. The problem is often framed in terms of the familiar "old versus new" conflict. And so the issue appears really to be one of demographics. The antiquated and obsolete social clubs and groups are in the process of dying off, replaced by more efficient and relevant Internet chat rooms and virtual communities. The Facebook generation doesn't need the Kiwanis. The social process of natural selection is at work, weeding out the elements of society that don't deserve to flourish.

After all, critics point to the shortcomings of all-male fraternal societies as cause of their own decline. Consider how a golf club like Augusta National has been subject to such scathing social commentary for the group's homogeneity. Shouldn't we then celebrate the death of such archaic "old boy" networks? Despite being afflicted by the sin and disruption that marks all human activities, civic groups like the Knights of Columbus and the Lions do much that is praiseworthy and beneficial for society. There is no doubt that flawed aspects of voluntary associations and fraternal societies have contributed in some part to their decline. The greatest share of blame, however, ought to be laid at the feet of the modernist view of individuality, which minimizes the importance of community and social structures.

In the words of theologian Stanley Grenz, "The modern world is an individualistic world, a realm of the autonomous human person endowed with inherent rights." While there are many elements of this modern world that are compatible with biblical Christianity, Grenz writes that "we must shake ourselves loose from the radical individualism that has come to characterize the modern mind-set."[33] And it is just this radical individualism that has undermined the vitality of civic and community groups, rendering them "irrelevant" in the minds of many. This was

33. Stanley J. Grenz, *A Primer on Postmodernism* (Grand Rapids: Eerdmans, 1996), 167–68.

hardly the view of the founders of America, who realized the importance of a vibrant civil society. The First Amendment implicitly promotes voluntary associations by stating that Congress shall make no law infringing the "the right of the people peaceably to assemble."

Chief Justice Warren Burger wrote that the right of association is a "fundamental" right, and in the Constitution, such rights, "even though not expressly guaranteed, have been recognized by the Court as indispensable to the enjoyment of rights explicitly defined."[34] This coheres well with the view of sphere sovereignty articulated by Dutch statesman and theologian Abraham Kuyper. Kuyper argued that social spheres enjoy independence or sovereignty, in that they are not created by the state but derive their authority and existence directly from God. He emphasized that this idea should be identified as "*sovereignty in the individual social spheres*, in order that it may be sharply and decidedly expressed that these different developments of social life have *nothing above themselves but God*, and that the State cannot intrude here, and has nothing to command in their domain. As you feel at once, this is the deeply interesting question of our *civil liberties*."[35]

And here we see the continuing importance and relevance of the structures of civil society, including voluntary associations like the Rotary and Optimist Club. These kinds of groups form an indispensable buffer between the individual and the State, fulfilling what Kuyper called the "organic life of society" as opposed to the "mechanical character of the government."

The proper view of civic groups is one that embraces the comprehensive nature of the human person as social individuals. We should embody attitudes neither of radical individualism nor of extreme communitarianism, but rather of balanced individuals within community. Civic groups and voluntary associations are anything but "irrelevant" within such a rich and complex view of human society. Indira Gandhi once said, "People tend to forget their duties but remember their rights."[36] In this case, it is our duty to exercise the right and the responsibility of association.

Indeed, the 2011 movie *Contagion*, which featured a star-studded ensemble cast, was successful in large part because it portrayed in a concrete, realistic, and believable way some of the deepest fears of human beings

34. Chief Justice Warren Burger, Judgment of the Court, in *Freedom of Expression in the Supreme Court: The Defining Cases* (Boston: Rowman & Littlefield, 2000), 270.

35. Abraham Kuyper, *Lectures on Calvinism* (Edinburgh: T&T Clark, 1899), 116.

36. Indira Gandhi, *Last Words* (New Delhi: Arnold-Heinemann, 1984), 25.

about the complexity of human community. All of us recognize, to one extent or another, the precious gift that life is, and we also recognize life's inherent fragility. This shared human understanding is one of the things that makes disaster stories—films in particular—so popular. They connect with some universal sense of the tenuousness of human social life and real threats, such as the recent scares surrounding possible pandemics like the Asian bird flu outbreak of 2005 or swine flu concerns of 2009.

As disease runs rampant on a global scale, the film shows how thin the bonds of civilization can be, as people desperate for survival descend quickly into mob violence, rioting, and looting. Again, there's something here that resonates deeply with us, as we all realize how quickly things can come to resemble a Hobbesian "state of nature," in which life is "solitary, poor, nasty, brutish, and short." What makes *Contagion* so powerful is that it successfully integrates the complex dynamics of globalization into the story, showing how quickly, given international travel and commerce, diseases might spread. In a very real way this film shows us how interconnected the world really is, as something that happens in Hong Kong (unlike Vegas, perhaps) doesn't stay in Hong Kong, but rather spreads throughout the world in a remarkably short period of time.

But while the film is clear about the dangers of globalized human relationships, it also teaches a more subtle lesson. Even as disease represents a danger that can have worldwide impact, such dangers remain the exception rather than the rule. Indeed, the film portrays quite well how global networks of information and exchange are absolutely foundational for our contemporary world. There are certainly institutional and human failures in the film, many of which are quite plausible, or even probable. But it is also clear that global interconnection is not simply negative, even though we often overlook the positive benefits.

Leonard Read illustrated this positive global dynamic powerfully in the essay, "I, Pencil," in which a common pencil narrates the back story, a "genealogy," of its production and dissemination to a near-universal level of familiarity, "to all boys and girls and adults who can read and write."[37] The Christian writer Lester DeKoster similarly invites us to consider the construction of the chairs in which we sit every day, and the complex web of human action that must be applied to such things to fit them for our use. "We are physically unable, it is obvious," he concludes, "to provide ourselves from scratch with the household goods we can now see from

37. Leonard Read, *I, Pencil* (Irvington-on-Hudson: Foundation for Economic Education, 1999). Available at: http://www.econlib.org/library/Essays/rdPncl1.html.

wherever you and I are sitting—to say nothing of building and furnishing the whole house."[38]

It's not simply diseases that we "give" and "catch" to and from other human beings around the world; it's also goods and services. This, too, displays something uniquely human. Certain kinds of animals migrate, to be sure, sometimes on a stunning scale. Consider the movement patterns of migratory birds, or the wide-ranging travels of various whales, for example. But the social nature of the human person, created in the image of God with a moral obligation to serve others through the use of reason and effort, is unique in the created order. So even while our material bodies are subject to disease and danger, very often from our interactions with other people, so too are these bodies served by the application of spiritual effort (as in prayer) and mental effort (as in scientific research) to find comfort amidst suffering and the best solutions possible to the wide range of human maladies.

In this way, ideas too are contagious, which is why they are often referred to analogously as "viral." There are certainly good ideas and bad ideas that are spread, just as there are goods and services as well as diseases and afflictions that are communicated throughout the world. But ultimately we must realize that we are in no way better off alone, or "solitary," as Hobbes puts it, which he quite rightly recognizes is connected to life also being "poor, nasty, brutish, and short." As human community becomes more developed on a global scale, we can see empirically as well as practically, that life is more often and increasingly (although with notable and lamentable exceptions) wealthy, pleasant, civilized, and long.

But in the face of a picture of peace like this, we must realize that violence, like other anti-social expressions of sins, is contagious in a sense. Researchers have released a report in the journal *Science* arguing that "the best model for violence may be that of a socially infectious disease."[39] So says Felton Earls, at Harvard Medical School, who led the study. Dr. Earls' study of the social implications of violence, in his words, "clarifies doubt that exposure to community violence is indeed part of the contagion process." This view of violence as a disease or contagion is

38. Lester DeKoster, *Work: The Meaning of Your Life—A Christian Perspective* (Grand Rapids: Christian's Library Press, 2010), 4.

39. "Witnessing gun violence significantly increases the likelihood that a child will also commit violent crimes," *Harvard Gazette*, May 26, 2005. Available at: http://news.harvard.edu/gazette/story/2005/05/witnessing-gun-violence-significantly-increases-the-likelihood-that-a-child-will-also-commit-violent-crimes/.

one that fits well with a traditional Christian view of sin. The theologian Neal Plantinga writes that an important recognition of sin is that it is "a dynamic and progressive phenomena. Hence, its familiar metaphors: sin is a plague that spreads by contagion or even quasi-genetic reproduction. It's a polluted river that keeps branching and rebranching into tributaries. It's a whole family of fertile and contentious parents, children, and grandchildren."[40]

The kinds of violence we see so often today are particular cases of a kind of sin with much biblical precedent. From the days of Cain, the world's first murderer, the instances of violence have only increased in frequency and depravity. The book of Genesis contains the words of Lamech, a descendant of Cain, who says, "I have killed a man for wounding me, a young man for injuring me. If Cain is avenged seven times, then Lamech seventy-seven times" (Gen 4:23–24).

What is the cure for such ills? The state plays an important role in the restraining of sin, and those who violate the law rightly ought to be punished. The enforcement of law by the government can act as a deterrent to various forms of unrest. But the external power of preservation can only function as a check on sin and violence, not as an ultimate solution.

The character of King Dahfu in Saul Bellow's *Henderson the Rain King* tells us about the cycle of violence perpetuated after the Fall. He says, "Brother raises a hand against brother and son against father (how terrible!) and the father also against son. And moreover it is a continuity-matter, for if the father did not strike the son, they would not be alike. It is done to perpetuate similarity . . . man cannot keep still under the blows." Dahfu continues and describes the essence of virtue in this fallen human condition: "A brave man will try to make the evil stop with him. He shall keep the blow. No man shall get it from him, and that is a sublime ambition. So, a fellow throws himself in the sea of blows saying he do not believe it is infinite. In this way many courageous people have died."[41]

And so for the answer of redemptive suffering, we must go to Jesus Christ, the Good Physician, who shows us through his life, death, and resurrection that the response to violence is not an increase in violence in the style of Lamech. Instead, we are called by Jesus to forgive each other "not seven times, but seventy-seven times" (Matt 18:22). The earthly

40. Cornelius Plantinga Jr., *Not the Way It's Supposed to Be: A Breviary of Sin* (Grand Rapids: Eerdmans, 1995), 53.

41. Saul Bellow, *Henderson the Rain King* (New York: Penguin, 1996), 214.

reversal of the escalation of sin and violence comes in the Christian life of forgiveness and reconciliation.

A good society is characterized by freedom, but it is freedom exercised toward virtue. This biblical teaching to do good even to our enemies gets at the root of virtue, the renewed heart capable of something far greater than a mere public morality.

All human structures are ultimately inadequate in the face of human sin. No government, economy, family, or society can survive if a critical mass of citizens do not exercise a particular level of self-government and restraint. If you change what people desire, you will change what the market tends to offer. The words of eighteenth-century preacher Samuel Cooper ring true, "Virtue is the spirit of a republic; for where all power is derived from the people, all depends on their good disposition. If they are impious . . . all is lost."[42]

But unfortunately the dynamics of community life, which are the source and school of civic virtue, are often cast simply in terms of the atomistic individual or the all-encompassing collective. A speech given by President Obama in which he seems to denigrate the entrepreneurial spirit of American enterprise caused a great deal of distress among many. "If you've been successful, you didn't get there on your own," said the president at a campaign event. "You didn't get there on your own," he reiterated. "If you were successful, somebody along the line gave you some help. There was a great teacher somewhere in your life. Somebody helped to create this unbelievable American system that we have that allowed you to thrive. Somebody invested in roads and bridges. If you've got a business, you didn't build that. Somebody else made that happen."[43]

It shouldn't be surprising that leading up to Election Day the president's articulation of his characteristic view of the American social compact took on sharper edges. Indeed, the president's sharp dichotomy in these and similar statements is what struck a negative chord with many. But even though the president's words here may have been designed to cater to a base more inclined toward collectivism, conservatives and independents should not respond by rejecting the kernel of truth contained in the president's remarks.

42. See James H. Hutson, ed., *Religion and the New Republic: Faith in the Founding of America* (Boston: Rowman & Littlefield, 2000), 172.

43. "Obama to business owners: 'You didn't build that,'" *FoxNews.com*, July 16, 2012. Available at: http://www.foxnews.com/politics/2012/07/15/obama-dashes-american-dream-suggests-nobody-achieves-success-alone/.

It is in fact true that businesses and entrepreneurs cannot be successful on their own. Indeed, none of us are autonomous or radically independent in this way. The president rightly pointed to the experience that all of us have had of someone nurturing us and helping us grow and develop. The family is the first institution where we experience this community of love, but we also find such expressions in different ways in churches, schools, and workplaces.

As for businesses, their success depends on cultivating a relationship of service and trust with their customers. This reality isn't groundbreaking to anyone who has experienced success in business (or any other field for that matter). The president also invoked the idea of "giving back," when he contended, "There are a lot of wealthy, successful Americans who agree with me because they want to give something back." This idea of "giving back" causes many of the president's ideological opponents to take umbrage. The concern is that such language depends on an idea of business as having first "taken from" in order to later "give back." This kind of analysis falls right into the "market" vs. "state" dichotomy that is so problematic.

Indeed, such an understanding doesn't do justice to the real dynamic between business and customer. The relationship is based on voluntary exchange, in which each party gives something to the other. It's true that in a just exchange nothing more is then owed by either party to the other. But it's also true within the larger context of human reality that we recognize the gracious nature of such relationships and that we can be thankful that we have the ability and freedom to give and receive. In this sense the idea of "giving back" can be understood on the basis of having first been *given to* rather than having *taken from*. "We sometimes speak as if the only way to 'give back' to society is by paying taxes, but any decent mechanic does more for society by fixing cars than by paying taxes," observes the political philosopher David Schmidtz.[44]

The political analyst Yuval Levin puts it this way: "We are all dependent on others. The question is whether we are dependent on people we know, and they on us—in ways that foster family and community, build habits of restraint and dignity, and instill in us responsibility and a sense of obligation—or we are dependent on distant, neutral, universal systems of benefits that help provide for our material wants without connecting us

44. David Schmidtz, *The Elements of Justice* (New York: Cambridge University Press, 2006), 91.

to any local and immediate nexus of care and obligation."[45] We all know at some level that we didn't get where we are on our own and that we have an ongoing responsibility and dependence on others for our continuing enjoyment of the goods of human existence.

Christians realize too that our independence and freedom is ultimately limited and dependent not simply on other people but on the grace of God. So there's a sense in which we do enjoy the "dignity of causality," as Blaise Pascal put it, through our own creaturely efforts. But there's also a real sense in which none of us exercise that causality on our own, independent of God or other people. "It is not dependence per se, which is a universal fact of human life, but dependence without mutual obligation, that corrupts the soul," writes Levin. What's needed, then, is a proper balance and perspective on this dynamic between independence and mutuality, individuality and community.

The president, as might be expected, often tends to emphasize what the government contributes to flourishing communities as he argues for his view of American society. To the extent that he downplays individual initiative and the merit of enterprise he does a real injustice to the reality of the situation. But we shouldn't let the president's overemphasis on the government's role in fostering and sustaining community lead us to abandon a more comprehensive, variegated, and richer vision of community and social life. A proper understanding of human community is a corrective to, not a symptom of, collectivist thinking.

45. Yuval Levin, "More Than Dependency," *National Review Online*, April 24, 2013. Available at: http://www.nationalreview.com/corner/346517/more-dependency.

2

Work, Culture, and Economics

"But not only did God make Sunday, He made Monday, too, and Tuesday, Wednesday . . . So if God made all those days, he's in all our days, not just the one you want to put him in."

—The Rev. Al Green

Amid the threat of a "double-dip" recession, and the ongoing plight of joblessness across America, recent Labor Day holidays have been bittersweet for many. For those who have the gift of employment, the right to work can seem more like a privilege. And for those looking for work, the hope of being hired soon can sometimes seem more like a fantasy. But it is precisely in this kind of challenging economic environment that we can most clearly see the blessing that work is, both to ourselves and to one another.

For ourselves, work helps give life meaning and purpose. Human beings are naturally productive, tending, when unimpeded, to use our minds and hands to make things, to be creative. The very term *manufacturing* comes from root words that mean "making by hand." Indeed, God has set up the world in such a way that work is a blessing, the way he provides for us to provide for ourselves and our families. The German theologian Dietrich Bonhoeffer in this context called work God's "order of grace," the regular means God has given to take care of our material needs. Anyone who has been out of work knows this to be true: having a job and receiving a paycheck is a great blessing.

But God has also given our work a spiritual meaning. The Apostle Paul exhorts us in this way: "Whatever you do, work at it with all your heart, as working for the Lord, not for men" (Col 3:23). That is, we are accountable to God for the opportunities he gives us to be productive, as well as for the energy and talents that we apply in our work. The first great commandment is to "Love the Lord your God with all your heart and with all your soul and with all your mind" (Matt 22:37). We are to love God in all we do. This includes that portion of our day which we spend at work. We are, quite simply, to show our love of God in our work.

It is one thing, however, to say that we are to love God in our work. It is quite another to do so. What does loving God in our work really look like?

It is here that the second great commandment comes to the fore: "Love your neighbor as yourself" (Matt 22:39). As the Christian writer Lester DeKoster puts it, at its core "work is the form in which we make ourselves useful to others."[1] It is in putting ourselves in the service of others that our work also finds meaning. For in making ourselves useful to others, we do for them as we would have them do for us. And this is, as DeKoster puts it, the great secret connecting work and the two great love commandments. For in making ourselves useful to others, we make ourselves useful to God. This is how we show our love for God: in serving others.

After all, that's how he shows his love for us. The incarnation is God's entrance into a life and death of service for human beings. The Apostle Paul makes this connection as he writes, "Each of you should look not only to your own interests, but also to the interests of others." He says this just before he points to the example of Christ as the one who serves others, "taking the form of a servant, being born in the likeness of men. And being found in human form, he humbled himself by becoming obedient to the point of death, even death on a cross" (Phil 2:4, 7–8 ESV). This is the good news of Jesus Christ, for our life and death, our rest and our work.

The early church father Augustine says, "Every human being, precisely as human, is to be loved on God's account."[2] For God loves us so much that he sent his only Son to die on the cross as an atoning sacrifice

1. Lester DeKoster, *Work: The Meaning of Your Life—A Christian Perspective* (Grand Rapids: Christian's Library Press, 2010), 1.

2. Augustine, *Teaching Christianity: De Doctrina Christiana* (New York: New City Press, 1996), 118.

for our sins. So let us love one another, this day and always, not simply in our leisure, but also in our labor.

WORK AND SERVICE

That human beings were created to be creators, to work, is undeniable. The anthropological concept of *homo faber*, man the tool-maker, attests to this basic aspect of what it means to be human. From a Christian perspective, we confess that human beings make things in a way that imitates their Maker. While God creates "out of nothing" (*ex nihilo*) and then orders and arranges it, we create in a creaturely way, dependent on God's primary acts of creation. All this is true about the human person, and it is good that it is so.

But ever since the fall into sin work has been bittersweet. This negative aspect of work is communicated to us in the biblical narrative in the form of a curse. As God says to Adam, "Cursed is the ground because of you; through painful toil you will eat food from it all the days of your life" (Gen 3:17). As fallen creatures we no longer relate to the world around us, whether the world of plants, animals, human beings, or spiritual truths, the way we did before.

So, on the one hand, work is a basic created good that God has given us to meet our temporal needs and fashion our souls in disciplined obedience. But, on the other hand, work often becomes toil—laborious, monotonous, repetitive, and unfulfilling. This dissatisfaction creates in us a deep and abiding sense that *things are not the way they are supposed to be*. As the book of Ecclesiastes reads, God has "set eternity in the human heart," such that the things of this world often pale in comparison with our attraction to spiritual things (Eccl 3:11). We imagine, we believe, we hope that there must be a better world to come.

We find this sense of brokenness in something as common as fishing. In a Michigan Radio story about the challenges facing the fishing industry in the state, veteran angler Ed Patnode mused that "we'd be rich if we could tap into the mind of a fish."[3] Sometimes the fish seem to like a particular color of lure, and if we could "just get that fish to talk and tell us why do you like pink, or can you tell us what days you're going to

3. Rebecca Williams, "Swimming Upstream: The mind of a fish (Part 5)," *Michigan Radio*, June 29, 2011. Available at: http://www.michiganradio.org/post/swimming-upstream-mind-fish-part-5.

bite pink on and what other factors are influencing your decision to bite this pink lure today," says Patnode, fishing would be a great deal easier. Patnode's notion that the challenges of fishing could be overcome if we could understand how fish "think" seems to point toward the possibility that human beings once did, and perhaps will again, relate to the rest of the world in a way that perceives how things really work.

And so while we live an existence marred by the curse, we still live. We still can work, even if that work is more troublesome and difficult than it would have otherwise been. The Dutch theologian and statesman Abraham Kuyper describes this dynamic between things being imperfect and yet still good in his doctrine of "common grace," an idea enjoying renewed attention with the publication in English of portions of his magnum opus on the subject. Kuyper writes that, after the fall, "we can arrive at the knowledge of things only by observation and analysis. But that is not how it was in paradise." Before the fall we read that Adam "named" the animals, by which we should understand that "Adam immediately perceived the nature of each animal, and expressed his insight into the animal's nature by giving it a name corresponding to its nature."

Things are far different today, however, as we see in the case of Ed Patnode and other fisherman, or any professional who deals daily with the natural world. Kuyper writes, "If we want to learn to understand a plant or an animal, then we must observe that animal and that plant carefully for a long time, and from what we observe gradually draw conclusions about their nature. This occurs apart from us ever learning to understand their essence."[4] Indeed, says Kuyper, "Even their instincts still remain a completely unsolved riddle for us," to the extent that we do not really know what causes lake trout to prefer pink lures to green or orange on any given day.

In this way the daily routine of work reminds us both of what we have lost and how we are still blessed. It reminds us that amidst the brokenness and blindness of sin, God has not abandoned this world. And so we are called, in our own limited and often wayward way: "Whatever your hand finds to do, do it with all your might" (Eccl 9:10). This is the nature of our "lot in life" and our "toilsome labor under the sun" until such time as we "shall know fully" (1 Co. 13:12) the extent of God's redeeming grace.

4. Abraham Kuyper, *Wisdom & Wonder: Common Grace in Science & Art* (Grand Rapids: Christian's Library Press, 2011), 57–58.

Indeed, in the parable of the sheep and the goats (Matt 25:31–46), Jesus differentiates between those who have done good to others by working well and those who have not. The king, taking the place of Christ in the parable, says that "whatever you did for one of the least of these brothers of mine, you did for me." Whatever good was done was counted as being done to the king, and whatever bad was done was counted the same way. And on this basis the king separates the righteous sheep and the unrighteous goats. The goats "go away to eternal punishment, but the righteous to eternal life." It is natural to think that the good the sheep do to others ("I was hungry and you gave me something to eat, I was thirsty and you gave me something to drink . . .") refers to special acts of kindness, things that are only done occasionally and usually within a charitable context.

Lester DeKoster provides a refreshing understanding of this parable. He writes that the good Jesus refers to includes these special acts of charity, but also refers to the service we do every day within the context of work. Consider that "God himself, hungering in the hungry, is served by all those who work in agriculture, wholesale or retail foods, kitchens or restaurants, food transportation or the mass production of food items, manufacturing of implements used in agriculture or in any of the countless food-related industries, innumerable support services and enterprises that together make food production and distribution possible."[5] The same goes for those who thirst, or who need clothing or shelter. "To work is to love—both God and neighbor!" concludes DeKoster.

One reflexive response to this claim is to argue that when we do work for money, when we profit from our labor, we are really serving ourselves and not others. Or we might say that our service to others is merely instrumental to our real selfish purposes. But from the context of Jesus' parable it's not clear at all that the sheep explicitly have in mind the idea that they were serving God through their service of others, or that all of what they did for others was simply voluntary and without monetary compensation. They even have to ask the king, "Lord, when did we do these things for you?"

The concept of work being at once remunerative and service-oriented is not totally foreign to us. We tend to think, at least generally, of those in "public service" as working for the good of others even though they receive a paycheck. The same typically goes for doctors and teachers, as well

5. DeKoster, *Work*, 13.

as for a host of other jobs. But if it is the case that these kinds of professionals can legitimately be said to serve others (even though they are paid to do so), why is not the same true for the entrepreneur, the waitress, the garbageman, the farmer, the babysitter, the bus driver, the manager, or the factory worker? The fact that our work is "salable," as DeKoster puts it, is one important piece of evidence that what we are doing is actually of use to someone, enough use, in fact, for them to compensate us for it.

This perspective on work and service as understood in the parable of the sheep and the goats also provides us with other norms for judging whether our work is true service or not. One measure, as we have said, is whether someone finds our work to be valuable enough to pay us for doing it. But given the corruption of human nature, people will pay us to do all kinds of things that are not good for them (or for us). So beyond mere "salability" of our work, we must judge it by its orientation and effects. Does our work actually help others? Is it for their good that this work is done? Does it foster independence or dependence? Does it humanize or dehumanize? Does it feed addiction or satisfy legitimate appetite? By necessity, then, things that are inherently harmful, such as the distribution of illegal drugs, pornography, or abortion, are ruled out of bounds. But there are innumerable other ways that otherwise valid service or work can be undermined by human sinfulness.

Even so, whether it is giving someone something to eat or drink, something to wear or somewhere to live, or any of the other myriad ways we serve one another in daily life, all legitimate forms of serving others, whether paid in wages or not, are valid ways to serve Christ. The key to this perspective, writes DeKoster, is to understand that our daily work is "the form in which we make ourselves useful to others, and thus to God."

Another famous story from the Bible is that of "The Prodigal Son," a tale that has resonated with parents across times and cultures. Like the parable of the sheep and the goats, the story illustrates some basic truths about work and stewardship that are often underappreciated. The basic plot of the story is straightforward: a rebellious youth sets off from home in search of worldly pleasures, and having wasted his father's money and reputation, eventually returns home in humility to a joyful welcome. Biblical commentators usually note that the parable appears in connection with two other stories in Luke 15, those of "The Lost Coin" and "The Lost Sheep."

The similarities in the stories are, in fact, quite striking, and as biblical scholars note, well worth attending to. But amid the important similarities of the stories, there are also significant differences that provide some important insights into the biblical vision of human stewardship, particularly our interaction with the material world, animal life, and other people.

So the stories should be read together, and understood as Jesus' answers to the complaint of the Pharisees that he "welcomes sinners and eats with them" (Luke 15:2). In each story the one who has lost something is understood as filling the role of God, who has "lost" something dear to him. The sheep, the coin, and the son represent God's people who have gone astray. These lost ones are the "sinners" whom Jesus welcomes. While those who lose things in these stories primarily represent God, the actions of these characters also shed light on how human beings are to conduct themselves as God's image-bearers.

In one story (which actually is the second parable of the three), Jesus describes a case in which a woman loses one of her ten silver coins. She takes quick action, lighting a lamp, sweeping the house and searching "carefully until she finds it" (Luke 15:8). In this case, that which is lost is a "coin," a Greek *drachma* worth about one day's wages. The woman is the one who "loses" the coin. There is no sense of agency imparted to the coin in this story; the coin, as a material object, is impersonal and inanimate. The coin is passive, receiving the action of the story. The woman *loses* the coin, *lights* a lamp, *sweeps* the house, *searches* carefully and finally *finds* the coin; the coin is passive; it is merely lost and found.

In another story (which Jesus tells first), a shepherd "has a hundred sheep and loses one of them" (Luke 15:4). Again we see the focus of the action on the shepherd (whom Jesus identifies directly with his listeners: "Suppose one of you has a hundred sheep . . ."). The sheep presumably wandered off, but it is after all only an animal, and so is impersonal. Even though animals are to be understood as active in some sense, it is an impersonal sense of agency, so that here again the action is ultimately attributed to the shepherd. The shepherd *loses* one of the sheep, *leaves* the ninety-nine, *goes after* the lost sheep, *finds* it, and *puts* it on his shoulders and *goes* home.

But the final story, that of the Prodigal Son (or even better to draw the connection with the other stories, "The Lost Son"), is much more complex than the other two. There are more characters. The action is dispersed, in the sense that agency is not simply attributed to the one who has lost something. In fact, in contrast to the other two stories, the one who drives the action in the story is the son rather than the father. Whereas the woman loses the coin and the shepherd loses the sheep, in this final story the son "got together all he had, set off for a distant country and there squandered his wealth in wild living" (Luke 15:13). To be sure, the son is lost to the father. But the focus here is on the personal agency of the son rather than that of the father.

We can imagine what this would have been like for the father. We can assume that he raised his son up in the fear of the Lord, that he trained his child "in the way he should go," with the hope that "when he is old he will not turn from it" (Prov 22:6). But when his son demands his inheritance and leaves home, the father seems to do nothing. He neither refuses to give his son what he asks nor prevents him from leaving. The text does not say so explicitly, but we can again presume that while the son is out in the world living wildly, the father is at home, attending to his household, and praying diligently for the son to return. We know the father has this hope because once the son decides to return home, "while he was still a long way off, his father saw him and was filled with compassion for him" (Luke 15:20). Once the son takes the initiative (*getting up* and *going to* his father), the father finally has some sense of agency: he *runs* to the son, *embraces* him, *kisses* him, and *orders* a celebration.

The contrast between the story of the Lost Son and the parables of the Lost Sheep and Lost Coin are striking on this level. In the case of human relationship to material objects, like coins, and impersonal agents, like animals, the stories account the moral agency completely to the human actors in the story. The woman and the shepherd *lose* their possessions and *work* diligently to find them again. But when the story involves human interrelations, there is an emphasis on the moral agency of every person in the story (including the elder son, whose role is often overlooked). The father definitely loses his son, but his diligence in finding him again is limited to means other than actively working to find him; he must instead diligently pray and watch.

Reading these three stories together teaches us many things about the nature of God's love for us, such that when we were lost, "While we were still sinners, Christ died for us" (Rom 5:8). But the stories also provide models for how we should relate to the different aspects of God's created order, from the material, to the animal, to the human. In each kind of relationship, humans have a definite role to play. In some cases we are called to work actively to achieve God's purposes in the world. In other cases, out of respect for human freedom and individual sovereignty, we have to engage in active searching for the lost things of this world by less direct means, such as prayer.

In a short essay on the relationship between work and prayer, C. S. Lewis points to the remarkable continuity between the two, and how prayer is in its own way an appropriate form of active searching. As Lewis writes of work and prayer, God "gave us small creatures the dignity of being able to contribute to the course of events in two different ways." With respect to primarily material reality, like coins and sheep, we can work, or "do things to it; that is why we can wash our own hands and feed or murder our fellow creatures." But with respect to spiritual realities, we exercise a different kind of creaturely causality, that of prayer, whose results are not always as predictable as in the physical order: "This is not because prayer is a weaker kind of causality, but because it is a stronger kind. When it 'works' at all it works unlimited by space and time."[6]

In these parables of the lost coin, sheep, and son, we see modeled in broad strokes the array of human causality, from work to prayer. These are, in fact, the two basic ways that God has instituted to accomplish his purposes in the world through human beings. In these stories, we find that the work and prayer of finding the lost things of the world are foundational for what it means to be a steward, an image-bearer, of God.

Clint Eastwood made headlines with his now infamous performance with an empty chair at the Republican National Convention in Tampa, and Scarlett Johansson delivered an impassioned plea to the Democratic proceedings in Charlotte. But it was a star of the small screen that provided the most substantive entertainment-industry contribution during the 2012 election season. Mike Rowe, the host of *Dirty Jobs* and narrator of *The Deadliest Catch* from The Discovery Channel, penned an open letter to the Mitt Romney campaign, highlighting what he calls a generational "change in the way Americans viewed hard work and skilled labor."

His work on *Dirty Jobs*, where he is a "perpetual apprentice," has allowed Rowe to see from the front lines of the workplace our national attitudes towards work. "Pig farmers, electricians, plumbers, bridge painters, jam makers, blacksmiths, brewers, coal miners, carpenters, crab fisherman, oil drillers . . . they all tell me the same thing over and over, again and again," he says. "Our country has become emotionally disconnected from an essential part of our workforce. We are no longer impressed with

6. C. S. Lewis, "Work and Prayer," in *God in the Dock* (Grand Rapids: Eerdmans, 1970), 106–7.

cheap electricity, paved roads, and indoor plumbing. We take our infrastructure for granted, and the people who build it."[7]

In a similar letter addressed to President Obama in 2008, Rowe wrote that "the ranks of welders, carpenters, pipe fitters, and plumbers have been declining for years, and now, we face the bizarre reality of rising unemployment, *and* a shortage of skilled labor." This is the so-called "skills gap," where jobs that require certain abilities or know-how remain unfilled even in the face of a vast number of otherwise available workers.

This gap points to the larger crisis we face in America, a cultural attitude toward work that Rowe has elsewhere called "dysfunctional." This shift is reflected in the attitudes toward work of younger people, often engendered by an educational system that promotes a singular vision of higher education at the expense of vocational and technical training: "I always thought there [was] something ill-fated about the promise of three million 'shovel ready jobs' made to a society that no longer encourages people to pick up a shovel," says Rowe.

There are a number of causes of this complex phenomenon, but at least part of the problem of work has to do with what we think work actually *is*. If all work ends up being is a paycheck, a necessary evil, a drudgery that only is worthwhile insofar as it allows us to find meaning elsewhere, then it becomes easy to see why our attitudes towards manual labor and hard work suffer.

What we need to recover, and Mike Rowe's warnings attest to this, is a view of work that celebrates it as not merely a necessary evil but rather an indispensible good. Work is, in fact, the basic form of stewardship that God has provided for human beings to serve one another and cultivate the created order. This isn't some easy task that might be checked off a list and dispensed with, but is rather a deeply meaningful responsibility laid upon each and every human person. As Gerard Berghoef and Lester DeKoster observe, "*The forms of work are countless*, but the typical one is *work with the hands*. The Bible has reference to the sower, to the making of tents and of things out of clay, to tilling the fields and tending the vine. Hand work makes visible the plan in the mind, just as the deed makes visible the love in the heart."[8]

7. Mike Rowe, "The First Four Years Are The Hardest . . ." *mikeroweWORKS.com*, September 2012. Available at: http://www.mikeroweworks.com/2012/09/the-first-four-years-are-the-hardest/.

8. Gerard Berghoef and Lester DeKoster, *Faithful in All God's House: Stewardship and the Christian Life* (Grand Rapids: Christian's Library Press, 2013), 11–12.

And indeed, the picture of work that we have here is not just a simple dichotomy between manual labor that ought to be disdained and mental labor that ought to be celebrated. All work has a spiritual dimension because the human person who works in whatever capacity does so as an image-bearer of God. "While the classic Greek mind tended to scorn work with the hands," write Berghoef and DeKoster, "the Bible suggests that something about it structures the soul." If we derogate work with the hands, manual and skilled labor, in this way, we separate what God has put together and create a culture that disdains the hard and often dirty work of cultivating the world in service of others. The challenge that faces the church and society more broadly then is to appreciate the spiritual meaningfulness of all kinds of work, to celebrate it, and to exhort us to persevere in our labors amidst the unavoidable troubles that plague work in this fallen world.

The Bible tells us that we reap what we sow, individually as well as corporately. If we sow a culture that disdains work, then we will reap a dysfunctional society that pits class against class, labor versus management, rich against poor, strong against weak. But if we sow a culture that celebrates all kinds of work as inherently valuable, as valid and praiseworthy ways of serving others and thereby serving God, we will reap a society that promotes flourishing in its deepest and most meaningful sense.

Besides the perennially sinful temptations to shrug off hard work, and particularly to avoid the "toil" with which we are cursed after the Fall into sin, people have often rationalized a worldview that tends to devalue the physical, the material, the *dirty*, and to idealize the spiritual. This tendency has worked itself out in the Christian tradition in various ways, from heresies like Gnosticism or Manichaeism, to more common phenomena like clericalism or secularism.

It was against a radical separation of the material and the spiritual that Cornelius Plantinga once wrote that "the things of the mind and spirit are no better, and are sometimes much worse, than the things of the body." He continues by asserting that a consequence of this perspective is that "it is not more Christian to play chess than to play hockey. It is not more Christian to become a minister than to become a muck farmer."[9]

Understood as a reaction to a kind of radical separation between material and spiritual realities, and the overvaluation of the latter, this kind of claim indeed has some merit. But it also is a dangerous claim, in

9. Cornelius Plantinga Jr., *Engaging God's World: A Christian Vision of Faith, Learning, and Living* (Grand Rapids: Eerdmans, 2002), 37.

that it can result in a worldview that simply conflates (or merely equates) the material and the spiritual.

The fact is, as Mike Rowe's concerns illustrate, we need to properly value the material, the physical, the work that preserves our natural life. But this doesn't mean that we need to buy in to some radically egalitarian view of all work as equal in every way. This certainly isn't the Reformational view. The Reformation, with doctrines like the priesthood of all believers and vocation, did make all legitimate callings equally dignified before God. There is no longer a hierarchical and qualitative split between offices as such. But there remained a kind of hierarchy of good, a proper way of coming to grips with the complex world and the complicated workings of special and common grace.

Consider, for instance, the reformer Martin Bucer, who labored in Strasbourg for many years and was influenced heavily by Luther and in turn exercised great influence on Calvin and the reformation in England. As church historian David Hopper puts it, "Vocation was, for Bucer, the necessary concomitant of a restored order of creation, to wit, a disciplined service and love of the neighbor—and all creatures—in this life, one freed, as in Luther, from concern for merit, but one integrated also into ongoing judgments about service to the well-being of the commonwealth."[10] This perspective necessitated some discrimination about better and worse ways of serving one another.

Bucer in fact held to a view of spiritual primacy, focused on the calling to ordained ministry, as the most significant way in which God's special, redemptive grace was communicated in human work. In the second position Bucer placed the civil magistracy, in part because of its duty and concerns for the care of religion, as well as for its responsibilities to maintain public order. But in the third position, behind soulcraft and statecraft, so to speak, Bucer placed farmers and others who work for the material well-being of their neighbors.

So, indeed, we can serve each other and thereby serve God either in the ordained ministry of the Word and Sacrament, or in muck farming, or in myriad other callings. But we must also affirm the dignity of all human beings as manifested in legitimate work without conflating the qualitative differences between means and ministries of special and common grace.

10. David Hopper, *Divine Transcendence and the Culture of Change* (Grand Rapids: Eerdmans, 2010), 133.

The reality that ministry as service of some sort is a lifelong calling rings harsh in modern ears accustomed to a model of retirement and relaxation at the achievement of a certain age. But in truth good work never ends. In an undiluted if unwelcome acknowledgment of new economic realities, the CEO of insurance giant AIG spoke candidly when he admitted that retirement ages in developed nations would need to be raised. "Retirement ages will have to move to 70, 80 years old," said Robert Benmosche. "That would make pensions, medical services more affordable. They will keep people working longer and will take that burden off of the youth."[11] While Benmosche's conclusions are firmly based in the calculus involving increases in life expectancies and declining birthrates, they also provide a timely occasion for reexamining popular attitudes toward work and retirement. Where work is seen merely as a necessary evil, it is natural to see retirement as a well-deserved escape from a lifetime of drudgery and toil. The biblical view of work, however, presents a somewhat different picture that shows us that the good work of service to others ought never end as long as we live.

Two examples from West Michigan help to illustrate the fact that God designed human beings to be blessings to others through their work and service. John Izenbaard of Kalamazoo, Michigan, turned 90 years old in April 2012, and under any proposed system would have long been eligible for retirement benefits. But Mr. Izenbaard has been working for 74 years at Hoekstra's True Value Hardware and has the same goal today as when he started there in 1936: "to be a 'blessing' for customers." When asked about the possibility of retirement, Izenbaard responded, "I look forward to coming to work. I really enjoy it."[12] Izenbaard's work infuses his life with meaning, as he uses his knowledge, experience, and skills to serve his neighbors.

Fred Carl Hamilton of Wyoming, Michigan, is a comparatively youthful 71 years old, but when faced with a disappearing retirement fund, he "realized he would have to get a job if he wanted to keep his house." Hamilton took an unconventional approach. Rather than looking for a local retail job, he decided to innovate. "I was walking around my

11. Boris Cerni and Zachary Tracer, "AIG Chief Sees Retirement Age as High as 80 After Crisis," *Bloomberg*, June 4, 2012. Available at: http://www.bloomberg.com/news/2012-16-03/aig-chief-sees-retirement-age-as-high-as-80-after-crisis.html.

12. Yvonne Zipp, "Now 90, the face of Kalamazoo hardware store has no plans to retire," *MLive.com*, May 15, 2012. Available at: http://www.mlive.com/business/west-michigan/index.ssf/2012/05/now_90_the_face_of_kalamazoo_h.html.

house thinking, 'There's got to be something I can create,'" said Hamilton. Experimenting over the course of three years, Hamilton created the Iron Bite, a tool for weight lifting equipment that secures weights to the bar by using "a spring-loaded push rod to let weight lifters gently pinch rings together and easily slide the device on and off the bar." Reflecting on the loss of retirement funds that prompted him to pursue a second career as an inventor, Hamilton says, "It's not all bad, because I always had a good job, and now I realize how people are struggling out there. And I can put people to work now."[13]

While these two stories show that work arises out of a range of possible motivations, from Izenbaard's intention to be a blessing in his work to Hamilton's desire not to take on a retail job like Izenbaard's, they both show that the divine institution of work orients us towards activities that serve others. Whether out of selfless altruism or simply the human instinct to be creative, work places us in a position to productively bless others with tangible goods and services.

Recognition of this fact about work challenges the standard conception of retirement as a time to focus on self-gratification after a lifetime of unfulfilling and meaningless toil. But it also casts doubt on a model that sees what a person does in their retirement years as finally achieving significance. The bestselling author Lloyd Reeb describes a halftime transition in life as moving "from success to significance."[14] Understood rightly, this kind of perspective can be helpful in reorienting our priorities toward service of others. Not all jobs are good jobs, and not all work is good work. If we are unable to see how our work serves other people, or how it might be anything but grinding and alienating, then an emphasis on significance can occasion a new outlook, a change in careers, or a move to different kinds of work, whether waged or not. But understood wrongly, this formula can reinforce the idea that work itself, even if successful in worldly terms, is of little or no importance. John Izenbaard would no doubt take some umbrage at such a suggestion.

In his book on the subject of work from a Christian perspective, Lester DeKoster goes so far as to call work "the meaning of your life." One of DeKoster's most powerful insights is that we don't need to look

13. Sheila McGrath, "Loss of retirement nest egg turns Wyoming man into inventor," *MLive.com*, May 25, 2012. Available at: http://www.mlive.com/byron-center/index.ssf/2012/05/loss_of_retirement_nest_egg_tu.html.

14. Lloyd Reeb, *From Success to Significance: When the Pursuit of Success Isn't Enough* (Grand Rapids: Zondervan, 2004).

beyond our daily work for significance in serving God and others: "It *is* your daily work, whatever your job, that does give meaning to your life, not because you will now decide to put meaning there but because God has already done so."[15] God has given us the order of work as the primary way in which we serve others, and thereby serve him.

Take a look at John Izenbaard and Fred Carl Hamilton. That's a vision of good work that never ends.

In the wake of the domestic credit crisis in America, the subsequent global economic downturn, and the various attempts to diagnose and correct the problems with today's business culture, politicians and pundits alike have been casting about for villains. Perhaps no one has filled that public role more prominently than the high-profile investment bank, Goldman Sachs. As John Arlidge of the UK newspaper *The Times* wrote, "Goldman's reputation is suddenly as toxic as the credit default swaps and other inexplicably exotic financial instruments it used to buy with glee."[16]

The firm was the target of a Saturday Night Live feature that included the advice to remove the words "gold" and "sack" from its name to improve a tarnished corporate image. Matthew Bishop, U.S. business editor at *The Economist* and co-author of *The Road from Ruin: How to Revive Capitalism and Put America Back on Top*, has said that "Goldman Sachs is a great firm—as good as you get on Wall Street and that's the problem." Things turned even worse for Goldman Sachs when the firm's leaders attempted to portray the bank's practices in a moral, even religious, light. In Arlidge's piece, Goldman CEO Lloyd Blankfein claimed that in his role at the bank he was doing "God's work."

At a panel discussion on morality and economics hosted at London's St. John's Cathedral, Lord Brian Griffiths, a Goldman Sachs advisor and vice chairman, reportedly said, "The injunction of Jesus to love others as ourselves is an endorsement of self-interest." This statement caused outcry not only among progressives, for whom Goldman Sachs is a favorite foil, but also from religious adherents across the political spectrum. Joseph Bottum, then-editor at *First Things*, expressed his skepticism of Griffiths' statement, observing (correctly) that Griffiths is "just not going

15. DeKoster, *Work*, xiv.

16. John Arlidge, "I'm doing 'God's work'. Meet Mr Goldman Sachs," *Sunday Times*, November 8, 2009.

to get much traction for the idea when he uses this phrasing."[17] In its January 2010 print issue, *Christianity Today* included Griffith's quote in its "Quotation Marks" sidebar.[18] *Res ipsa loquitur*: what we have here by representatives of Goldman Sachs is a craven attempt to get theological cover for very base human greed.

But a closer, more charitable look at Griffiths' comments reveals some things that casual dismissal does not. First, to Bottum's point regarding the ineffectiveness of Griffith's phrasing, it bears noting that the coverage of the panel discussion seems to have inaccurately reported Griffith's statement. According to the transcripts, Griffiths actually said not that Jesus' command was an "endorsement" of self-interest, but rather that it was an acknowledgment of self-interest as a motivating factor in human behavior.[19] Said Griffiths, "I think that the injunction of Jesus to love our neighbours as ourselves is *a recognition* of self-interest" (emphasis added). This is a somewhat different claim than the one attributed to him in various news reports.

Second, the proximate context of Griffiths' remark is a distinction he was making between self-interest (a broader category) and selfishness (a narrower category). Indeed, Griffiths was trying to communicate this distinction in dialogue with comments from another panelist, Adair Turner, Chair of Britain's Financial Services Authority, who introduced Adam Smith into the discussion. Griffiths says he was trying to "be just a little less academic," and notes that Smith's point "is that self-interested actions, they may sometimes be selfish, produce good results but I don't think of self-interest as something bad."

The theological background to Griffiths' claim is the broad Augustinian understanding of rightly ordered loves, the so-called *ordo amoris*. We are to love ourselves; self-love is recognized, acknowledged, and even endorsed, when understood correctly. But this self-love must be rightly ordered relative to other loves, the highest of which is God. From this perspective, Jesus' injunction to "love your neighbor as yourself" links

17. Joseph Bottum, "Endorsement of Self-Interest?" *First Thoughts*, November 6, 2009. Available at: http://www.firstthings.com/blogs/firstthoughts/2009/11/06/endorsement-of-self-interest/.

18. "Quotation Marks," *Christianity Today*, January 2010. Available at: http://www.christianitytoday.com/ct/2010/january/15.11.html.

19. Panel Discussion, "Regulation, Freedom and Human Welfare," St. Paul's Institute, October 20, 2009. Available at: http://www.stpauls.co.uk/documents/st%20paul's%20institute/regulation%20freedom%20and%20human%20welfare%20transcript.pdf.

the right level of love for ourselves with the level of love for other people. We are, all of us, created in God's image and bear equal dignity, and we therefore have equal claims to be loved. Self-love, self-regard, and self-interest are to be *ordinate*, rightly ordered relative to other loves, regards, and interests.

At this level, Griffiths' exegesis is nothing novel, and only the inaccurate citation of Jesus' instruction as an "endorsement" rather than a "recognition" makes it appear controversial. As C. S. Lewis writes, reflecting especially on the Gospels, "If there lurks in most modern minds the notion that to desire our own good and earnestly to hope for the enjoyment of it is a bad thing, I submit that this notion has crept in from Kant and the Stoics and is no part of the Christian faith."[20]

But perhaps more importantly, the attention paid to these passing remarks by Griffiths misses his larger point, which he spent much more time discussing at the event. This larger point could be characterized thusly: "To me as a Christian, I think that we should be committed not only to, as I said, laying the basis for prosperity; but also being seen to serve our society in all sorts of ways, and I think the hallmark of the Christian lifestyle is generosity." We have here an emphasis on giving and charity rather than selfishness and self-seeking.

The picture we get from looking at the larger context of the panel discussion and Griffiths' comments is not of a greedy banker seeking unwarranted justification in the Scriptures, but of a serious and committed Christian, attempting to wend his way through the difficult trials of a life called to discipleship. In his final thoughts to the audience, Griffiths says, "I think we all have to ask ourselves—in whatever institution we work—what is your moral compass and what is my moral compass? There will always come a time when you and I will have to stand up and be counted, and sometimes that is very difficult, can be very embarrassing and can be very painful—but I think that is what we have to do, and this evening has confirmed for me the need to examine my own moral compass more and more."

This is another way of saying that we need to learn more and more to properly relate love of ourselves and our interests to that of our fellow human beings, and subordinate all of these loves to God himself. I can think of no better way to summarize the life of Christian discipleship.

20. C. S. Lewis, "The Weight of Glory," in *The Weight of Glory and Other Addresses* (New York: Touchstone, 1996), 25–26.

But indeed, one of the complaints often rendered against the market economy is that it encourages selfish behavior. This picture of the marketplace is that of a kind of war of all against all, with each participant out only to maximize his or her own individual benefit. As American social gospel advocate Walter Rauschenbusch contended in his *Christianizing the Social Order*, "The trader has always been the outstanding case of the man who plays his own hand and sacrifices social solidarity for private gain." This characteristic, claimed Rauschenbusch, has been exaggerated in the modern era, such that "the trading class has become the ruling class, and consequently the selfishness of trade has been exalted to the dignity of an ethical principle. Every man is taught to seek his own advantage, and then we wonder that there is so little public spirit."[21]

There are a number of reasons that this simplistic depiction of the motivation and practice of market participants is problematic. The features of the market economy actually require those who would selfishly seek their own narrow interests to orient their activity to the good of others. As the economist Walter Williams puts it succinctly, "In a free market, you get more for yourself by serving your fellow man. You don't have to care about him, just serve him."[22] Even Adam Smith, who codified the recognition of this truth into economic theory, realized that benevolence was morally superior to selfishness, but he also saw that the sharp edges of selfishness are typically blunted through market interactions. The incentives that underlie the possibility of mutually beneficial exchange also tend to align interests rather than simply to bring them into conflict.

But beyond the level of structural incentive, it is also the case that market actors are typically oriented towards the good of others in another, even more fundamental way. If you were to inquire of people why they get out of bed to go to work every day, high up on the list of answers would be something like this: "To provide for my family." In this way the economic sphere is not a realm of disconnected individuals whose hearts are curved in upon their own individual interests. Instead, the market is a meeting place of those who come to serve others through work in order that they might provide for the good of those to whom they are intimately bound.

In a very real sense, then, when we act in the marketplace we are not acting as abstracted individuals, but rather as human persons embedded

21. Walter Rauschenbusch, *Christianizing the Social Order* (New York: Macmillan, 1914), 173.

22. See John Stossel, *Give Me a Break* (New York: HarperCollins, 2009), 244.

in a deep social and moral reality. We act in our callings as representatives of the interests of others. The father sacrifices a day in which he otherwise might seek his own limited good to head to the assembly line so that he might bring home a paycheck to provide for his family: to put a roof over their heads, food on the table, and clothes on their backs. A mother takes an extra shift at the hospital so that she might be able to get something special for her child this Christmas. These kinds of sacrifices are so common and so familiar that we often forget just how remarkable they are. Families all over the world make significant sacrifices every day in the time and effort that parents (and sometimes children) expend in the marketplace.

This more complex and realistic vision of economic life is what inspired the Dutch theologian Herman Bavinck when he wrote that the "moral calling of work does not hover above us in the air and is no abstract theory, but lies embedded in life itself, in the family. Through the family God motivates us to work, inspiring, encouraging, and empowering us to work. Through this labor he equips us to survive not for the sake of satisfying our lusts but for the sake of providing for our family before God and with honor, and also to extend the hand of Christian compassion to the poor."[23]

It is morally significant, then, how we define our interests and where we place our happiness. As the economist Paul Heyne noted, "While self-love or self-interest is certainly capable of producing selfish behavior, it need not do so." Instead, said Heyne, "self-interest is not the same as selfishness, and the narrow pursuit of private purposes has no necessary connection with greed, materialism, or a lack of concern for others."[24] We might, in this way, choose to align our economic interests with those of our families, our churches, and those who are materially impoverished. The marketplace is in reality, rather than in abstract theory, a place where this sacrificial love of neighbor is realized, a love which is in no way inconsistent with self-interest, rightly understood.

A popular response to the perception of out-of-control selfishness among financial elites became the "Occupy" movement across the globe. Indeed, the widespread Occupy Wall Street movement and its offshoots have posed a difficult question to churches and religious leaders about the proper way to critically engage broader cultural movements. All too

23. Herman Bavinck, *The Christian Family* (Grand Rapids: Christian's Library Press, 2012), 129.

24. Paul Heyne, *"Are Economists Basically Immoral?" and Other Essays on Economics, Ethics, and Religion* (Indianapolis: Liberty Fund, 2008), 60, 31.

often, church leaders offer open arms to such trends, which is how we find anachronistic assertions that such heroes of the Christian tradition as John Calvin, St. Francis, and John Wesley would in fact be active supporters of the Occupy movement. In other cases, as in London's St. Paul's Cathedral and New York's United Methodist Church of St. Paul and St. Andrew, churches have had to respond in some way as protestors show up on their doorsteps. New York's Union Theological Seminary is "in full solidarity with the protestors," according to seminary president Serene Jones.[25] Around the same time Union welcomed back Cornel West to its faculty, "to a place where his scholarly commitments and his activism don't live in two different worlds," said Jones.[26]

It is true of course that the Christian gospel has inherently social implications, and that in some cases direct political action and social activism are entailed, at least for individual Christians working out of their own convictions, if not always for the institutional church itself. It makes sense, then, that the consciences of some Christians are deeply pricked by the message emanating from the Occupy movement and have wholeheartedly thrown their lot in with the cause of the so-called "99 percent." This is in part why religious activists like Jim Wallis and Shane Claiborne have positively engaged the Occupy movement.

But involvement in and support of the Occupy protests do not represent a normative way for Christians of all convictions to engage the world. We are not all called to identify ourselves with the rebelliousness of the perpetually outraged. In identifying the institutions of the church with these protest movements ecclesial leaders risk overlooking the most important occupiers: those Christians who occupy the pews every Sunday morning and pursue various occupations throughout the week. The range of cultural engagement by Christians is therefore coextensive with the panoply of morally legitimate activities in the world. This has been true from the church's earliest beginnings. As the early apologist Tertullian observed with respect to the Christian presence amidst the pagan Roman Empire, "We sojourn with you in the world, abjuring neither forum, nor shambles, nor bath, nor booth, nor workshop, nor inn, nor

25. Serene Jones, "Protest 101: What Happens When a Seminary Is Occupied?" *Huffington Post*, November 16, 2011. Available at: http://www.huffingtonpost.com/serene-jones/occupy-seminary-protest-chaplains_b_1097972.html.

26. Laurie Goodstein, "Cornel West to Take a Job in New York," *New York Times*, November 16, 2011. Available at: http://www.nytimes.com/2011/11/17/nyregion/cornel-west-returning-to-union-theological-seminary.html?_r=0.

weekly market, nor any other places of commerce. We sail with you, and fight with you, and till the ground with you; and in like manner we unite with you in your traffickings—even in the various arts we make public property of our works for your benefit."[27]

Abraham Kuyper gave voice to the impetus for this Christian diaspora into the varied vocations of life with his articulation of the consequences of God's sovereignty. "Christ's church on earth and God's child cannot simply retreat from this life," he wrote. "If the believer's God is at work in this world, then in this world the believer's hand must take hold of the plow, and the name of the Lord must be glorified in that activity as well."[28] What this means is that there are Christians who already occupy Wall Street every day in their occupations as businessmen and women, bankers and investors, traders and executives, secretaries and receptionists, janitors and security guards. The church's responsibility to these "occupiers" is to provide them with the moral and spiritual formation necessary to be faithful followers of Christ every day in their productive service to others.

A group of business and ministry leaders in the UK articulated this in a recent letter to *The Times* of London, in which they observed, "Many Christians today work within mainstream business, attempting to be 'salt and light'. Others run organizations . . . that are committed to using business and finance to bring social benefits, raise living standards and create jobs." Through these kinds of efforts such business leaders "are part of the broader effort of the Church to reform capitalism by going to the root of the problem: the human heart."[29]

Christians therefore must occupy the world in their occupations, doing all their work as Christians, whatever it is, "whether in word or deed," as the Apostle Paul instructs, "in the name of the Lord Jesus, giving thanks to God the Father through him" (Col 3:17). In this way the church finds its most significant and transformative cultural engagement through its affirmation of the daily work of Christians who already occupy Wall Street (and all streets).

27. Tertullian, *Apology*, in *Ante-Nicene Fathers*, vol. 3 (Grand Rapids: Eerdmans, 1980), ch. XLII.

28. Abraham Kuyper, Foreword to *De Gemeene Gratie*, vol. 1 (Amsterdam: Höveker & Wormser, 1902). Translated by Nelson D. Kloosterman.

29. Letter to the editor, *The Times*, November 8, 2011. Available at: http://www.fivetalents.org.uk/church-and-finance-uncomfortable-companions.

CULTURE AND STEWARDSHIP

The responsibility of stewardship is intimately linked to the Cultural Mandate of Genesis 1, the duty to cultivate the earth. What isn't often recognized is the diverging character of the various theological interpretations of stewardship. These divergences are summed by two major views on the definition of stewardship, characterized respectively by the words "preservation" and "production." As illustrated below, the preservationist position, while biblically based, does not do justice to the fullness of scriptural witness.

The first position, understood as the preservationist view of stewardship, is manifest in the Evangelical Environmental Network's *Evangelical Declaration on the Care of Creation*.[30] This view emphasizes the pristine state of creation before the fall into sin, and understands this "garden" to be the ideal toward which we are to bend our efforts. The failure of humankind lies principally in its inability to "both sustain creation's fruitfulness and preserve creation's powerful testimony to its Creator." The stewardly role of humankind can essentially be seen as maintenance of the created status quo. The dominant image of the earth in this view is that of "garden," a fruitful botanical paradise.

The second position is evident in the *Cornwall Declaration on Environmental Stewardship*.[31] This view emphasizes "productivity" and "proliferation." The "productivity" view of stewardship stresses the unity between the biblical mandate both to "be fruitful and increase in number" and to "rule over the fish of the sea and the birds of the air and over every living creature that moves on the ground" (Gen 1:28). The adherents to the Cornwall Declaration affirm human "potential, as bearers of God's image, to add to the earth's abundance," and recognize the identity of human beings as both "producers and stewards." If the preservationist view idealizes the "garden," we can characterize the productive view's dominant image of the created ideal as "city."

The parable of the talents contained in Matthew 25 helps illustrate the difference between these two positions. Jesus tells the story of a man who goes away on a trip, and leaves his servants in charge of varying amounts of wealth. While the owner is away, the first two men double the

30. Evangelical Environmental Network, *Evangelical Declaration on the Care of Creation*. Available at: http://www.creationcare.org/blank.php?id=39.

31. Available at: http://www.cornwallalliance.org/articles/read/the-cornwall-declaration-on-environmental-stewardship/.

money entrusted to them through productive activity, as each "put his money to work." The third servant, however, buries the money, so that it could be preserved and saved to be given back to the master upon his return. When the master returns, he praises the productive servants, but rebukes the servant who merely maintained his master's wealth, saying, "You wicked, lazy servant! . . . You should have put my money on deposit with the bankers, so that when I returned I would have received it back with interest" (Matt 25:26–27). Jesus uses this parable in part to illustrate the moral imperative for human beings to be productive stewards with the gifts we are given. This applies to the mandate of the created world no less than to monetary wealth or spiritual gifts. As Jesus relates elsewhere, the basic principle of stewardship is, "from the one who has been entrusted with much, much more will be asked" (Luke 12:48).

Theologians have sometimes used the doctrine of *tertiary creation* or *sub-creation* to get at this reality. Primary creation is understood as God's creation of the world out of nothing. Secondary creation refers to God's forming of this material into various shapes and creatures, especially as described in Genesis 1. By contrast, tertiary creation points to the creative action of human beings, acting as image bearers of God and in the power of his Spirit, who bring out the created potentiality of the world into new forms, shapes, and technologies. Such things as art, houses, and airplanes fit into this category.

It is in the recognition of this mandate to be productive and creative stewards that the "productive" view of stewardship is preferable to the "preservation" view. Thus, the Cornwall Declaration "views human stewardship that unlocks the potential in creation for all the earth's inhabitants as good."

The preservationist view of stewardship often contains biblical truth as far as it goes, but it stops short of recognizing the full witness of Scripture. Instead, it offers a truncated and inadequate view of stewardship, which can lead to destructive policies. For instance, the preservationist view sees fallen humans primarily as destructive polluters, as menaces to the rest of creation. In this way, preservationists find that environmental degradations "are signs that we are pressing against the finite limits God has set for creation. With continued population growth, these degradations will become more severe." This line of reasoning can even lead into support for various forms of population control.

By contrast, the "productive" view of stewardship does not oppose the fruitfulness and multiplication of human beings (as present in Gen 1:28) with the interests of the rest of the created world. Only by embracing humankind's role as productive and creative stewards in all matters will we collectively hear the words of Jesus, "Well done, good and faithful servant! You have been faithful with a few things; I will put you in charge of many things. Come and share your master's happiness!" (Matt 25:21)

Let's consider what productive stewardship might look like in a particular example. At the conclusion of the 1985 hit *Back to the Future*, Michael J. Fox's character Marty McFly is shocked to learn that cars in the future don't run on gasoline. Instead, Doc Brown shoves trash from a nearby garbage can, including a banana peel, into the Mr. Fusion Home Energy Reactor, which powers the DeLorean time machine. And although cars won't be running on nuclear power by 2015, we should be shocked and disappointed if the future didn't realize the promise of alternative sources of energy.

Other feature films like *An Inconvenient Truth*, courtesy of former Vice President Al Gore, and the 2004 box-office hit *The Day After Tomorrow* have revolved around the topic of climate change. Indeed, global warming has been the occasion for policy debates in Washington and around the world, and the basis for a hotly contested international agreement, the Kyoto protocol. But what connects this scene from *Back to the Future* with these other movies? No, the answer isn't that all three are just science fiction. Instead, the shared focus is on renewable and clean sources of energy as alternatives to the burning of fossil fuels, including gasoline.

American evangelicals, long credited with having a powerful and vigorous voice in national politics, have weighed in on the issue. The Evangelical Climate Initiative (ECI), backed by such evangelical celebrities as Rick Warren and Jim Wallis, stated, "Climate change is happening and is being caused mainly by human activities, especially the burning of fossil fuels."[32] The declaration also included a call for the federal government to "pass and implement national legislation requiring sufficient economy-wide reductions in carbon dioxide."

That the ECI does not speak for all evangelicals became clear following the release of a letter disputing many of the ECI's conclusions, signed by another group of prominent evangelicals including Chuck Colson and James Dobson. Because of the missive, the National Association of

32. See Evangelical Climate Initiative, "Climate Change: An Evangelical Call to Action" in David P. Gushee, *The Future of Faith in American Politics: The Public Witness of the Evangelical Center* (Waco: Baylor University Press, 2008), 276. Available at: http://christiansandclimate.org/statement/.

Evangelicals (NAE), an umbrella group representing fifty-two denominations and over 30 million Christians, refrained from endorsing the ECI statement. Even so, the moral and spiritual authority that climate change politics has gained from the ECI is significant and noteworthy.

Many environmental activists, including the ECI, attribute global warming to human activity, most prominently to the burning of fossil fuels. But if filling our cars with gas and heating our homes with petroleum represent such a grave and tremendous threat, for Christians a fundamental and as yet ignored theological question emerges: Why did God create oil?

The answer is to be found in an examination of the role of fossil fuels and the explosion of wealth production in the industrial revolution. The advent of the internal combustion engine made transportation easier, cheaper, and more reliable, so that goods could be traded more efficiently and quickly across larger and larger areas. Today the long-haul trucking industry remains a critical component of the infrastructure for the distribution of goods throughout the continental US.

Fossil fuels were created by God as a natural resource for human beings to use wisely and to steward well in the culturing of the world, as mandated in Genesis 1:28. It would be much more difficult to "fill the earth and subdue it" if we didn't have cars and planes and ships to carry us about, and furnaces to warm our homes in intemperate climates. *An Inconvenient Truth* made famous the so-called "hockey stick" graph which depicted a sharp rise in temperature into the atmosphere over the last century. But there's another rather remarkable "hockey stick" chart that is far less well-known.

The lifeblood of our modern economy is based on fossil fuels. It would seem, then, that oil, natural gas, and other petroleum products exist to be used by human beings. But just like any other resource, these fuels are to be used responsibly. This is a basic insight provided by the Christian concept of stewardship.

On this view, fossil fuels would thus have the created purpose of providing relatively cheap and pervasive sources of energy. These limited and finite resources help raise the standard of living and economic situation of societies to the point where technological research is capable of finding even cheaper, more efficient, renewable, and cleaner sources of energy.

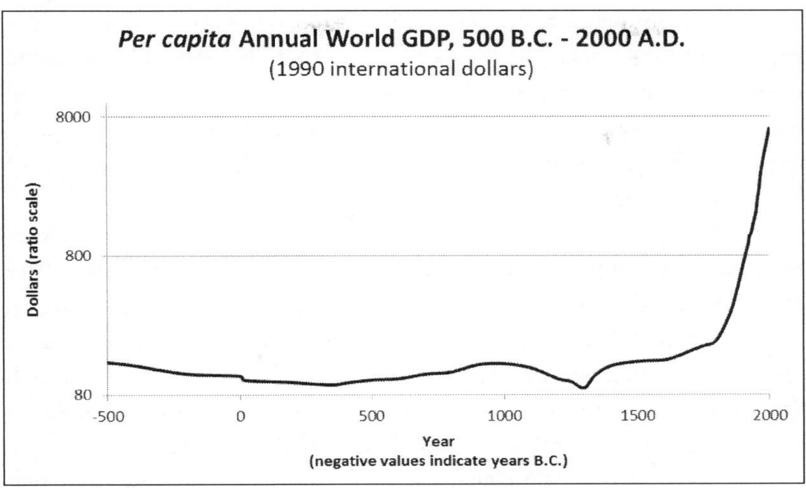

Source: Victor V. Claar, "The Urgency of Poverty and the Hope of Genuinely Fair Trade," *Journal of Markets & Morality* 16, no. 1 (Spring 2013). GDP figures taken from J. Bradford DeLong, "Estimates of World GDP, One Million B.C.—Present." http://delong.typepad.com/print/20061012_LRWGDP.pdf.

Simply put, oil, gasoline, and coal, are part of what has made it possible for economies to advance from agrarian to industrial systems. This change has already occurred throughout the industrialized West, but many other nations are only at the beginning stages of this transition. Howard W. French, a journalist for *The New York Times*, writes that China, which has about one-fifth of the world's population, in 2005 accounted "for about 12 percent of the world's energy demand, but its consumption is growing at more than four times the global rate."[33]

So although today the US is the world's largest consumer of fossil fuels, the transition to industrialized economies and the advent of a new "car culture" in places like China and India guarantee that global demand for cheap and accessible fuel will only increase in the future. If the purpose of petroleum fuels is to pave the way for their own obsolescence, it's becoming clearer day by day that this means the embrace of nuclear power.

But as America begins to enter a post-industrial, information and service-driven economy, the same spirit of alarmism that sounds the warnings about global warming has prevented a major alternative source

33. Howard W. French, "A City's Traffic Plans Are Snarled by China's Car Culture," *New York Times*, July 12, 2005. Available at: http://www.nytimes.com/2005/07/12/international/asia/12china.html.

of energy from being realized. In a 2005 editorial, Patrick Moore, a co-founder of Greenpeace in the 1970s, says that "by the mid-1980s, the environmental movement had abandoned science and logic in favor of emotion and sensationalism." He notes that "environmental activists," like Greenpeace and Friends of the Earth, "continue lobbying against clean nuclear energy."

Moore concludes that "nuclear energy is the only nongreenhouse gas-emitting power source that can effectively replace fossil fuels and satisfy global demand."[34] Despite the impression you might get from campaigns like the "What Would Jesus Drive?" initiative, sponsored by the Evangelical Environmental Network (EEN), a founding member group of the ECI, the number one source of fossil fuel consumption in the US is coal, not gasoline. Just how many coal-powered SUVs have you seen lately?

According to the US Department of Energy, coal provides over half of the electricity flowing into American homes, and as Moore writes, "More than 600 coal-fired electric plants in the United States produce 36 percent of U.S. emissions—or nearly 10 percent of global emissions—of CO2."[35] But even though coal represents such a significant source of energy for the US, it has not been fashionable among environmental activists to pursue the only currently feasible replacement source of energy, nuclear power.

One relatively overlooked aspect of President Obama's State of the Union address in January of 2010 was the promise of "building a new generation of safe, clean nuclear power plants in this country." In pursuit of this vision, the president announced that he was tripling to more than $54 billion the amount of guaranteed loan money made available by the government for the development of new nuclear plants. What's needed more than increased funds from the government, however, is the streamlined approval of license applications already pending at the Nuclear Regulatory Commission (NRC).

Addressing what's been called a licensing "bottleneck" and loosening up the nuclear power market in the United States needs to be the top priority for a federal government focused on addressing the paired challenges of economic development and environmental stewardship. Letting nuclear

34. Patrick Moore, "'Environmental movement has lost its way," *Miami Herald*, January 30, 2005.

35. Patrick Moore, "Going Nuclear," *Washington Post*, April 16, 2006. Available at: http://www.washingtonpost.com/wp-dyn/content/article/2006/04/14/AR2006041401209.html.

power compete on a level playing field, without either direct government subsidy or delay, would position the American economy for future success. Over the last decade the federal government has run up record-setting deficits, fighting wars in Afghanistan and Iraq and more recently pushing stimulus money to pull the American economy out of a crippling recession. This dire economic situation makes quick action to move toward this "new generation" of nuclear power vitally important. The promise of nuclear energy is a key way to balance the responsibility entrusted to us by God to be good stewards of our economic as well as natural resources.

Back in 2004 the Copenhagen Consensus examined what it considered the top 10 challenges and solutions facing the world, and it ranked all the climate change proposals as "bad projects," because of the economic devastation that would be wreaked by solutions like cap-and-trade, carbon taxes, and the Kyoto protocol. The basis for this judgment is the economic reality of "opportunity costs." The money spent on compliance with carbon reduction policies are consumed in functionally retrograde ways, reducing the economic progress that would be enjoyed in the future.[36]

Nobel laureate Vernon L. Smith, a professor of economics and law at George Mason University, writes, "Earlier generations have the responsibility of leaving subsequent generations a capital stock that has not been diminished by incurring premature abatement costs." Copenhagen Consensus participant Thomas C. Schelling, a professor at the University of Maryland, puts it this way, "Future generations will be much richer than current ones, and it thus makes no sense to make current generations 'pay' for the problems of future generations." Common to each of these proposals judged "bad" by the consensus, as well as to the major proposals pending in Congress, is that they pit economic development against the reduction of greenhouse gas emissions.

Not so with nuclear energy. Indeed, various congressional energy proposals aimed at reducing emissions through carbon taxes or cap-and-trade measures include the assumption that over the next twenty years nearly 100 new nuclear power plants will be built, each one representing a significant source of new jobs and long-term energy stability. The first project to receive funding under President Obama's loan promise was a pair of new nuclear reactors at a Southern Company plant in Burke, Georgia, which will produce enough power to run 550,000 homes.

36. Bjørn Lomborg, ed., *Global Crises, Global Solutions* (New York: Cambridge University Press, 2004).

Meanwhile these reactors are estimated to create about 3,000 onsite construction jobs and around 850 permanent operations jobs.

As the Cornwall Declaration on Environmental Stewardship observes, "A clean environment is a costly good." And fossil fuels have helped provide the economic capital to begin to pay the price of this costly good. The human stewardship of oil and other petroleum-based fuels entails a responsibility to use the economic opportunities they afford to find and integrate other renewable, sustainable, and cleaner sources of energy, especially represented by the promise of nuclear power, into our long-term supply.

As we've seen, one dominant biblical image of the productive vision of stewardship is the movement from garden to city. And this transition, paired with an economy wedded to fossil fuels, is perhaps on display in no sharper relief than in the case of Detroit, Michigan. The economic, political, and cultural challenges facing the city of Detroit are well-known, and have received international coverage in recent years. And while hope springs eternal, there are still signs that the city's culture of stifling bureaucracy and corruption will be difficult to reform. Nowhere is this simultaneous promise and peril of Detroit's future more clearly evident than in the countless urban gardens that have sprung up throughout the city.

These areas of growth, in the form of cooperatives, community programs, and individual plots, represent a significant avenue for the revitalization of the city. The benefits of urban farming are manifold. Otherwise unproductive vacant lots, which have been estimated to number close to 100,000, are put to an economically and socially positive use. Urban farmers learn skills and discipline necessary to have long-term economic success. At farmer's markets, you can see what amount to independent businesses creating small but significant economic opportunity. In an environment that often appears to offer little hope, and where the false allure of drugs and crime is pervasive, this is especially important for the city's youth.

In some cases urban gardens are born out of necessity, as struggling families look for ways to grow food cheaply and earn some extra money. It's not uncommon to hear of stories like that of Yvette King, who as a 17-year-old student participated in the East Warren Avenue Farmer's Market to make about $100 per weekend. And Cornelius Williams of Vandalia Gardens Urban Farm helped found the "G.R.O.W.

Collaborative," which assists those already engaged in urban farming to transform abandoned lots into productive farmland.[37]

In these kinds of efforts we see the spark of human creativity and responsibility shine through in the face of adversity. This creativity reflects in a human way the creativity of the divine. The biblical account of creation includes the blessing to humankind, "Be fruitful and increase in number; fill the earth and subdue it" (Gen 1:28). This blessing has been understood to refer to human cultural work in all kinds of areas, including the cultivation of the land and the raising of crops. We find God's specific injunction to Adam to reflect this aspect of cultivation quite clearly: "The LORD God took the man and put him in the Garden of Eden to work it and take care of it" (Gen 2:16). And as the Bible begins with human beings caring for a garden, it ends with restored humanity living in a city, the New Jerusalem (Rev 21). Indeed, the New Jerusalem unites garden and city: "Then the angel showed me the river of the water of life, as clear as crystal, flowing from the throne of God and of the Lamb down the middle of the great street of the city. On each side of the river stood the tree of life, bearing twelve crops of fruit, yielding its fruit every month. And the leaves of the tree are for the healing of the nations" (Rev 22:1–2).

This biblical dynamic, moving from garden to city, provides an image of the kind of work humankind is to be doing in this world. It is the story of every city and every town, and it is a story that is especially relevant for a place like Detroit that is trying to refashion itself. There are perils, of course, and perhaps there are none greater than the political culture of regulation, entitlement, and corruption that has marred the city for decades. The city government must not crush this nascent urban gardening movement through superfluous regulation and the instinctive reflex to government control. This has already happened in the case of Neighbors Building Brightmoor, which maintains gardens on city-owned lots. Reit Schumack, who heads up the group, says that new city regulations will, among other things, prevent him from organizing a youth group as he has done in the past to grow food and sell it at a farmer's market.[38] "It's a beautiful self-sustaining program where 15 kids

37. "Urban farming takes root in Detroit," *APM Marketplace*, October 8, 2009. Available at: http://www.marketplace.org/topics/business/urban-farming-takes-root-detroit.

38. Sarah Hulett, "Detroit gardeners frustrated by new rules for city lots," *Michigan Radio*, May 13, 2011. Available at: http://www.michiganradio.org/post/detroit-gardeners-frustrated-new-rules-city-lots.

are busy the entire growing season, make money, learn all kinds of skills, and really, I can't do this. This is forbidden, what I'm doing," Schumack said.

In his 1974 song "Funky President," James Brown, the Godfather of Soul, encouraged people "to get over before we go under" in the midst of economic recession. The song, with a subtitle as suitable today as it was then ("People It's Bad"), could serve as an anthem for the urban farmer in Detroit. Brown urges, "Let's get together and get some land, raise our food like the man." Urban farms, these little plots of liberty in the city, represent one important way forward for Detroit. If James Brown were the mayor, we know he would "change some things around here." Let us hope and pray that the city government in Detroit will follow his lead and make the regulatory and political environment one in which urban farms can flourish.

In the attempts to develop the latent possibilities of creation, the rapid advance of technological achievement increasingly places human beings in a tenuous moral position. On the one side, we have an obligation to be productive and innovative. On the other, we must respect the divinely-imposed limits, our creaturely finitude, and our propensity to twist good things to evil purposes. The public debate regarding genetically modified (GM) food, for instance, has for the most part been driven by practical considerations, but the phenomenon calls for greater moral reflection. For those on the side of GM food, the economic and social benefits far outweigh any possible negative consequences. In this vein, *Reason* magazine science correspondent Ronald Bailey points out, "With biotech corn, U.S. farmers have saved an estimated $200 million by avoiding extra cultivation and reducing insecticide spraying. U.S. cotton farmers have saved a similar amount and avoided spraying 2 million pounds of insecticides by switching to biotech varieties."[39]

On the other side is a group which believes the possible threats posed by genetic engineering far outweigh the projected benefits. Representative of this position are Martin Teitel and Kimberly Wilson, who write, "Genetic engineering is an unasked-for technology dependent on new and inadequately controlled techniques, and it is a technology based

39. Ronald Bailey, "Dr. Strangelunch," *Reason*, January 2001. Available at: http://reason.com/archives/2001/01/01/dr-strangelunch.

on the release of organisms into the environment whose aggressive but dimly understood reproduction threatens the entire ecosystem."[40]

The flip side of concern about the earth's climate and global sustainability is angst about population growth. Where these issues collide most prominently is in the question of food. Can the earth's food supply possibly keep pace with a global population estimated by some to top 8 billion by the year 2020 and 9 billion by 2030? A recent article in the journal *Science* examined the challenge of sustainably feeding a new generation of inhabitants. As the authors pose the problem:

> A threefold challenge now faces the world: Match the rapidly changing demand for food from a larger and more affluent population to its supply; do so in ways that are environmentally and socially sustainable; and ensure that the world's poorest people are no longer hungry. This challenge requires changes in the way food is produced, stored, processed, distributed, and accessed that are as radical as those that occurred during the 18th- and 19th-century Industrial and Agricultural Revolutions and the 20th-century Green Revolution. Increases in production will have an important part to play, but they will be constrained as never before by the finite resources provided by Earth's lands, oceans, and atmosphere.[41]

These are complex issues that defy simplistic analysis. But one aspect of the population and sustainability challenge that is nearly universally acknowledged is the need to increase crop yields on finite, and increasingly limited, arable land. And at the forefront of these efforts are companies dedicated to altering crops to accentuate desirable characteristics through genetic modification.

That's one reason why agricultural giant Monsanto was selected as *Forbes* magazine's company of the year in 2009. Robert Langreth and Matthew Herper write, "By marrying conventional breeding with genetic engineering, Monsanto aims to produce more food for less money on the same amount of land." According to Monsanto CEO Hugh Grant, these traditional methods "allow crop scientists to create hundreds of seed varieties tailored to different soils and weather. Monsanto's research budget is now split equally between genetic engineering and conventional

40. Martin Teitel and Kimberly Wilson, *Genetically Engineered Food: Changing the Nature of Nature* (Rochester, VT: Park Street Press, 2001).

41. H. Charles J. Godfray, et al., "Food Security: The Challenge of Feeding 9 Billion People," *Science* 327, no. 5967 (12 February 2010): 812–18.

breeding." As Langreth and Herper report, "If you have incredibly brilliant biotech and extraordinarily average seed, you will end up with average crop yields," Grant says. "The thing the [genetic engineering] does is protect that preprogrammed yield."[42]

The limits of all these arguments about GM food are essentially the same: they argue primarily, if not solely on the basis of pragmatic concerns. While these arguments are attractive, especially to American common sense, they are neither comprehensive nor adequate in and of themselves. Pragmatic considerations certainly have an important place in the discussion, but only one posterior to ethical and theological considerations.

The theological background of ethics is essential for this discussion, because religious groups have begun to weigh in on the issue and lend their moral credibility to the discussion. For example, the Ecumenical Consultative Working Group on Genetic Engineering in Agriculture, a coalition comprised of members from various mainline Christian denominations and para-church organizations, authored a study which concludes, "It has yet to be demonstrated that agricultural genetic engineering, as it exists in the current system, safeguards the common good, human dignity, the sacredness of life and stewardship."[43] The Interfaith Center for Corporate Responsibility (ICCR) has a working group which critically addresses the issue of GM foods.[44] So far, a significant chorus of voices of religious communities has come out decidedly against GM foods.

We need to bring the focus back one or two steps to the theological foundations for any ethical decision about the activity of engaging in genetic modification. In general, a biblical-theological framework provides some important general affirmations of the genetic engineering movement with regard to *food*. This reality is in some respect directly related to the truth of human exceptionalism, the priority of human life over and against that of animals and particularly plants. This same reality, the dignity of the human being created in the image of God, likewise entails sharp limits on genetic-modification of human beings.

42. Robert Langreth and Matthew Harper, "The Planet Versus Monsanto," *Forbes*, January 18, 2010. Available at: http://www.forbes.com/forbes/2010/0118/americas-best-company-10-gmos-dupont-planet-versus-monsanto.html.

43. "Faith-Based Conceptual Framework on Genetic Engineering in Agriculture," available at: http://archive.maryknollogc.org/ecology/ecug_gea.htm.

44. "Goals and Objectives," available at: http://web.archive.org/web/20041101040340/http://www.iccr.org/issues/waterfood/goalsobjectives.php.

The first reality under consideration is the general mandate in Genesis 1 to be creative and productive stewards. The effect of the Fall and the curse in Genesis 3 follow, along with some brief observations about the reality and implications of human salvation in Jesus Christ with an implicit eschatological perspective.

Creation

> Then God said, "Let us make man in our image, in our likeness, and let them rule over the fish of the sea and the birds of the air, over the livestock, over all the earth, and over all the creatures that move along the ground."
>
> So God created man in his own image, in the image of God he created him; male and female he created them. God blessed them and said to them, "Be fruitful and increase in number; fill the earth and subdue it. Rule over the fish of the sea and the birds of the air and over every living creature that moves on the ground." (Gen 1:26–28)

These three verses form a complex and interrelated picture of the original state of humanity. Created in the image of God, human beings are placed in dominion over "all the earth, and over all the creatures that move along the ground." In this way, v. 26 speaks to the placement of human beings as God's earthly representatives. Within the original Ancient Near Eastern (ANE) context of this passage, the language of "image-bearing" would have been immediately understandable. When a vassal or representative of the king spoke or acted with the authority of the king, he was said to "bear the image" of the king, a physical representation of the king and his authority. Verse 27 narrates the creation of human beings alluded to in the previous verse, and the placement as God's image-bearers, representatives of the divine King.

There are, of course, no rights or privileges without responsibility, so on the heels of the creation of human beings and their placement in dominion, we find the corresponding responsibilities and blessings laid out in v. 28. Verse 28 is most often understood in terms of "stewardship," and here again we run up against the political and social structure of the ANE. A steward was one who was in charge of a household or kingdom during the ruler's absence. Humans, in exercising their exalted place of stewardship, are to be productive and creative rulers of the earth. This is the norm of human existence and the standard to which we are called. The creation account continues:

> Then God said, "I give you every seed-bearing plant on the face of the whole earth and every tree that has fruit with seed in it. They will be yours for food. And to all the beasts of the earth and all the birds of the air and all the creatures that move on the ground—everything that has the breath of life in it—I give every green plant for food." And it was so. (Gen 1:29–30)

For Christians, moral questions about the validity of genetic-modification of creatures are raised within the framework of stewardship. On the biblical account, God placed human beings created in his image in dominion over the earth, as stewards of the world's natural resources, including plants and animals. God placed Adam in the Garden of Eden "to work it and take care of it" (Gen 2:15).

Verses 29 and 30 are not usually included in an examination of the previous three verses, but given the topic under discussion they could hardly be excluded. Indeed, we see here that the plants are originally given and intended to provide for the life of the rest of creation, especially those creatures with the "breath of life." The original purpose for plants was to be food for humans (and animals) and in this way to sustain life. This will become important as we deal with the implications of sin and the Fall on creation.

Fall

> To Adam he said, "Because you listened to your wife and ate from the tree about which I commanded you, 'You must not eat of it,' "Cursed is the ground because of you; through painful toil you will eat of it all the days of your life. It will produce thorns and thistles for you, and you will eat the plants of the field. By the sweat of your brow you will eat your food until you return to the ground, since from it you were taken; for dust you are and to dust you will return." (Gen 3:17–19)

With the Fall into sin created relationships were upset, marred by enmity and distress. Because of the sin of the first couple, we have here in these verses a portion of the curse for violation of God's command. The effect here primarily is pointed toward the earth and the ground, out of which the plants in Genesis 1:29–30 grow. Part of the curse on human sinfulness is the difficulty that marks human efforts at cultivation in a fallen world. Humans are bound to the earth and plantlife for their survival because of the relationship God sets up in Genesis 1:29–30, but because of the Fall this previously harmonious relationship is changed into opposition. After the Fall, plants no longer function in the way they were intended at creation. Now plants will only sustain human life through difficult labor. Humans must work to bring out the life-giving power of plants to sustain themselves. Luther, in his commentary on these verses of Genesis, writes that because of this curse, the earth "does not bring forth the good things it would have produced if man had not fallen . . . It produces many harmful plants, which it would not have produced, such as darnel, wild oats, weeds, nettles, thorns, thistles. Add to these the poisons, the injurious vermin, and whatever else there is of this kind. All of these were brought in through sin."[45] We don't need to agree with Luther about the details of discontinuity and disharmony brought about by the Fall to see that scarcity, blight, and toil are fundamental realities in the fallen world.

Redemption and Consummation

Luther also notes, along with Paul, that "the creation was subjected to frustration, not by its own choice, but by the will of the one who subjected it, in hope that the creation itself will be liberated from its bondage to decay and brought into the glorious freedom of the children of God" (Rom 8:20–21).[46] Here we have a hint at the reversal of the curse on the human-earth relationship. Paul continues in this section to address the "firstfruits of the Spirit" which believers have received after the life, death, and resurrection of Jesus Christ. Our task as believers is to bear witness to the saving work of Jesus Christ. This work has begun to reverse the effects of sin and the curse, first and especially in the lives of believers, but also through the grateful work of believers, who are seeking to live up to their calling as faithful stewards.

The original purpose of plants was to provide sustenance for life, as is illustrated in Genesis 1:29–30. With the redemptive work of Christ in view, Christians are called to, in some way at least, attempt to realize and bring out the goodness of the created world. Genetic modification of

45. Martin Luther, *Lectures on Genesis*, vol. 1, Luther's Works (Saint Louis: Concordia Publishing House, 1999), 204.

46. See Luther, *Lectures on Genesis*, 204.

food can be a worthy human endeavor within the context of the created purpose of plant life to provide sustenance for human beings. It is important to note that many of the groups which oppose genetic modification of food also (rightly) decry the phenomenon of starvation in various parts of the world. As GM advocate Ronald Bailey notes, "If the activists are successful in their war against green biotech, it's the world's poor who will suffer most. The International Food Policy Research Institute estimates that global food production must increase by 40 percent in the next 20 years to meet the goal of a better and more varied diet for a world population of some 8 billion people."

The creation needs to be cultivated in such a way as to support and sustain human life. To do so efficiently is prudent, and genetic modification of food, like irrigation channels, plows, and mechanized tractors, is yet another technology that attempts to bring out of the land in some small measure its created bounty. Genetic modification changes nature at a more minute level, but such changes aren't materially different than any of the other various environmental or technological modifications that farmers have been making use of for millennia.

It is within the context of this world corrupted by sin and death that famine and hunger reign. And as long as we live in this world of sin, hunger, poverty, and sickness will remain (Matt 26:11). But as stewards of God's creation, human beings are called to work to mitigate the effects of sin wherever possible. So in the realm of agriculture and food, the call to bring forth the fruitfulness of the earth endures from creation to our fallen world. Efforts to minimize the effects of the curse in our lives do run the risk of aggravating our offense against God if they lose sight of our responsibility as stewards behind an emphasis on our liberties as autonomous tyrants.

Thus our stewardship must be cast in terms of obedience to God's will. As biblical theologian Eugene F. Roop writes, "While virtually all things are possible in God's garden, not all things are beneficial, and some things are not permitted. Nevertheless, we are genuinely free."[47] We are free to make use of the land, for good or ill.

The biblical account makes it clear that plants were given to provide sustenance for the creatures of the world with "the breath of life" (Gen 1:29–30), including human beings. And so as stewards of God's

47. Eugene F. Roop, *Let the Rivers Run: Stewardship and the Biblical Story* (Grand Rapids: Eerdmans, 1991), 28–31, quoted in *NIV Stewardship Study Bible* (Grand Rapids: Zondervan, 2009), 6.

creation we have wide latitude to, as Roop puts it, continue "finding new ways to nurture the soil back to life." Increasing crop yields through technological advances like genetic modification appear to be well within the boundaries of God's ordained freedom for human stewardship.

A chastened view of stewardship recognizes that we are only caretakers, called to an important task, but nevertheless dependent on the power of God to make the new heavens and the new earth. While growing more food for the earth's inhabitants will not eradicate hunger this side of Christ's return, we can understand our own efforts here as reflections, however blurry and indistinct, of the new creation. It is with God's own rule manifested in heaven that we will finally realize the day in which the Tree of Life will bear its fruit, and "no longer will there be any curse" (Rev 22:3).

Human Genetic Modification

There is sometimes a sort of negative visceral reaction to talk about genetic modification of any sort. This is due in large part to the fear of a reprisal of Nazi eugenics or some other sort of gene modification program which goes to the very center of who we are as human beings. It is appropriate therefore to make a brief observation regarding the applicability of the preceding arguments to any form of gene modification of humans, cloning, or embryonic stem cell research. To put it bluntly: these arguments aren't applicable.

The preceding analysis deals with the earth in general, but plants in particular. Of special note has been the created purpose of plants to provide for the sustenance of beings with the "breath of life." We have briefly touched on the doctrine of the image of God, or the *imago Dei*. This doctrine invalidates any facile application of arguments for genetic modification of plants to an argument for the genetic modification of humans. Quite simply, human beings, as God's image-bearers, are placed in a position of unique authority over creation, but also bear in themselves inherent dignity which places the worth of human beings as far greater than that of plants, or even animals. This doesn't devalue the rest of creation; but it rightly orders creation with humanity at its head. This inherent value of the human person is what Jesus points to when he states, "you are worth more than many sparrows" (Matt 10:31). The *imago Dei* precludes the argument from the purpose of plants to be applied in a similar fashion to human beings. It's also worth noting that nothing in the above framework justifies the genetic manipulation of animals or the creation of human/animal chimeras. Furthermore, nothing in this framework presumes any particular policy outcome in the realm of law, and so, for instance, concerns about the use of property rights as a means to tyrannize or monopolize particular industries ought to be considered.

The preceding is a brief sketch of an overview of a biblical-theological framework from which to view the particular arguments in favor of and opposed to genetically modified foods. In general, we can observe that the default position in this regard should not be simply to maintain the status quo of a fallen creation. The ICCR argues on a misuse of the precautionary principle that no genetically modified food should be made available until long-term independent safety testing shows that it is safe for health and the environment. Instead, the default position should be in favor of innovations which have a realistic possibility of substantively increasing the fruitfulness of the earth, and the burden of proof should be to prove that it is unsafe.

We have also seen that gene modification has the possibility of working to begin to reverse, or at least to ameliorate, some of the effects of the curse in Genesis 3, which should temper concerns like those of the Ecumenical Consultative Working Group on Genetic Engineering in Agriculture about "the common good, human dignity, the sacredness of life and stewardship." Concerns in these areas, informed by this theological framework, would in fact lead us to be in favor of gene modification for plants.

Does this mean that we should abandon all regulation of any sort and simply allow whatever is new and better to run free until devastating consequences become apparent? Absolutely not. The Fall affects human beings as well as the rest of creation, and even regenerate human beings are fallible and capable of horrible errors. What we need instead is a dialogue informed by the theological realities of fallen creaturely existence and by which we can begin to measure some of the claims both for and against genetically modified foods. Only when the reality of the created purpose of food and humankind's role in making plant life fruitful is realized will the pragmatic discussion on genetically modified food be appropriately framed.

The Hunger Games trilogy penned by Suzanne Collins has proven to be hugely successful, and deservedly so. The tale of post-apocalyptic love, poverty, war, and oppression poignantly captures the fundamental injustice of tyranny. As the film premiere of the first book dominated the box office, it's worth reflecting on what can be learned about faith and freedom from *The Hunger Games*.

As for faith, reporter Jeffrey Weiss has rightly noted that there's precious little in terms of explicit religiosity in *The Hunger Games*. Weiss wonders, "So what about religion? There isn't any. Not a prayer. Not an oath. The word 'god' does not so much as appear in any of the books."[48] That isn't to say that the world of Panem is populated by humans who have moved beyond religion in a fundamental sense. What it does show, rather, is the depth of the depravity the world where these Hunger Games are played. For the people of Panem, at least those in the classes of the governing elites, their stomachs are their god.

Thus there is, in fact, a sort of religion in Panem, a civil religion characterized by hedonism, the pursuit of pleasure as the greatest good. As Weiss writes of the world of Panem, "There's no ritual that isn't totally grounded in some materialistic purpose." And the Hunger Games are the high feast of Panem's civil religion. The games are a yearly ritual designed to show outlying districts of the nation how dependent they are on the good graces of the Capitol for their continued existence. As the vile President Snow relates, "It was decreed that each year, the 12 districts of Panem should offer up a tribute of one young man and woman between the ages of 12 and 18 to be trained in the art of survival and to be prepared to fight to the death." The districts must annually serve up these tributes to fight, kill, and mostly to die in the spectacle of savage violence, fickle fate, and uneven odds. The games are broadcast throughout the nation, and at once sicken and satiate the sensibilities of the masses.

Panem's is a secular faith that sacrifices the children of the districts as atonement for the original sin of political rebellion. As Snow makes clear, the Hunger Games are in fact part of the constitutional mandate for the nation, intended to remind the oppressed in the districts of the costs of political resistance. The analogues between Panem and ancient Rome are clear, from the "bread and circuses" nature of the Hunger Games (*panem* is Latin for "bread"), to the sensuousness of the ruling elites in the Capitol. But in place of the Christians who so often wet the sands of

48. Jeffrey Weiss, "Starving for Religion in 'Hunger Games,'" *RealClearReligion*, March 26, 2012. Available at: http://www.realclearreligion.org/articles/2012/03/26/starving_for_religion_in_hunger_games.html.

the arenas with their blood in ancient Rome are the children of Panem, who go to pay each year for the sins of their forebears.

Katniss, Peeta, and the rest of the tributes from each district are in this way kinds of secular scapegoats, bearing the sins of the rebel districts, and through the atoning sacrifice of their deaths prolong the lives of their friends and families for one more year. When Katniss volunteers to go to the Games in place of her younger sister, we encounter a moment rich with theological significance. We might be reminded of the free sacrifice offered by Christians like Maximilian Kolbe, the Franciscan friar who took the place of another prisoner condemned to die by starvation in Auschwitz. Ultimately these sacrifices are images of the one true sacrifice, the scapegoat for all sin, Jesus Christ, who "'himself bore our sins' in his body on the cross, so that we might die to sins and live for righteousness" (1 Pet 2:24).

The idea of freedom that is dominant throughout the world of the Hunger Games mirrors the materialism of the society's secular faith. When Peeta expresses his frustration at his impending doom, he speaks in the only terms he knows, that of ownership. "I just keep wishing I could think of a way to show them that they don't own me. If I'm gonna die, I wanna still be me," he says. Panem is a sick society, its allure and beauty merely superficial, a thin covering over the moral decay at the heart of the Capitol. The ruling classes of Panem are thus like "whitewashed tombs, which look beautiful on the outside but on the inside are full of the bones of the dead and everything unclean" (Matt 23:27).

The Hunger Games have been criticized by some for their depiction of Panem as faithless and oppressive. But what these criticisms miss is that Collins' story is ultimately about the injustice of such a world and the corresponding moral imperative to work, even to fight, to improve it. Indeed, the patent illegitimacy of any government whose existence depends on the oppression of its people, particularly its most vulnerable members (whether defined by class, creed, or color), is manifest throughout Collins' books. If Panem is what a world without faith and freedom looks like, then Collins' books are a cautionary tale about the spiritual, moral, and political dangers of materialism, hedonism, and oppression. As Collins teaches us, a society whose foundations are built on the bones of innocent children is reprehensible, and this is a timely lesson for the world today.

So we are not today in the post-apocalyptic world of the Hunger Games or the Walking Dead, or any of the other myriad narratives that make up this compelling genre. So what basis for hope do we then have? The question of hope in relation to material and spiritual goods is one that clearly distinguishes the Christian perspective from that of the pagan world. Suzanne Collins' futuristic Hunger Games trilogy pivots on this distinction, and as commentator Robert Joustra recently observed, "At the root of that genre, of all fantasy, of story and of imagination, is hope."[49]

The film version of the first installment of the Hunger Games series has a scene that nicely explicates the pagan view of hope in Panem. President Snow, the oppressor-in-chief of the regime of elites running the Capitol, has a question for the lead Gamemaker. Snow asks the Gamemaker why he thinks there is a winner at all. "Hope," Snow answers. "It is the only thing stronger than fear," he says. "A little hope is effective, a lot of hope is dangerous. A spark is fine, as long as it's contained." This dialogue shows how hope is used as a means of social control. It turns out, of course, that this manipulation of hope as a weapon is not so easy; President Snow's effort ends up turning against him.

There is a kind of dichotomy between the material and the spiritual world that runs through Collins' depiction of Panem. This dualistic perspective is in radical disjunction to what might be called a sacramental worldview, which recognizes the various and ubiquitous dispensations of divine grace behind everything, even something as mundane and as necessary as bread. On this view of the world as infused with divine grace, as Dietrich Bonhoeffer writes, "It is true that work is commanded, but the bread is God's free and gracious gift. We cannot simply take it for granted that our own work provides us with bread; rather this is God's order of grace."[50]

But as Weiss has also contended, the large scale absence of God and religion from the scene in the Hunger Games serves a narrative purpose. Indeed, one could argue that the post-apocalyptic Panem is a uniquely *American* world, in which the pragmatic tyrannizes the theoretical, the future, the ultimately *hopeful*.

So there is this compellingly complex paradox between what we might call bread and hope from the Christian perspective. On the one side, bread is necessary sustenance for our physical life, and an appropriately worldly evaluation comprehends a measure of hope in relation to this aspect of our existence. As the Apostle Paul writes, "Whoever plows and threshes should be able to do so in the hope of sharing in the harvest" (1 Cor 9:10). But when disordered, our material hopes become

49. Robert Joustra, "Our Dystopian Rut," *Cardus Daily*, April 11, 2012. Available at: http://www.cardus.ca/blog/2012/04/our-dystopian-rut.

50. Dietrich Bonhoeffer, *Life Together and Prayerbook of the Bible*, vol. 5, Dietrich Bonhoeffer Works (Minneapolis: Fortress Press, 1996), 77.

temptations. In the words of the tempter, "tell these stones to become bread." On the other side, as Jesus answers definitively, "Man shall not live on bread alone, but on every word that comes from the mouth of God" (Matt 4:3–4). God knows that we need bread, and we aren't to focus on the acquisition of bread as an ultimate goal.

So one way of understanding the difference between the pagan and the Christian perspective on bread is to follow Jesus' depiction of the situation: "Do not worry, saying, 'What shall we eat?' or 'What shall we drink?' or 'What shall we wear?' For the pagans run after all these things, and your heavenly Father knows that you need them. But seek first his kingdom and his righteousness, and all these things will be given to you as well."

This Christian perspective reorients and revalues bread, putting it within the broader context of spiritual goods and eschatological hope. Dietrich Bonhoeffer writes that the Christian's eternal hope in the resurrection and the new heavens and new earth provides us with the basis for risk and responsibility in this life. Consider Bonhoeffer's contention that the "world is the seedbed of eternity."[51] The pagan answer to the question of hope focuses on bread first, and only afterwards (and perhaps never) on spiritual or moral matters. The Christian answer seeks God's kingdom, realizing that primarily the kingdom is "not a matter of eating and drinking, but of righteousness, peace and joy in the Holy Spirit" (Rom 14:17). Christian hope frees us for responsible action in this world. Our heavenly joy gives us the freedom to get our hands dirty in this world, the "seedbed of eternity."

ECONOMY AND SOCIETY

The economic downturn of recent years, "The Great Recession," as it has been popularly called, has spawned a plethora of responses in the public square. This period of large-scale economic instability, initiated on the global scene with the collapse of the housing market in the United States and continuing through the sovereign debt crises affecting a number of nations in the developed world, has given rise to a cottage industry of blame, with opinion columns, feature-length commentaries, and trade books meting out their form of retributive justice. Sometimes the pen of the press must reach where the sword of the state is unwilling (or unable).

51. Dietrich Bonhoeffer, *Barcelona, Berlin, New York: 1928–1931*, vol. 10, Dietrich Bonhoeffer Works (Minneapolis: Fortress Press, 2008), 521.

But beyond the question of whether Wall Street, Main Street, or Pennsylvania Avenue deserve the lion's share of blame, the conflux of social and economic factors resulting in the crisis has left the public square openly wondering about the viability of the free market. The one thing that all the critical voices responding to the ongoing economic turmoil in the world agree on is that capitalism has some serious, if not fatal, flaws.

A global public opinion poll released earlier this year speaks to the pervasiveness of such conclusions. The poll, conducted by the Canadian research firm GlobeScan, displayed, as *The Economist* summarized, "another, perhaps more serious form of damage: falling public support for capitalism."[52] In the United States, for instance, the percentage of respondents who agreed that "the free-market system is the best" fell from 80 percent in 2002 to 59 percent in 2010.[53] The results for Canada in 2010 were roughly the same, with the only significant difference being that a larger percentage of Canadians were more tempered in their agreement (39 percent of Canadians agreed "somewhat" while only 20 percent agreed "strongly"). The biggest loser of the recent financial crisis, it seems, may well turn out to be global capitalism itself.

And yet we must not allow the very real and very pressing dilemmas facing us individually and communally to overshadow the equally real successes that market economies have engendered. As the recently launched Live58 project, an "action-based, global alliance of Christians, churches and world-class poverty-fighting organizations working together to end extreme poverty in our lifetime," rightly observes, the number of people living in extreme poverty in the world has been cut in half in the last two decades alone. This kind of amazing economic development has been made possible in the framework of economic globalization, and it is this reality that provides such organizations the practical hope of realizing the goal to "end extreme poverty in our lifetime."[54]

And so while technical and particular solutions offered in the context of debates over public policy have their place, the most promising avenue for reform of our economic system is to be found in restoring

52. "Capitalism's waning popularity," *Economist*, April 7, 2011. Available at: http://www.economist.com/node/18527446.

53. "Sharp drop in American Enthusiasm for Free Market, Poll Shows," GlobeScan, April 6, 2011. Available at: http://www.globescan.com/news_archives/radar10w2_free_market/.

54. See Scott C. Todd, *Fast Living: How the Church Will End Extreme Poverty* (Colorado Springs: Compassion International, 2011).

the various spheres and institutions of social life to their rightful place in pursuit of their rightful purposes. After briefly outlining a comprehensive vision for social life, I will focus in more detail on the economic realm and some concepts that have been largely lost, or underappreciated, and that need to be recovered in order to reform economics. These themes will be explored under the rubric of two sets of pairs: sustainability and stewardship, and service and shalom.

Putting Economics in Its Place

The history of Christian social thought has consistently emphasized the normative nature of God's commands for all of human existence, and since at least the time of the Reformation these commands have been usually understood in terms of four basic structures of social life: the family, culture, the church, and government. The consistency with which Christian thinkers from a variety of traditions have identified areas of life roughly corresponding to these structures speaks to the definitive nature of this framework. These basic institutions, or their correlates, can be found in thinkers as diverse as the Puritan Richard Baxter (1615–1691), the German jurist Friedrich Julius Stahl (1802–1861), the Dutch Reformed theologian and statesman Abraham Kuyper (1837–1920), and the Lutheran pastor and theologian Dietrich Bonhoeffer (1906–1945). Sometimes the relationship between these institutions is defined in different ways, such that the realm of the family is understood within the larger context of "society" (as in the case of Kuyper), or there is overlap between the realm of the family and the realm of culture (as in the case of Baxter). Likewise these structures are often identified by different names, whether "spheres" in the case of Kuyper or "mandates" in the case of Bonhoeffer. The reformer Martin Luther and his followers preferred to speak of three "estates," or of the "orders of creation," while Reformed thought tends to use the language of "institutions" to describe these realities.

But in all cases there is a characteristic sensitivity to the variegated nature of human social life. No one sphere or institution exists at the expense of all the others. And so it is within the context of this larger framework of social thought that Christian reflection on economic aspects of life must be situated. All of these institutions together, when they are working properly and in harmony, create the conditions in which individuals and larger communities can exist and flourish. Each sphere or institution has its own particular task for which it is fitted, a basic purpose that it must fulfill.

So, for instance, the family is the structure that is primarily concerned with manifesting the biblical blessing, "Be fruitful and multiply" (Gen 1:28). As the area of life concerned with cultivation of created realities, particularly (although not exclusively) related to meeting material needs, the cultural sphere is where we work out the corollary cultural or dominion mandate: "Fill the earth and subdue it. Rule over the fish in the sea and the birds in the sky and over every living creature that moves on the ground." The realm of government is the institution fitted for keeping civil order in a fallen world, tasked as the Apostle Paul puts it, "to bring punishment on the wrongdoer" (Rom 13:4). The Belgic Confession, a doctrinal authority in the Reformed tradition, understands the responsibility of the civil government to fulfill God's intention for the "world to be governed by laws and policies so that human lawlessness may be restrained and that everything may be conducted in good order among human beings" (Art. 36).

These three spheres of life constitute what is usually understood as the channels of God's common or preserving grace, focused particularly on the basic ongoing needs for human life together. The church represents the institution in which God communicates his special, saving grace. The church has the responsibility to respond faithfully to the Great Commission, in the words of Christ to "go and make disciples of all nations, baptizing them in the name of the Father and of the Son and of the Holy Spirit, and teaching them to obey everything I have commanded you" (Matt 28:19–20). Again, as the Belgic Confession puts it, the church "engages in the pure preaching of the gospel; it makes use of the pure administration of the sacraments as Christ instituted them; it practices church discipline for correcting faults" (Art. 29).

The purpose of this brief primer on Christian social thought is to properly orient the following discussion about economic aspects of human life. Each of these institutions has their own unique and sovereign role to play in promoting human flourishing. As has been noted, different thinkers have related and ordered the various institutions in different ways, but unanimously Christian social thought has recognized the pluriformity of the structures of social life. The fact that the Greek root word for economics (*oikonomia*) originally referred to the ordering of a household speaks to the basic importance of marriage and the family, for instance. But in no case is any one of these spheres to be understood as ultimately independent of the others. The Lutheran writer Ryan C. MacPherson speaks to the basic interdependence of these institutions, focusing particularly on the family and the government, as he observes, "What harms the family will ultimately ruin society and civil government, and vice versa; similarly, what strengthens the family ultimately will improve society and civil government."[55]

The variety of social institutions finds unity in the relationship of the individual person to each of these aspects of life. That is, the individual person is to be understood as relating simultaneously in various ways to each one of these spheres. Sometimes Christian thinkers speak of a variety of different "callings" or "vocations," such that a single person might have one calling to be a father, another to be a citizen, and another to be a dockworker. But a better way of thinking about the unity of these diverse relations is to understand that as Christians we have a single calling, to follow Christ, which manifests itself in a variety of human relationships. Thus, an individual person might have a calling to follow Christ in various ways, as a sister, a teacher, a small group leader, and a coach.

With this understanding of calling with relation to the various social spheres, we can properly locate those aspects of our individual callings that relate to economic matters. Just as no single institution is to tyrannize or impose itself upon the others, no single aspect of our vocation is to exclude or usurp the proper place of the others. The devolution of social life is typically attributable to the overreach of one institution into the rightful realm of others, either through outright tyranny or as a stopgap response to the failure of another institution.

What is usually understood as economic relates to the sphere connected to the cultural mandate. In particular, our economic relationships are intended to be the regular means by which God provides us with "our daily bread" (Matt 6:11), the process of transforming part of the natural world, like grain, to something necessary for human survival, like bread. This natural relationship between work and material sustenance is made explicit when the Apostle Paul issues this rule: "The one who is unwilling to work shall not eat" (2 Thess 3:10).

55. Ryan C. MacPherson, "The Natural Law and the Family," in *Natural Law: A Lutheran Reappraisal* (St. Louis: Concordia Publishing House, 2011), 202–3.

Sustainability and Stewardship

The first pair of concepts that must be recovered in order to reform our economic relationships to accord with this basic purpose, to properly orient our focus on material wealth, production, and acquisition, are those of *sustainability* and *stewardship*. When sustainability enters contemporary discourse on economic matters, it is usually from the perspective of preservation of some aspect of the natural world, like rivers, forests, and animals. But sustainability is not simply a norm for environmental concerns. It is, in fact, a normative value that has been consistently ignored or overlooked in much economic practice today.

More consistent consideration of sustainability as a norm for economic exchange would have some very important implications. The massive growth in levels of both public and private debt in the United States, for instance, are evidence that the economic growth enjoyed over that same period of time are in some very real sense artificial and unsustainable. For 2011, for instance, in both the United States and Canada, government expenditure accounted for nearly forty percent of GDP (38.9 and 39.7 percent, respectively). But in the US, in recent years roughly 40 percent of that government expenditure has been above and beyond what has been taken in via taxation. This means that since 2009, the percentage of GDP represented by deficit spending by the federal government has been between 9–10 percent (10.01 percent in 2009; 8.82 percent in 2010; 10.91 in 2011).[56] This represents a significant element of ostensible economic growth that is patently unsustainable, since such deficits are, as one political economist put it recently, "future taxes."[57]

On the consumer side, a commitment to sustainability entails a lifestyle that is not financed by chronic reliance on unsecured debt, like credit cards. That the message of sustainability has struck a chord in North America is evidenced by the popularity of common sense financial strategies like those offered by Dave Ramsey. For corporations, the idea of sustainability is concomitant with the basic economic lesson of forgoing the lure of short-term profits that destroy the foundational store of capital. But for executives with a generous benefits package in reserve, focusing solely on maximizing quarterly profits can seem attractive. When

56. "Government Spending Chart," http://www.usgovernmentspending.com/downchart_gs.php?year=&chart=G0-fed&units=p

57. Michael Munger, "The Budget Deal is DAFT," *Duke Today*, December 16, 2010. Available at: http://today.duke.edu/2010/12/munger_oped.html

sustainability is a virtue, the corporate equivalent of eating the seed corn is no longer a viable option.

This is why the corollary to sustainability is the concept of stewardship. Based on the fundamental relationship between the Creator and humankind made in the image of God, the idea of stewardship is a basic way that human beings relate to the world. A steward is one who has been entrusted with something by someone else. As the Apostle Paul writes, "Now it is required that those who have been given a trust must prove faithful" (1 Cor 4:2). The steward has the authority and responsibility to discharge his or her duties with faithfulness.

In this sense we can affirm that stewardship must be expanded and applied beyond the standard areas of the environment and financial generosity. This is a point that has been made comprehensively and persuasively in connection with the scriptural witness by the *NIV Stewardship Study Bible*. Each human being has a stewardship responsibility over some aspect of creation, small or large. Rudy Carrasco, a veteran of urban and global ministry initiatives, puts it strikingly,

> Every single person on the face of the planet is created in God's image. Everybody has the same heavenly Father. Everybody has capacity, talent, and ability. Everybody has responsibility. Everybody has stewardship responsibility . . . You have a responsibility to be a steward of the resources under your control because you have a heavenly Father who has put great things inside of you and that's waiting to be called out and developed and extracted.[58]

The social implications of this perspective are enormous. There is no such thing as a human life that is not valuable, that is not able to contribute to the common good in a qualitative or quantitative way. Human beings, as a matter of economic policy, should be viewed as intrinsically creative, dynamic, free, and responsible. Welfare policy, where and when it must be implemented, should be designed to remove impediments to self-sufficiency and encourage individuals and families to actively care for and develop whatever stewardship responsibilities they possess.

Service and Shalom

The idea of stewardship requires some orientation, however. The purpose for which things have been entrusted to us must have some content

58. See PovertyCure at: http://www.povertycure.org/voices/rudy-carrasco.

in order for us to understand the means to achieve divinely-mandated goals. In this sense we must understand stewardship as oriented toward the norm of service, which defines the function of economic enterprise. The basic purpose of business must therefore be redefined. In a fine book about the purpose of business from a Christian perspective, Jeff Van Duzer, a dean and professor of business and economics at Seattle Pacific University, writes that business and economic relationships matter to God because people matter to God. "What is the proper purpose of business? To what end should a company be managed if it is to best glorify God?" asks Van Duzer. "A business exists *to serve*," he answers.[59]

For too long a view has held dominance that has portrayed profit as a purpose or end, rather than as a means or a consequence. That is to say, the pursuit of profit is acceptable when it is couched within the broader framework of and constrained by the norm of service of others. Make no mistake: profit remains indispensible. As Van Duzer writes, "Profit is not easy to come by, and generating profit is critical to the health of the organization. It just isn't the purpose—the why—of the business."[60] Profit is, in fact, a meaningful signal that the product or service a business provides is actually valued by its customers and clients. When people value what a business does for them enough to pay for it, indeed, enough to pay an amount that allows the business to be profitable, this is a very clear indication that, at least from the perspective of the client (who is in the best position to judge), a real service is being performed. As Lester DeKoster writes, "We find work to do, in fact, only because what we do is useful, that is salable, to another."[61]

In this way work in the economic areas of life becomes one of the ways that we are called to fulfill the second great love commandment, "Love your neighbor as yourself" (Mark 10:31). But in order to understand fully how faithful service in economic relationships contributes to human flourishing, to *shalom*, it must be established how loving our neighbors in these concrete ways relates to the first great love commandment: "Love the Lord your God with all your heart and with all your soul and with all your mind and with all your strength" (Mark 10:30).

DeKoster makes the compelling case that by serving others, in the varied economic roles present in modern life, human beings actually

59. Jeff Van Duzer, *Why Business Matters to God (And What Still Needs to be Fixed)* (Downers Grove: IVP Academic, 2010), 151.

60. Van Duzer, *Why Business Matters to God*, 170.

61. DeKoster, *Work*, 7.

fulfill God's ordained purposes for our lives. "Work," he writes, "is the form in which we make ourselves useful to others." But this usefulness to others is significant in part because "God himself chooses to be served through the work that serves others."[62] So by faithfully serving others we make ourselves useful to God. It is for this reason that Martin Luther observed that "all people placed in the position of neighbors . . . have received the command to do us all kinds of good. So we receive our blessings not from them, but from God through them. Creatures are only the hands, channels, and means through which God bestows all blessings."[63] It is this perspective on work, business, and economic relationships that clarifies how this sphere of activity contributes in a distinctive fashion to the comprehensive Christian vision of social life.

First World Problems

It has become more common in recent years for Protestants to draw on the tradition of social teaching offered by the Roman Catholic Church, if for no other reason that, in the words of Lutheran theologian Carl Braaten,

> the Roman Catholic Church has produced a comprehensive body of social teachings on most issues of human concern. Even when we do not agree with the Roman Catholic application of natural law in every case of moral dispute, there is much to admire about a church that knows where it stands on the critical issues of the day and offers cogent arguments to explain its teachings.[64]

In the contemporary context of the crisis facing capitalism, it is worthwhile recalling that two decades ago in his encyclical *Centesimus Annus* John Paul II wondered about the prospects of capitalism in a global context. In answer to the question whether capitalism is "the model which ought to be proposed to the countries of the Third World which are searching for the path to true economic and civil progress," he answered affirmatively, if the term "capitalism" would be understood as referring to "an economic system which recognizes the fundamental and

62. DeKoster, *Work*, 9.

63. Martin Luther, *The Large Catechism*, in *The Book of Concord: The Confessions of the Evangelical Lutheran Church*, ed. T. G. Tappert (Philadelphia: Fortress Press, 1959), 368.

64. Carl E. Braaten, "A Lutheran Affirmation of Natural Law," in *Natural Law: A Lutheran Reappraisal*, 8.

positive role of business, the market, private property and the resulting responsibility for the means of production, as well as free human creativity in the economic sector."[65]

This assessment rings true from the perspective of those in the developing world today. It is instructive that on many accounts the attitudes in the developing world are much more optimistic about capitalism's prospects than those in developed nations. Where the previously mentioned GlobeScan poll shows stagnation and decline in positive attitudes toward the free market in developed countries, "the Chinese and Brazilians, 67 per cent of whom regard the free market system as the best on offer, are now more positive about capitalism than Americans, while enthusiasm in India now equals that in the USA, with 59 per cent rating the free market as the best system for the future."

A system within which service is valued, stewardship is expected, and sustainability is pursued is that which will tend to produce a more accurate earthly reflection of heavenly *shalom*. What J. Daryl Charles says of democracy, therefore, is equally as true of democratic capitalism. "Democracy," he writes,

> wherever found, as a form of government cannot maintain itself effectively over the long term merely through its political and procedural resources; it is dependent on the larger web of human culture, of which religious faith and moral first principles are key elements that provide the enduring basis for a normative ethical code.[66]

It is certainly the case that the structural and procedural elements of the market economy like those highlighted by John Paul II are critical to its contribution to human flourishing. But no such elements are incorruptible. So while structural reform and policy solutions are necessary, the more foundational and ultimately more critical and long-lasting reform will occur through the work of moral formation and acculturation in and through all the spheres of human life.

What will the fate of free enterprise be in the First World? The dilemma of prediction and forecasting has been a hallmark of modern economic theory and practice. Is economics a purely descriptive science or do

65. John Paul II, encyclical letter *Centesimus Annus* (May 1, 1991), 42.

66. J. Daryl Charles, *Retrieving the Natural Law: A Return to Moral First Things* (Grand Rapids: Eerdmans, 2008), 299.

prescriptions attend to it, either implicitly or explicitly? Does the descriptive element of economics cover what has already happened, and to some extent what is currently occurring, or does it also involve making predictions about what will happen? And what are we to think of the status of economics as a science if it does not involve making claims that might be objectively falsifiable? No matter what one thinks of the answers to these questions, or the questions themselves, the biblical accounts show that the questions of the past, present, and future are intimately connected. Biblically speaking, the question "Where have you come from?" is linked with the question "Where are you going?" (see Gen 16:8). In attempting to outline the possible futures of the economy in America, we must first take stock of where we are and where we have come from. This exercise will help temper the certainty which we may be tempted to have about the future of free enterprise in the United States, and it will likewise help clarify some of the critically important factors that will help determine the course of the domestic—and by extension the global—economy.

As for where we are today, there seems little doubt that we are in the midst of crisis, both with respect to the economy itself as well as to the broader intellectual and philosophical underpinnings of that economy. As Charles McDaniel of Baylor University wrote recently, the complexity of the economic crisis must be understood as a contributing factor to the doubt about the viability of the American system of enterprise: "Comprehending the technical jargon—derivatives, credit default swaps, reference entities—associated with the present crisis has been a significant part of the problem. We are fast exiting the period when laymen could describe the workings of financial markets and even the assets in which they are invested with clarity." Indeed, he writes, "Economic downturns are inevitable in capitalist economies, but the seemingly arbitrary determinations of who wins and who loses in the present flux have shaken confidence in the system."[67]

The British evangelical Os Guinness provides a visitor's account of the current state of affairs in American society, which he describes as an "America failing to live up to its past and its potential," and contends that "America's deepest crisis is the crisis of sustainable freedom."[68] By

67. Charles A. McDaniel, "Reviving Old Debates: Austrian, Post-Keynesian, and Distributist Views of Financial Crisis," *Journal of Markets & Morality* 15, no. 1 (Spring 2012): 38.

68. Os Guinness, *A Free People's Suicide: Sustainable Freedom and the American Future* (Downers Grove: InterVarsity Press, 2012), 16.

"sustainable freedom" Guinness identifies a dynamic inherent to sinful humanity ever since the Fall: human success and prosperity brings along with it the temptations to rely on oneself and one's own resources.

This is, in fact, one of the civilizational realities we see most clearly in the cyclical rise and fall of the Old Testament people of Israel. The America of today differs in many ways from the Israel of the ancient world, not least in that the contours of the political state and the religious assembly are not coextensive. But the temptations that follow upon affluence remain the same because fallen human nature does not change across time and space. Human beings are born sinful, and thus we become experts at taking God's good gifts, such as wealth, health, and creativity, and perverting them. We "invent ways of doing evil" (Rom 1:30).

That the United States has been blessed with great prosperity is beyond argument. Even critics of the American system of government and economy admit that the system of free enterprise has been unmatched in its ability to generate wealth. As Hunter Baker notes, this reality has occasioned a shift in the polemic against free enterprise. Pointing to John Kenneth Galbraith's argument in *The Affluent Society*, which "implicitly conceded that earlier critics of the free economy had been wrong in their repeated assertions that competitive capitalism failed to yield broad benefits to the public," Baker observes that "critics of the free market now argue more on the basis of inequality and relative deprivation instead of on the basis of absolute deprivation."[69]

Where the fairness of the unequal outcomes characteristic of market economies can no longer be assumed, the burden of proof shifts to those who would defend the merits of free enterprise. Two recent and notable books, from Arthur C. Brooks and Rev. Robert A. Sirico, presidents of the American Enterprise Institute and Acton Institute, respectively (the latter where I serve as research fellow), seek to do exactly that. In *The Road to Freedom: How to Win the Fight for Free Enterprise*, Brooks deals directly with the need to cast the positive case for free enterprise in explicitly moral, rather than simply pragmatic, terms.[70] He argues that the idea of earned success is absolutely critical to a moral culture that supports sustainable economic freedom. In his recent book, Sirico likewise examines the moral roots of the free enterprise system, and

69. Hunter Baker, "Reflections on Social Justice, Government, and Society," *Journal of Markets & Morality* 15, no. 1 (Spring 2012): 145–47.

70. Arthur Brooks, *The Road to Freedom: How to Win the Fight for Free Enterprise* (New York: Basic Books, 2012).

argues that "when civilizational virtues are eroded from within, people lose the capacity to defend the good things those habits enabled previous generations to achieve."[71] We are living today on civilizational capital that is rapidly being depleted.

This becomes apparent in many ways, and notably by examining a book first published thirty years ago, and in many ways an intellectual forebear of the work of both Brooks and Sirico: Michael Novak's *The Spirit of Democratic Capitalism*. Novak's book appeared in the early years of the "Reagan revolution," a high water mark in many ways for both popular and intellectual appreciation for the free economy. In this book, Novak showed that what he called democratic capitalism depended not merely on having the right laws or electing the right people, but most importantly, on a diverse and complex mix of cultural assumptions and moral institutions. Thus, he observed, "Democratic capitalism is not a free enterprise system merely. Its political system has many legitimate roles to play in economic life, from protecting the soundness of the currency to regulating international trade and internal competition." But in my view even more importantly, Novak continued, "Its moral-cultural system also has many legitimate and indispensable roles to play in economic life, from encouraging self-restraint, hard work, discipline, and sacrifice for the future to insisting upon generosity, compassion, integrity, and concern for the common good."[72] The economic historian Dierdre McCloskey has explored this moral-cultural matrix deeply in her significant work on what she calls the "bourgeois virtues."[73]

What we have increasingly seen over the last century, however, is the predominance of a view that our personal, familial, ecclesial, economic, and political lives can be neatly segmented and hermetically-sealed. Even if we often do not consciously choose to do so, many of us live our lives in ways that tend to align with such a secular mentality. This is one aspect of the moral shift from what Gertrude Himmelfarb called "Victorian virtues" to "modern values."[74] The virtues were objective standards that

71. Robert A. Sirico, *Defending the Free Market: The Moral Case for a Free Economy* (Washington: Regnery, 2012), 2.

72. Michael Novak, *The Spirit of Democratic Capitalism* (New York: Touchstone, 1982), 57–58.

73. Dierdre N. McCloskey, *The Bourgeois Virtues: Ethics for an Age of Commerce* (Chicago: University of Chicago Press, 2007).

74. Gertrude Himmelfarb, *The De-Moralization of Society: From Victorian Virtues to Modern Values* (New York: Vintage, 1996).

held true for all persons in all circumstances, while modern values are highly subjective and transient goods, depending primarily on individual occasion and circumstance.

In her recent book, *How the West Was Lost*, the Oxford-educated and Zambian-born economist Dambisa Moyo traces many of the proximate causes of the global economic crisis starting in 2008, often called "the Great Recession."[75] She comes to the stark conclusion that the choice facing the United States is essentially binary between two types of socialism: either a "socialist state" that is "well engineered and designed" and that "can finance itself," or "the worst form of welfare state, one borne of desperation that rapaciously feeds on itself."[76] Without radical constitutional and political effort to create the former, she fears the latter is what the United States is haphazardly lurching towards.

Moyo's point of departure is that the economic power of the developed West, headed by the United States, is rapidly being matched, and indeed will soon be surpassed, by that of the developing "Rest," headed by nations like China and India. There are two basic reasons for this. First, the West has stumbled. This is largely because of the economic downturn in America (driven largely by the sub-prime lending bubble) and the broader public debt crises faced by Western countries, including the United States and European nations like Greece, Spain, and Portugal. Second, the Rest have made significant economic gains, particularly in terms of GDP. These phenomena have significantly altered the balance of economic power on a global scale, and this, Moyo argues, means that the future we face is much different than we would have assumed only a short time ago.

The strongest part of Moyo's narrative is her description of these trends. She subjects the major players in the global economy to a standard (in her words "canonical") macroeconomic analysis, focusing on labor, capital, and total factor productivity (TFP), "a catch-all phrase which encompasses technological developments as well as anything not captured by the capital and labour inputs, such as culture and institutions."[77] One drawback of this technical economic approach as it is employed by Moyo (an Oxford-trained economist) is that it does not focus adequately on the value added by "culture and institutions." Instead, Moyo generally fo-

75. Dambisa Moyo, *How the West Was Lost: Fifty Years of Economic Folly—And the Stark Choices Ahead* (New York: Farrar, Straus, and Giroux, 2011).

76. Moyo, *How the West Was Lost*, 104.

77. Moyo, *How the West Was Lost*, 8.

cuses only on "technology" as the driver of TFP. The results of this focus come to fruition in her conclusions about the best course of action for Western societies.

Focusing particularly on the American economic landscape, Moyo makes a strong case that the policy decisions to incentivize homeownership in a way that tended to misallocate capital and publicly "guarantee" risky mortgages were a significant factor in driving up the housing market bubble. The effects on the other side of the "bust" are still being felt, but it is clear that over time America became increasingly comfortable with unsustainable levels of public and private debt. "The direct consequence of the subsidized homeownership culture," writes Moyo, "was the emergence of a society of leverage, one where citizen and country were mortgaged up to the hilt; promoting a way of life where people grew comfortable with the idea of living beyond one's means." More succinctly and pointedly, she rightly observes, "Debt, as a way of Western life, has become an addiction."[78]

One of the consequences of this addiction to debt is that the advantages and successes enjoyed by the West, and primarily America, in the post-war period of the twentieth century have been squandered and minimized as increasingly rich developing nations have become the financiers of the Western debt culture. This is a culture that goes far beyond the housing market and is clearly evident in the intergenerational entitlement promises made by government to its citizenry. Moyo goes so far as to describe "government and some corporate defined-benefit pension schemes" as "little more than Ponzi schemes."[79]

While Moyo's narrative is lucid and relatively convincing (as far as it can be, given the breadth of trends and times this book purports to cover), the prescriptions based on her descriptions are highly problematic. To be fair, Moyo has taken on an enormous project in this book: she attempts to synthesize more than five decades of global economic trends, with special attention to contemporary contexts that are still not well understood, and then on this basis to provide a helpful framework for a positive way forward for the West—all in under 200 pages of text! It should be unsurprising, then, that Moyo does not make her comprehensive case convincingly. There are just too many questions and problems that she cannot address adequately.

78. Moyo, *How the West Was Lost*, 37, 49.

79. Moyo, *How the West Was Lost*, 83.

For example, it is clear that the West ought to be concerned about the soundness of its economic order, but it isn't at all obvious that the relative success of the Rest should be viewed as threatening. Even if we assume that China, for instance, can continue its economic growth apace (which is a rather large and unsubstantiated assumption), Moyo does not successfully make the case that this must come at the cost or the expense of the already-developed world. The best she can do is show that the U.S. will be "relatively" weakened when compared to the Rest. This might not be such a bad thing. The U.S. has *de facto* become the world's sole economic and political superpower, which brings with it responsibilities that many Americans would be more than happy to share with other nations. Indeed, there is a sense that America has been asked to do too much for too long for the world's stability, security, and growth, and that it is high time for other nations to step up and contribute their fair share.

The most confusing and problematic elements of Moyo's vision for avoiding the West's "savage economic decline" come when she advises that America in particular should "hand more power to the state." It is at this level of analysis and prescription that Moyo's project simply fails. Her narrative assumes that the United States gained economic prominence by its characteristic approach to social life, a balance between the responsibilities of government and the rights of individual citizens. But likewise, she simply assumes that the Great Recession shows the long-term unsustainability of this Western approach and the superiority of state-led capitalism. Thus, she says, assuming current trends, "it is almost certain that America will move from a fully fledged capitalist society of entrepreneurs to a socialist nation in just a few decades." Given these assumptions, the way forward is clear: America must adopt the form of state-led capitalism that has apparently worked so well for the Chinese in recent decades. The choice then is between "better" and "worse" socialism, since, as Moyo puts it, "there is, after all, nothing inherently wrong with a socialist state *per se* if it's well engineered and designed and can finance itself."[80] In her view, only an economy driven by the expertise of those vested with political power and with "the political mettle to drive the decisions that they need to take to keep their societies afloat" can flourish going forward. The totalitarian implications of this view are frightening, and her credulous faith in the benevolence of government-led economies ignores some of the basic insights

80. Moyo, *How the West Was Lost*, 193.

of public choice theory. Human beings do not miraculously become saints when elected to public office.

Nowhere does Moyo give serious credence to an alternative explanation and prescription: China has been relatively successful because it has increasingly imitated the West. Why then would the West's solution be to become more like China, rather than to return to its own foundations of a "capitalist society of entrepreneurs"? Moyo is surely right that there is something gangrenous in the body politic in the Western world. But her diagnosis and prognosis are not compelling insofar as they gloss over the normative value of basic differences in culture, in assumptions about human nature, and in visions of social life that distinguish the worldviews of the West and the Rest. Is the West relatively weak because of or in spite of the fact that its nations have historically "embedded in their very foundations that the rights of the individual supersede all"?[81]

If the West is lost, it will ultimately not be on account of federal deficits or trade imbalances, inflation, or intellectual property, but rather because it has lost its faith in and commitment to its founding ideals, its established traditions, and its calling to live out the experiment in ordered liberty. But Moyo's dichotomous future for America only holds true if we assume that the fight for the moral-cultural system that gives life to free enterprise is beyond repair. Whatever their pessimism about the future, the works of Guinness, Brooks, and Sirico do not read merely as chronicles of civilizational decline, but rather as calls to reform efforts on a massive scale.

Lord Acton observed that "liberty is the delicate fruit of a mature civilization." The delicacy of this fruit lies in large part in the fact that the institutional structures of freedom do not sustain themselves independently of the moral character of the people. And so whatever the fate of free enterprise in America, it is not a destiny apart from the broader renewal of our social life and institutions. As Guinness writes, "Each sphere—business, law, education, entertainment and so on—must be reordered to serve the wider public good, and principles such as individual self-reliance, local self-government and state government must again be given their proper roles." Or as John Paul II concisely stated in *Centesimus Annus*, "Economic freedom is only one element of human freedom."[82] The reformation of American economic life is part and par-

81. Moyo, *How the West Was Lost*, 171.

82. John Paul II, *Centesimus Annus*, 39.

cel of the reformation of American social life, and such reformation, as with all true and lasting revitalization, begins with each individual within their own immediate areas of influence, however great or small: the home, the school, the workplace, the house of worship, and the polling booth. This is a reformation of freedom that can begin without tarrying for any broader political movement or social change, but which also has the potential for far more substantive and lasting impact.

With the latest presidential campaign in America, the traditional question of the coherence of the Republican Party has again come to the fore. Like clockwork, it seems, political commentators predict "the end of Republican fusionism," which has been a defining feature of the conservative movement for decades. Andrew Sullivan has lately contended that Mitt Romney represented "the last, dying gasp of Republican fusionism," which Sullivan identifies as consisting of the intersection of "free market capitalism, social conservatism, and anti-Communism."[83] But four years ago columnist Robert Tracinski celebrated the passing of William F. Buckley Jr. as ushering in fusionism's demise. Indeed, wherever you locate the origins of the fusionist project, whether before or after Barry Goldwater's campaign in 1964, from that time on the alliance has often been seen as tenuous at best.

Columnist David Brooks also recently turned his attention to the relationship between social and economic conservatism in his piece, "Going Home Again."[84] The subject of Brooks's piece is the journalist Rod Dreher, author of 2006's much-discussed *Crunchy Cons*, which has the verbosely descriptive subtitle: *How Birkenstocked Burkeans, gun-loving organic gardeners, evangelical free-range farmers, hip homeschooling mamas, right-wing nature lovers, and their diverse tribe of countercultural conservatives plan to save America (or at least the Republican Party)*. The book includes a ten-point "Crunchy Con Manifesto," with propositions like, "Small, Local, Old, and Particular are almost always better than Big, Global, New, and Abstract," and, "Beauty is more important than efficiency."[85]

83. Andrew Sullivan, "The End of Republican Fusionism?" *The Dish*, January 6, 2012. Available at: http://dish.andrewsullivan.com/2012/01/06/ron-paul-in-new-hampshire/.

84. David Brooks, "Going Home Again," *New York Times*, December 29, 2011. Available at: http://www.nytimes.com/2011/12/30/opinion/going-home-again.html?_r=0.

85. Rod Dreher, *Crunchy Cons* (New York: Crown Forum, 2006).

Brooks' piece updates Dreher's story since the publication of *Crunchy Cons*, and follows Dreher's decision to move to the small town of St. Francisville, Louisiana. The choice came about following the death of Dreher's younger sister Ruthie after a struggle with cancer and her experience in the Louisiana community. Late last year Dreher and his family moved to St. Francisville—choosing, as Brooks puts it, "to accept the limitations of small-town life in exchange for the privilege of being a part of a community." Brooks concludes the piece by describing Dreher as representative of one of "the two great poles of conservatism" inspired by the likes of Russell Kirk and Robert Nisbet, that of "communitarian conservatism." Brooks writes of the "creative tension" generated by the fusion between communitarian and "market" conservatism, identified with Milton Friedman. "In recent decades, the communitarian conservatism has become less popular while the market conservatism dominates. But that doesn't make Kirk's insights into small towns, traditions, and community any less true, as Rod Dreher so powerfully rediscovered," Brooks concludes.

But as we see from some developments since Dreher's move to Louisiana, the contributions of the "creative tension" of fusionism are threatened when either end of the spectrum considers itself fundamentally incompatible with the other. The reality is rather that economic or market conservatism and social or communitarian conservatism are more than simply compatible; they are also deeply interdependent in many often overlooked ways.

Indeed, it was not very long into Dreher's sojourn into small-town America that the limitations of the small, local, old, and particular became painfully obvious. As if on cue, less than a month into his new community, Dreher complained of the "frustratingly slow" Internet access in his house. You can perhaps imagine the gravity of the situation: "We had to cancel Netflix, because we can't stream. My iPad apps can't update, and have been permanently hung up for weeks (I've rebooted the iPad several times, to no avail). Skyping is very spotty. You can't watch any online video, even YouTube, without transmission being interrupted." Dreher is savvy enough to realize how these complaints sound, and defends himself on the grounds that "given the line of work I'm in—media—I have to have reliable broadband access to do my job efficiently."[86] It seems when

86. Rod Dreher, "Small town, small broadband," *The American Conservative*, January 11, 2012. Available at: http://www.theamericanconservative.com/dreher/small-town-small-broadband/.

it comes to our professions, sometimes efficiency does trump simplicity after all. So much for Slow Journalism.

Dreher's frustration in this situation illustrates in microcosm how deeply the contemporary communitarian conservative impulse relies on the technological innovations made possible by global trade. Perhaps it's just the vestiges of Dreher's cosmopolitan acculturation, but we can hardly imagine him being satisfied professionally and vocationally if his potential readership were restricted to readers of the local paper. As it stands, the development of and dissemination of access to the Internet have broadened rather than constricted the freedom of people like Dreher to live where they choose, in large cities, suburbs, or small towns. At a website like the American Conservative, where Dreher's writings now find a home, his readership is potentially global. Smaller is better, except when it comes to audience.

Just reflect for a moment on the delicious irony of the following: The existence of a Crunchy Con Facebook group; the online journal *New Pantagruel* (highlighted by Dreher in his book as being at the intellectual vanguard of crunchy conservatism), partially supported by Google ads; the availability of *Crunchy Cons* for sale on Amazon. A simple glimpse at what a Facebook server farm looks like, or the reach of the Google network, or the stock profile of Amazon should be sufficient to destroy any myths about the independence of crunchy conservatism from global markets. Dreher could presumably shrug off the networks of modern telecommunication, drop off his iPad at the nearest electronics recycling centre (the closest Best Buy seems to be in Baton Rouge), and use a typewriter and the US Postal Service to issue his dispatches from the wilderness. What happened instead (rather predictably) is that Dreher seemed to intimate that the federal government should deliver reliable high-speed Internet to the hinterlands: "The Internet really has become a necessity for economic development, just as electrification was a century ago."

But the resistance of communitarian conservatives to turn Luddite is evidence of at least an inchoate recognition of the good represented by the advance of global technologies. Even the most dedicated advocates of communitarian conservative values at some level realize that the flourishing they experience is, to a great extent, made possible by global markets. As Dreher puts it, "You don't realize how much our modern way of economic life depends on reliable high-speed Internet service, until you don't have it."

After the end of the Cold War, the centripetal force that anti-Communism represented to the original fusionist project has been replaced by the dynamic influence of globalization. Globalization has thus functioned as a centrifugal force for fusionism, as there is a major separation between communitarian conservative views of global trade and those of market conservatives. In the words of the Crunchy Con Manifesto, "We appreciate slow food . . . . We believe in Fair Trade over Free Trade." But even as the irony of the Internet illustrates the deep dependence of communitarian conservatives on technological innovation, largely made possible by global markets, market conservatives are no less dependent on the insights of social conservatives.

Russell Kirk famously excoriated libertarians as "chirping sectaries" and "the sour little remnant," who hold to "the notion of personal freedom as the whole end of the civil social order, and indeed human existence."[87] Such libertarians who absolutize individual freedom are better identified as libertines, given Christian insights about the relationship of the human person to the moral order. But part of the problem of ongoing commentary on the fusionist program has been the failure to recognize both that Kirk was absolutely right about the impossibility of connections between the libertarians he describes and true conservatism, as well as the reality that such libertarians are not merely identical with advocates of free markets and economic conservatism. Market conservatism is not reducible to libertinism. But neither do Crunchy Cons corner the market on communitarian conservatism.

Markets do not in fact exist in a vacuum, but are shaped for good or ill by the mores of their actors and institutions. And in this the Crunchy Con Manifesto is certainly correct: "Modern conservatism has become too focused on money, power, and the accumulation of stuff, and insufficiently concerned with the content of our individual and social character." As social conservatives remind us, institutions like the family and church play critical roles in forming a virtuous citizenry. As Elias Boudinot, a delegate to the Continental Congress and one of the founders of the American Bible Society, once observed, "Good government generally begins in the family, and if the moral character of a people degenerates, their political character must soon follow."[88]

87. Russell Kirk, "Libertarians: the Chirping Sectaries," *Modern Age* (Fall 1981): 345.

88. Elias Boudinot, "Oration before the Society of the Cincinnati in the State of New Jersey," in *The Life, Public Services, Addresses and Letters of Elias Boudinot*, vol. 2 (Cambridge, MA: Riverside Press, 1896), 365.

Churches, too, play an absolutely indispensible role in providing the moral formation necessary for Christians to contribute to the common good. Churches do this in many ways, but primarily through the proclamation of the gospel and its implications for Christian discipleship. For instance, the eighth commandment, "You shall not steal," when understood in its broadest implications, provides a basis for the Christian approach to responsible stewardship of material blessings. As the Heidelberg Catechism explicates this commandment, it requires not only that we avoid explicit theft and hidden cheating, but also that the Christian does "whatever I can for my neighbor's good" and that "I work faithfully so that I may share with those in need."

Business activity that provides goods and services truly is, in this way, an enterprise that does good and serves others. This is why John Wesley famously said that the "first and great rule of Christian wisdom, with respect to money," was the dictum, "Gain all you can." But he immediately noted that this rule was qualified: "Gain all you can *by honest industry*."[89] If market conservatives help us to remember that we are to gain all we can, communitarian conservatives help us remember that we are to do so honestly, and that morality is not reducible to mere legality.

Churches thus can serve as catalysts for orienting activity within markets toward the common good, providing the moral formation necessary for actors within markets as well as showing the moral boundaries to the logic of the market. Amy Sherman, director of the Sagamore Institute's Center on Faith in Communities, recently described the efforts of local church members in Pittsburgh, inspired by the preaching of their pastor, to launch Grace Period, a non-profit focused on addressing the problem of payday lending, with a mission "to educate the community about the danger of using predatory lenders and offer a more reasonable alternative for borrowers."[90]

As our recent financial crisis shows, these connections between morality and markets are critically important. Perhaps now more than ever communitarian and market conservatives need each other's insights to mutually test their respective assumptions and the practical implications of their views. One of the main criticisms of the market economy leveled

89. John Wesley, "The Use of Money," in *The Works of the Reverend John Wesley*, vol. 1 (New York: Emory and Waugh, 1831), 444, emphasis added.

90. Amy Sherman, "An Ichthus in a Sea of Loan Sharks," *Christianity Today*, December 6, 2011. Available at: http://www.christianitytoday.com/thisisourcity/7thcity/loansharks.html.

by people of faith is that the market thrives on competition, incentivizing the voracious and oppositional features of human existence. Walter Rauschenbusch captured this concern in his classic exposition of what he called "the law of tooth and nail" in *Christianizing the Social Order*. "The moral instinct of men has always condemned competitive selfishness," he wrote, "just as it has always admired the moral beauty of teamwork."[91]

The moral cogency of the argument against competition is enhanced in a framework where the goods that are sought after are static. Whether conceived of in terms of market share or the size of a firm, business and political leaders often use language that makes it seem as if economic gain comes at the expense of others. Indeed, this is an economic perspective with a lengthy historical pedigree. As the New Testament scholar Craig Blomberg writes, this is sometimes called a "theory of limited good," and it was characteristic of the biblical world: "Most people were convinced that there was a finite and fairly fixed amount of wealth in the world, and a comparatively small amount of that to which they would ever have access in their part of the world so that if a member of their society became noticeably richer, they would naturally assume that it was at someone else's expense."[92]

This theory of limited good has been known by many names and taken many forms. The Austrian economist Ludwig von Mises called it "Montaigne's fallacy," after the famous early modern French essayist Michel de Montaigne, and according to which, as Mises put it, "human intercourse cannot consist in anything but the spoliation of the weaker by the stronger."[93] The Spanish Jesuit Juan de Mariana (1536–1624), who likewise possessed remarkable wit and intellectual courage, also picked up the idea from the ancient philosopher Plato that "one man's profit is another's loss." This, said Mariana, is one of the "fundamental laws of nature," and meant that "one man's loss is another man's gain. There is no way around that fact."[94]

91. Rauschenbusch, *Christianizing the Social Order*, 172.

92. Craig Blomberg, "Neither Capitalism nor Socialism: A Biblical Theology of Economics," *Journal of Markets & Morality* 15, no. 1 (Spring 2012): 208.

93. Ludwig von Mises, *Economic Freedom and Interventionism* (Irvington-on-Hudson: Foundation for Economic Education, 1990), ch. 46, "Economics as a Bridge for Interhuman Understanding."

94. Juan de Mariana, *A Treatise on the Alteration of Money* (Grand Rapids: CLP Academic, 2011), 85.

It would not be until some of the more historically recent insights into the nature of subjective valuation of goods, innovation, and technological progress that the idea of the amount of wealth in the world as a static thing, a "zero-sum game," began to be effectively challenged. But as Charles Murray of the American Enterprise Institute reminds us, this destructive view of economic life is still with us: "Americans increasingly appear to accept the mind-set that kept the world in poverty for millennia: If you've gotten rich, it is because you made someone else poorer."[95]

But if economic activity is conceived of as at its core consisting of mutually-beneficial exchanges, then "human intercourse," to use Mises' description, need not fundamentally manifest in "spoliation of the weaker by the stronger." And, indeed, if the measures of economic activity are expanded to include realities beyond market share and relative inequalities, we can see that competition, rightly conceived, can be a force for much good in the world. Market economies tend to reward those who serve others well and meet the needs and wants of their customers. If the competition among various market players is cast as competing to surpass one another in providing increasingly excellent goods and services, then it becomes easy to see the virtue of competition. As the economic educator and entrepreneurial leader Manuel Ayau put it, in a market economy, in a "very real sense, we all compete to enrich others."[96]

Conservatism at its best recognizes the fundamental relationship between appreciation for markets and economic freedom on the one side, and morality and social responsibilities on the other. Far from a temporary alliance, this deep and real connection guarantees that the essence of the fusionist program, despite calls to the contrary, will continue to animate the future of conservative social thought.

The comparative orientation at the heart of competition can certainly work itself out in destructive ways. As Thomas Aquinas noted, when we observe good in others that surpasses what we possess ourselves, there are two basic responses. One is to grieve at the good another possess, to envy it, and very often out of a malicious spirit to seek its destruction. This, says, Aquinas, "is always sinful," for "to do so is to grieve over what

95. Charles Murray, "Why Capitalism Has an Image Problem," *Wall Street Journal*, July 30, 2012. Available at: http://online.wsj.com/article/SB10000872396390443931404577549223178294822.html.

96. Manuel F. Ayau, *Not a Zero-Sum Game: The Paradox of Exchange* (Guatemala: Universidad Francisco Marroquín, 2007), 44.

should make us rejoice," that is, "our neighbor's good."[97] But on observing a good which our neighbor has that we do not possess can also spark a different reaction: zeal for virtue and self-improvement. Observing a relative lack in ourselves, we can be moved to address the lack not by tearing others down but by addressing our own flaws and weaknesses. This zeal is praiseworthy especially when the sought-after good is spiritual, but it can also receive moral approbation when temporal goods are sought after judiciously and prudently.

Where the market economy can engender a spirit of competition, Christians must work to assure that the competitive spirit is expressed in, and when necessary transformed into, a zeal for doing good for others. As the Apostle Paul urges in another context, we should seek to excel one another in serving others: "Outdo one another in showing honor" (Rom 12:10 ESV). When competition is construed as seeking ways to love one another better, it becomes a virtue of the market economy that ought to be celebrated rather than scorned.

97. Thomas Aquinas, *Summa Theologica* (New York: Benzinger Bros, 1947), II.ii.36.2.

3

Church Authority, Moral Formation, and Public Witness

"The church has an unconditional obligation toward the victims of any societal order, even if they do not belong to the Christian community."

—Dietrich Bonhoeffer

Some time ago the congregation to which I belonged considered launching a large building project. It's an increasingly common circumstance in North America. The merits of this particular plan are no less worthy than those used to justify other church building projects. The fact is, my congregation is getting too big for its physical facilities, at least as they are currently used.

Given the number of members in the congregation, the square footage of the church building was probably on the low end when compared to facilities used by other North American congregations. But I can't help wondering whether our frame of reference is too narrow. Why should we only compare our needs to those of other North American churches?

What about the church in other countries, especially in the developing world? Sometimes congregations share one Bible. Often there are no pews to sit in, no ornate gold goblets with which to commune. Many communities don't even have a building in which to worship.

In North America the conflict we face is largely between spending our leisure or disposable income on ourselves and spending it on others. If a congregation determines that a particular building project is a legitimate need for its ministry, it shouldn't hesitate to pursue the plan. But it should also actively consider the situations of Christians around the world. Instead of an "either/or" framework, let's work with a "both/and" attitude.

Jim Wallis has made famous the claim during his political advocacy that "budgets are moral documents." If this is the case for governments, it is that much truer for churches. What might a moral church budget look like? Obviously there is a great deal of room for prudential judgment. But a place to start might be to apply the principle of the tithe to building projects. If, for example, a needed building was projected to cost $1 million, the local congregation could pledge an additional $100,000 to building and mission projects directed externally, whether in the surrounding neighborhood, regionally, nationally, or internationally.

Certainly church action should respect the principle of subsidiarity and prioritize the local. But because American and Canadian dollars often have greater buying power in developing nations, smaller amounts can go much further than they would in North America. A tithing guide certainly should not be a ceiling to aid for Christians abroad, but it might be a workable starting point for widening the perspective of our churches. This widening of perspective would be just the start, however, as responsible giving also requires helping in a way that doesn't harm. All too often, as Steve Corbett and Brian Fikkert write, our helping actually hurts.[1] What's most important about changing perspective, however, is that it directs the church's gaze outward rather than inward.

Whatever our various churches in different situations choose to do, we should look to the example of the churches in Macedonia, who were blessed with plenty. As Paul writes of the need in Jerusalem, the Macedonian church "gave as much as they were able, and even beyond their ability. Entirely on their own, they urgently pleaded with us for the privilege of sharing in this service to the saints" (2 Cor 8:3–4).

Let us pray that we might be so generous.

1. Steve Corbett and Brian Fikkert, *When Helping Hurts: Alleviating Poverty Without Hurting the Poor . . . And Yourself* (Chicago: Moody, 2009).

CHURCH AUTHORITY

In the context of Christian giving and stewardship, a teaching that often comes under scrutiny is this Christian practice of "tithing," by which ten percent of a believer's income is dedicated to God. Non-Christians, and non-religious folks in general, sometimes have difficulty understanding just how tithing goes. Is this a loan that Christians expect to receive back from God with interest? Is it a down-payment on something that will appreciate over time?

Some versions of evangelicalism in America tend toward an affirmative answer to these kinds of questions. You reap what you sow, they say, and when you sow the seed of the tithe with God, he'll reward you handsomely. The focus on giving here is finally and fully on what the givers get back.

Often those who reason in this way will make an appeal to the prophet Malachi, who records this message from God: "Bring the whole tithe into the storehouse, that there may be food in my house. Test me in this," says the LORD Almighty, "and see if I will not throw open the floodgates of heaven and pour out so much blessing that you will not have room enough for it" (Mal 3:10).

The teaching that we give in order to get even more is really a perversion of the biblical message. It's a message associated with a particular form of evangelicalism in America, the so-called "health and wealth" gospel, or the "gospel of prosperity." We shouldn't understand the passage in Malachi, directed at the covenant people of Israel toward the end of the Old Testament monarchy, to so easily and directly refer to the situation of the American church.

The focus on the good brought to ourselves in the act of tithing is one that corrupts the purpose of the giving itself. There is an analogy to the proper view of marriage that fits here. When you truly love someone, you don't get married to make yourself happy. Instead, you marry another person so that you might be able to make them happy. Your own happiness comes about not because you were aiming for it, but in a way precisely because you weren't. Your own happiness is a by-product, a consequence, of maintaining the proper end, the good of your spouse. If, by contrast, you get married simply in order to make yourself happy, the relationship becomes mercenary, and your true happiness is made that much more unlikely.

C. S. Lewis illustrates how this dynamic works in relationship to a variety of purposes and their consequences. "Aim at Heaven and you will get earth 'thrown in': aim at earth and you will get neither." There are some things that we can only get by not trying to get them directly. "It seems a strange rule," says Lewis, "but something like it can be seen at work in other matters. Health is a great blessing, but the moment you make health one of your main, direct objects, you start becoming a crank and imagining there is something wrong with you. You are only likely to get health provided you want other things more—food, games, work, fun, open air."[2] This rule applies to our happiness in the context of marriage as well. If you love and aim at the good of your spouse, you will get your own happiness "thrown in." In the same way, whatever benefits we claim to receive from tithing, whether spiritual, emotional, or financial, these are not to be the reason that we give. We give out of obedience to God's word.

The biblical basis for the tithe is primarily found in the Old Testament narratives about the divinely-ordered life of ancient Israel. For instance, when Melchizedek, the King of Salem, blessed Abram the Bible tells us that "Abram gave him a tenth of everything" he had recovered during battle (Gen 14:20). This provides Christians with an example of a righteous action that is later explicitly referred to in the New Testament (Heb 7:4–10).

When we give a tithe to God, we testify that everything we receive is a blessing from the Lord. He is the giver of all good gifts, and we are stewards of his creation, for "the earth is the LORD's, and everything in it" (Ps 24:1). So when we tithe or give other offerings to God, it isn't the case that we're simply giving him something of our own. We're demonstrating that everything ultimately belongs to God and that part of our first responsibility as stewards is to give a portion back directly.

This is not to say that there are not good reasons beyond simple obedience to give to the church and to other charitable organizations. Evangelical activist Ron Sider estimates that if all Christians gave a full ten percent of their income, "there would be enough private Christian dollars to provide basic health care and education to all the poor of the earth. And we would still have an extra $60–70 billion left over for evangelism around the world."[3]

2. C. S. Lewis, *Mere Christianity* (New York: HarperCollins, 2001), 134.

3. Ron Sider, *The Scandal of the Evangelical Conscience: Why Are Christians Living Just Like the Rest of the World?* (Grand Rapids: Baker, 2005), 118.

While evangelism should never be an afterthought or relegated to "leftovers," Sider's point is true enough. If American Christians were to focus on the simple obedience of giving back to God what is really his in the first place, the church would have the resources to do great things. But we should give not primarily because of the good we expect it will do the church, or others, or ourselves (although these may be valid considerations for *how* we give). Ultimately we should give because, as the children's song goes, the Bible tells us so.

So we, as Christians, have an obligation to give. But the questions remain *where* and *how*? Some details about the state of charitable giving in America are in order. Even though charitable giving has declined nationwide during the Great Recession, the amount of funding to church and other religious and faith-based organizations increased.[4] Although people are giving less overall, religious charities are seeing greater donations. But this makes the second trend even more striking: while "church" and "religious organizations" are getting a larger share of a smaller pie, local congregations are seeing donations decline.

This is the basic picture we get from a study released annually by Empty Tomb, Inc., which looked at numbers for 2008 in its twentieth annual report.[5] Sylvia Ronsvalle, executive vice president of Empty Tomb, says that the 2008 data "suggests it's possible that fewer people are seeing churches as the primary conduit for meeting the larger (charitable and evangelistic) need." For various reasons, people seem to increasingly view places other than their local congregations as the place where their charitable dollars ought to go.

This seems to be another bit of data showing that Americans in general, and Christians in particular, are becoming increasingly dissatisfied with a host of social institutions. Churches and denominations are no exception. If we look at the numbers for 2008, the general level of trust in social institutions declined significantly over a thirty-year period. As related by the General Social Survey, which has tracked polling data for more than three decades, those expressing a "great deal" of confidence

4. Stephanie Strom, "How Much Less Did You Give Last Year?" *Bucks*, June 9, 2010. Available at: http://bucks.blogs.nytimes.com/2010/06/09/how-much-less-did-you-give-last-year/.

5. Matt Vande Bunte, "Study reveals church giving at lowest point since Great Depression," *MLive.com*, October 23, 2010. Available at: http://www.mlive.com/living/grand-rapids/index.ssf/2010/10/study_reveals_church_giving_at.html.

in organized religion fell from 32 percent in 1976 to 20 percent in 2008.[6] Every other major social institution (except the military) also saw declines during that same period, including the "scientific community" (48 to 40 percent), banks and financial institutions (40 to 19 percent), and the press (29 to 9 percent).

The fact that people are more often bypassing their local congregations as places to support financially is troubling, and for churches it ought to signal that their budgets are often out of step with the concerns of their congregants. If churches do not have spending priorities that are aligned with the convictions of their members, it is to be expected that this will show up in the balance sheet. This shows that there is some basic accountability inherent in the donor/charity relationship, and while that model may not be the best way of characterizing the relationship between the individual member and the local congregation, there can be some positive results from doing so.

For one thing, if the congregation pulls back its support because it feels that its priorities are not represented in the church's spending, this can be an important check on the temptation for church leaders to be bad stewards of the church's finances. Empty Tomb's analysis of its data emphasizes a "long-term turning inward of congregations," which is to say that congregations are increasingly spending more money on themselves and their own institutional maintenance than on evangelism and outwardly-focused works of service. Consider here the cautionary tale of Robert Schuller's Crystal Cathedral in Orange County, Calif., which filed for bankruptcy in 2010 amid financial and ministerial turmoil. Multi-million dollar building campaigns, designed to accommodate the perceived desires of affluent Americans, can quickly go off-track when funding for missionaries, benevolence ministries, and poverty programs suffer.

If local churches hope to take up their rightful place of priority in their congregation's charitable giving, then they will need to show that they are being faithful and obedient stewards of their mandate. In many cases that will mean a revitalization of the office of deacon. As Lester DeKoster and Gerard Berghoef contend in their *Deacons Handbook*, the deacon is the "executive agent for good stewardship in the Church." Consider here the positive example of Redeemer Presbyterian in New York City. Redeemer Pastor Tim Keller speaks of the importance of the church having "an

6. Nate Silver, "Americans Losing Their Faith in Faith . . . And Everything Else," *FiveThirtyEight*, March 12, 2009. Available at: http://www.fivethirtyeight.com/2009/03/americans-losing-their-faith-in-faith.html.

excellent diaconate that works with those in need within our community."[7] Berghoef and DeKoster write, "A congregation well furnished with plant, facilities and staff is a richly leafed tree. How well that congregation, through its diaconate, cares for its own needy and for the poor within its reach is one key measure of the fruit which this tree bears."[8]

There are corresponding responsibilities at work here, and if the problem of declining donations to local churches is to be resolved then both parties need to meet their obligations. First, individual Christians need to see their local church as the first place where their charitable donations go. This is part and parcel of what it means to be visibly connected to others as the Body of Christ. And they need to trust and hold accountable the leadership of the church, especially the diaconate, for the good stewardship of those funds. Second the church leaders and administrators, especially the deacons engaged in the face-to-face and front-line ministry work, need to be committed to using those funds entrusted to them in a manner obedient to the gospel imperative. The deacons must be, in Berghoef and DeKoster's words, "seeing eyes, hearing ears, and serving hands of the congregation."

In this relationship between a community of "cheerful givers" (2 Cor 9:7) on the one hand and faithful stewards on the other, we see the biblical picture of a people who lets its "light shine before others, that they may see your good deeds and glorify your Father in heaven" (Matt 5:16).

In this way, even though charitable giving to religious and faith-based non-profits has increased, local congregations are still feeling the pinch. As the effects of the Great Recession continue to ripple outward, many churches are having a difficult time meeting their budgets. There has been an uptick in foreclosures of church properties across America, and this is in addition to the budgetary belt-tightening that congregations are performing in order to stay solvent.[9] And as local governments face shortfalls as well, bureaucrats are increasingly casting

7. "Interview with Tim Keller on Generous Justice," *The Gospel Coalition*, October 26, 2010. Available at: http://thegospelcoalition.org/blogs/kevindeyoung/2010/10/26/interview-with-tim-keller-on-generous-justice/.

8. Gerard Berghoef and Lester DeKoster, *The Deacons Handbook: A Manual of Stewardship* (Grand Rapids: Christian's Library Press, 1980), 11, 13.

9. Shelly Banjo, "Churches Find End Is Nigh," *Wall Street Journal*, January 25, 2011. Available at: http://online.wsj.com/article/SB10001424052748704115404576096151214141820.html.

covetous eyes on properties that do not generate tax revenue.[10] These are all factors in an economic context that bodes ill for the fiscal future of many American churches.

It would be natural to assume that as the economy shrinks, when people lose their jobs and see their income decrease, the pool of support available to churches also gets smaller. And it is true, as we just mentioned, that over recent years giving to local congregations has declined. But this decline is all the more noteworthy when it is juxtaposed with the reality that giving to religious organizations and causes has overall *increased*, rather than decreased, during the recent economic downturn. What this suggests is that church-goers are less and less satisfied with how their congregations are spending money. So as money available for charitable causes decreases, so has giving to local churches.

Many churches simply took on commitments that were too ambitious during times of plenty. Multi-million dollar building and expansion projects may seem appealing when the economy is growing and property values are increasing. But when bubbles burst on Wall Street, and the effects flow outward onto Main Street, expensive investments in ostentatious brick-and-mortar projects begin to seem imprudent, even foolhardy. When congregants are barely able to pay their own mortgages or are losing their own homes, the local church's building debt becomes a burden that chafes and is cast off, or at the very least ignored.

This aspect of the fiscal crisis facing many churches illustrates the fundamental interconnectedness of civil society. The poet John Donne once wrote, "No man is an island, entire of itself; every man is a piece of the continent, a part of the main." This is as true for institutions as it is for individuals. Churches as well as governments depend on the economic activity of their members for their ongoing maintenance and support. In an important sense this reflects the biblical model for the relationship between the priesthood and the tribes in ancient Israel. The Levites, for instance, were forbidden to have tribal land of their own and were entirely dependent on the tithe of the rest of the nation. This is the system that God set in place to support the system of public worship: "A tithe of everything from the land, whether grain from the soil or fruit from the trees, belongs to the LORD; it is holy to the LORD" (Lev 27:30).

10. Adelle M. Banks, "Cash-Strapped Cities Look To Tax Churches," *Huffington Post*, January 21, 2011. Available at: http://www.huffingtonpost.com/2011/01/21/cashstrapped-cities-look-_n_812400.html.

But despite the Christian mandate to give to the church, if the individual members are suffering, then the whole body suffers, too, and there is less to sustain churches. In this way, this economic downturn and its cascading effects throughout society remind us of the solidarity of our social life. We are all dependent upon others, to a greater or lesser extent, and this is a reality that points our way forward through the various threats and dangers we negotiate today.

One such danger is that in hard times we lose this sense of relationship and interdependence. We are tempted to turn against one another for our own survival, carving out our space for existence at the cost of our neighbors. It is this survival instinct that is at work when local governments turn a programmatic focus on vulnerable churches as a means to boost flagging property tax revenue. This is a phenomenon that was at work even before the current downturn, and it has only been exacerbated as cities and municipalities face tough budget choices. In many cases it is more expedient to place pressure on a church to close its doors than to make cuts to pet spending projects and line items.

In the aftermath of the Great Recession many churches have closed and will close their doors for good, just as many businesses and many homes have done. In some cases this is deserved, in others less so. But the challenge of this economic downturn can be an opportunity for churches, as well as individuals, businesses, and governments, to learn again the lessons of fiscal discipline, thrift, and stewardship that are the hallmarks of sustainable economic growth and social flourishing. These are lessons that we all must learn and put into practice if we are to enjoy a brighter future as we move toward realizing the common good.

But even with all the challenges to local congregations that we've outlined here in mind, American Christians still must keep in mind their vast relative affluence as compared to the rest of the world. The North American church is wealthy, a reality that has not been substantially affected by the economic downturn. American Christians are, both individually as well as corporately, still rich even if we don't always feel that way.

"Remember, with great power, comes great responsibility." With these words, Uncle Ben counsels Peter Parker, the alter ego of the super hero Spiderman, on how to deal with his newfound superhuman strength. These words imply a sense of stewardship, of a duty to use our abilities, powers, and knowledge for the common good. This idea of stewardship is a recurring biblical theme, and one that Jesus summarized best when he said: "From everyone who has been given much, much will be demanded;

and from the one who has been entrusted with much, much more will be asked" (Luke 12:48). This applies especially to Jesus' church, which has been given the gift of salvation and tasked with proclaiming the good news.

But how exactly do we do that in a contemporary context? Dietrich Bonhoeffer, the German theologian, once wondered, "How are we to live as Christians today?"[11] In the context of the church in North America, the answer to this question is increasingly recognized as one of stewardship.

Christians in the United States and Canada live in societies that rank among the richest in the history of human civilization. According to the World Bank, in 2004 the United States ranked third in Gross National Income per capita (according to Purchasing Power Parity) and Canada ranked sixteenth. Former Fed Chairman Alan Greenspan has said that Americans have "the most extraordinarily successful economy in history."[12]

To a large extent Christians have been a part of the success of the North American economies. And with those material blessings comes the corresponding responsibility to use them for the advancement of the gospel. Paul implores Christians, "as we have opportunity, let us do good to all people, especially to those who belong to the family of believers" (Gal 6:10).

There is no lack of economic need around the world, as any justice or mission group will tell you. And North American Christians, to a staggering degree, have the ability to provide for the material needs of Christians abroad. International efforts at relief can become representative of authentic acceptance of the true "catholicity," or universality, of the Christian church. The Christian church extends beyond every national and ethnic border. All this is done in recognition of the communion of saints, and as the Westminster Confession of Faith states, Christians are bound to relieve "each other in outward things, according to their several abilities and necessities. Which communion, as God offereth opportunity, is to be extended unto all those who, in every place, call upon the name of the Lord Jesus."

All of this gets at the proper motivation for Christians to give. But what do we make of various initiatives championed by well-meaning Christians to help those in poorer nations? One such popular program is that of "fair trade," and the foremost fair trade product is coffee. Indeed,

11. This is the basic question of his classic *Discipleship*, vol. 4, Dietrich Bonhoeffer Works (Minneapolis: Fortress Press, 2003).

12. Peter Grier, "Rich-poor gap gaining attention," *Christian Science Monitor*, June 14, 2005. Available at: http://www.csmonitor.com/2005/0614/p01s03-usec.html?s=itm.

the fair trade coffee campaign is gaining traction beyond its early beachhead on college campuses and grungy latté shops. Increasingly, the campaign is finding new adherents in religious organizations, which are busily issuing guidelines for consumers. In churches and synagogues all over America, the once ideologically innocent coffee klatch has become a forum for international trade policy. Prominent religious advocates of fair trade include outreaches of Lutheran World Relief, the Presbyterian Church (USA), and the United Methodist Committee on Relief. These groups, among other things, advise churches to "offer gift baskets of fairly traded coffee and tea for new members, as Christmas presents, or on other occasions."[13] Catholic Relief Services has also launched efforts to boost fair trade coffee consumption among the nation's 65 million Catholics.[14]

People of faith are working with groups like Global Exchange, a San Francisco-based human rights organization, which claims, "Agriculture workers in the coffee industry often toil in what can be described as 'sweatshops in the fields.'"[15] The fair trade movement, encouraged by victories among the religious and in corporate America, has ambitions that range all over America's supermarket. Fair trade techniques are based on convincing the consuming public and working through the market to achieve their goals. This approach is vastly superior to relying solely on governmental subsidies, which has historically been the chosen means of influencing agriculture policy for many like-minded activists.

The main difficulty with this, however, lies in the fact that these campaigns rely on guilt-tripping people who drink coffee, rather than arguing from sound economic principles. The rhetoric of the fair trade movement attacks "big business" coffee companies, and favors smaller, cooperative farms. In addition to using such rhetoric as "sweatshops in the fields," Global Exchange implicitly blames consumers and big business for the "crisis" with an explanation that does not explain: "Many small coffee farmers receive prices for their coffee that are less than the costs of production, forcing them into a cycle of poverty and debt."

The "middlemen" involved in coffee importation into the United States are often called "exploitative." Big business coffee is asserted to

13. "Ensure a better life for others," *UMCOR*. Available at: http://develop.gbgm-umc.org/umcor/work/hunger/fair-trade/.

14. In-Sung Yoo, "Faith Organizations Throw Weight Behind 'Fair Trade' Coffee Movement," *USA Today*, December 2, 2003.

15. Global Exchange, "Coffee." Available at: http://www.globalexchange.org/fairtrade/campaigns/coffee.

involve "a lengthy, and expensive, cast of middlemen between the coffee farmer and the consumer." Most people, and not just economists, refer to this as a supply chain, the system by which food is delivered from field to table. The fair traders' answer to the "sweatshop on the fields" situation is simple: fix the price of coffee at a level that will provide an adequate standard of living for the farmer. Currently they affirm that this fair level ranges between of $1.30 and $1.40 per pound, depending on type and quality of the bean.

Such artificial and arbitrary measures fly in the face of economic reality. The law of supply and demand is, or at least should be, the primary player in regulating the price of coffee, which is bought and sold like any other commodity. The economic price mechanism takes into account a variety of factors that an artificial price standard cannot hope to deal with justly. Indeed, fair traders ignore one of the main reasons coffee growers face price drops: worldwide production has greatly expanded, especially in Southeast Asia. Increased supply equals lower prices given a static demand.

From 1995 to 2002 Brazil increased coffee exports by more than 200 percent. Colombia has shown a slight decline in production over the same period, while Vietnam's production has almost tripled. So the three largest exporters of coffee in the world had all either nearly maintained or significantly increased their production during that seven-year period. Worldwide coffee production peaked in 2002 and because of a long buildup of surplus. For a number of years there was simply too much coffee on the market. But fair trade price fixing simultaneously subsidized more coffee production rather than encouraging investment in other commodities or industries.

Even though the U.S. is one of the largest importers of coffee in the world, per capita consumption of coffee has declined steadily, dropping from 38.8 gallons in 1960 to 22 gallons in 2000. This is indicative of a downward trend in global demand, which, combined with increased supply, is a major cause of the plummet in coffee prices. More recently prices have rebounded, in part because of the flexibility of the market to respond by reallocating production to other industries as well as shifts in consumer demand.

Most troubling is the fact that the fair trade movement effectively pits the poor against the poor. It's a case of coffee farmers in the fair trade co-ops versus conventional farmers. Those who sell coffee in the traditional commercial manner are forced to compete with those who are artificially enabled by the fair trade movement to maintain production through such guilt-driven, market-based subsidies.

The Apostle calls us to live godly lives, to "keep these instructions without partiality, and to do nothing out of favoritism" (1 Tim 5:21). This stems from our proper reflection of God's holiness and justice, "For God does not show favoritism" (Rom 2:11). While these words are spoken especially in regard to salvation history, they have application to our morally-informed economic lives. Religious groups especially should reevaluate their position with respect to fair trade in the interest of true justice. The fair trade movement needs to take into consideration the poor who are left out of their arbitrarily constructed system of privilege.

The fair trade movement's only response to this disparity is to argue for a complete standardization of its price-fixing methods. Global Exchange thus calls for "a total transformation of the coffee industry, so that all coffee sold in this country should be Fair Trade Certified." The success of this sort of endeavor will never be comprehensively effective, especially in a free economy like the United States.

The Christian economist Victor Claar examined fair trade as a potential solution to global poverty in a recent comprehensive study. He concluded, "The moral shortcoming of the fair trade movement is that it keeps the poor shackled to activities that, while productive, will never lead to poverty reduction on a large scale—or even a modest one."[16] Rather than attempting vainly to maintain the status quo, the fair trade movement should look for other, more innovative ways to provide resources for the world's poor. As Claar notes, one of the more effective ways to achieve this would be to reduce domestic subsidies for commodities like sugar. A great deal could be accomplished if the energy of advocacy for fair trade were redirected to the problem of domestic agricultural subsidies and protectionism.

Likewise direct investment and targeted micro-finance opportunities abound. As Claar writes, "We should help poor countries wisely grow their stocks of human and physical capital, all the while bearing in mind that markets and their prices send the best available signals regarding where our efforts can have the greatest impact."[17] Ronald J. Sider outlines ideas about micro-enterprise development that offer better solutions

16. Victor V. Claar, *Fair Trade? Its Prospects as a Poverty Solution* (Grand Rapids: PovertyCure, 2012), 53.

17. Claar, *Fair Trade?*, 57.

than fair trade advocacy.[18] Those who care about small coffee growers might invest capital and enable farmers to grow crops that are in higher demand. Micro-loans which empower people in developing nations to invest in the opportunities that they see for themselves in their own circumstances, using their own local knowledge and expertise, are far more promising than subsidies from the developed world which, however well-meaning, dictate standards, practices, and industries from afar. In his work, Peter Greer, the president and CEO of HOPE International, has worked effectively to empower the global poor in ways that respect their dignity, responsibility, and comprehensive development.[19]

In all these ways, those who choose to stay in the coffee growing business would see less competition and, in theory, rising prices resulting from decreased supply. How much better than fair trade price fixing and guilt trips, which demand partiality for a select group of the poor!

The challenge of the implicit favoritism and partiality found in "fair trade" initiatives is a particular instance of the kinds of tribalism that is characteristic of fallen humanity. There's a sense in which even the language of the "First World" and the "Third World," which has fallen out of favor, or the "developed" and the "developing" world, can reinforce the strangeness of those in other parts of the world. There's an implicit superiority in the posture taken between the "haves" and the "have-nots," such that those in the West are burdened with saving "the rest."

We often seek to exclude the *other* on the basis of skin color, gender, economic status, language, or some other social characteristic. These cultural categories are often imported into church settings, and a real danger is conflating or identifying such standards based on fallible human practices with gospel truth and the dictates of divine revelation. H. Richard Niebuhr recognized a significant truth when he explored what he called the "social sources of denominationalism," although his example shows the perils of trying to unravel those views which are culturally-derived and those which are revelationally-normative.[20]

Certain ways of "doing church" or "being the church" or even of casting the ecclesiological question, can lead to drawing lines where they

18. Ron Sider, *Rich Christians in an Age of Hunger* (Dallas: Word Publishing, 1997), 233–36.

19. See Peter Greer and Phil Smith, *The Poor Will Be Glad: Joining the Revolution to Lift the World out of Poverty* (Grand Rapids: Zondervan, 2009).

20. H. Richard Niebuhr, *The Social Sources of Denominationalism* (New York: H. Holt, 1929).

perhaps ought not to be drawn. Models of pastoral ministry can reinforce certain stereotypes about who we ought to think of as our neighbors. The missiologist and theologian John H. Armstrong has wondered about the pastoral office in the modern world. He writes,

> For a long time I have had serious doubts about many of the models of pastoral ministry used and promoted in the West. These models range from academic and biblical teacher models to chief counselor and care-giver. In my estimation they all fail the biblical test at some crucial point, and some fall even further short than others. Worse still these various models generally hinder the church from being the church in the best sense. Until these models are radically altered I do not believe that we will see the kind of renewal that we need in the church in America.[21]

He goes on to critique what he sees as two primary models: the scholar/teacher and the CEO/manager. Armstrong raises some very important issues, and he indirectly attempts to redefine the terms of the pastor's calling. He writes that "the pastor can only complete the work Christ gave to him when he has *taught and prepared the people so that they can be engaged in the mission of Christ, namely service*."

A great contributing factor to the problems Armstrong examines in the contemporary role of the pastor stem from an improper view of the importance of pastoral ministry. In the following, I'll assert some biblical truths against the conception that all vocations are equal in a radical and thoroughgoing sense. This error, in terms of individual vocations, is expressed in the idea that the calling of a plumber, poet, or president is just as important, valuable, or eternal in service to the kingdom of God as that of a pastor. The correlative to this is the idea that service in various spheres of life, business, education, family, are equally important as service in the church. I mean this to refer to what might be called an *egalitarian* view of vocation, which makes no distinction in any sense between various callings and their value.

The source of error, despite its historical interest and value, is perhaps less important than its current popularity. We might describe it as the democratization of vocation or the egalitarianism of calling. The point here is not to denigrate the valid and important vocations that Christians live out every day in this world. It is rather to properly balance the value of these callings, the fidelity to which has its own eternal consequences

21. John H. Armstrong, "Getting the Role of Pastor Right Again," *Reformation & Revival*, August 15, 2005.

for individuals, with the task of the minister of God's Word, the care of a community of souls.

Today, in many ways and certainly compared to the past, the task of ministry has been largely stripped of its respect and dignity. No doubt in many cases this is due to the failings of the ministers themselves. But in other cases, an anti-authoritarian spirit is at work in the church, unbending in the face of rebuke, unyielding to prophetic testimony. The tendency for this to manifest itself is likely in some part related to the form of church polity, as in some necessary sense, a congregational polity is more prone to produce pastors who preach messages comfortable to their congregants. All this stands in opposition to the observation of the puritan Richard Baxter, that "God hath hitherto made use of the qualifications of the Ministers as the special means for the welfare of his Church."

But of what importance is this church? Is it not merely just another sphere of human redemptive activity? Clearly not. There is no single straight line separating the realms of common grace and special grace, as if the former is *worldly* and the latter merely *churchly*. But the distinction between common and special grace remains, and the significance of the church as an institution lies, in large part, on its unique responsibility to be a structural vehicle of divine grace, primarily through preaching and administration of the sacraments. Armstrong gets at this when he writes, "Pastors must stress mission to the world over separation from the world. As the Christendom model increasingly fails this will becomes more and more obvious. This means we must become less and less interested about who is in and who is out. Baptism and the Lord's Supper are meant to provide the real boundary markers and churches that recover their proper place will be better able to pursue mission."

Abraham Kuyper has one of the most helpful discussions of these matters in his distinction between common and special grace as well as in the distinction between the church as *organism* and *institution*. As he writes with regard to the typology of grace, "Scripture does not arrange both of those—the way of salvation and natural life—like two ticket windows next to each other, but continually weaves them together like threads, giving us a view of the world, its origin, its course within history, and its ultimate destiny, within which, as though within an invisible framework, the entire work of salvation occurs."[22] Likewise Kuyper distinguishes between the church as an *organization* (institution) and an *organism*, showing how the

22. Abraham Kuyper, *Wisdom & Wonder: Common Grace in Science & Art* (Grand Rapids: Christian's Library Press, 2011), 83–84.

two are intimately related without confusion or conflation. Kuyper derives from the Apostle Paul an image of the church as "rooted and grounded," rooted in the organic life of the Christian as renewed in the image of Christ, but grounded in the structures of the institutional church. This image "unites organism and institution, and where Scripture itself refuses to allow any separation, it weaves them together."[23]

There is a real sense in which the radical priority of Christ and his church for the identity of the Christian life is made again and again in the Bible. Consider, for instance, the contrast between natural and spiritual relationship in the following encounter between Jesus and his family. When challenged that he had been ignoring the call of his family members, Jesus replies, "'Who is my mother, and who are my brothers?' Pointing to his disciples, he said, 'Here are my mother and my brothers. For whoever does the will of my Father in heaven is my brother and sister and mother.'" (Matt 12:48–50)

In an important sense, the cross of the Christian life is a testimony to the priority of the spiritual over the natural, the eternal over temporal. This priority of the spiritual over the natural does not merely reorder the Christian relationship to the family. There's a sense in which it *restores* the natural order of the family that had been disrupted in the Fall. In this way, special grace is seen as *restoring* or *transforming* natural relationships into what they ought to have been in a sinless world. Thus the church, in both its organic or institutional form, is not merely just another valid sphere for living Christian life, along with family, business, or politics. It precedes all of these in importance for every Christian, because of its spiritual unity and solidarity as the body of Christ.

So even though we should recognize that all legitimate callings are equally valid ways of following Christ, it does not follow that all spheres are not equally important in every sense, or that all vocations are equally commendable in every way. Let us never forget the pastoral task of the minister of the Word, the shepherd who feeds Christ's sheep (see John 21:15–19), is most important, weighty, serious, and worthy vocation to which a person can ever be called. As the Belgic Confession puts it, "everyone ought, as much as possible, to hold the ministers of the Word and elders of the church in special esteem, because of the work they do" (Art. 31). The recognition of the priority of special over common grace need not derogate the ministries of common grace, even though this is

23. Abraham Kuyper, *Rooted & Grounded: The Church as Organism and Institution* (Grand Rapids: Christian's Library Press, 2013), 5.

all too often what happens in practice. But neither ought we conflate the ministries of common and special grace such that we see the task of "minister" and "muck farmer" as radically equal in every sense before God and human beings.[24]

The reformational doctrine of the priesthood of all believers should not be construed to mean that the ministerial task is just as important as the task of the plumber, as if the gospel and waste water are of equal dignity. Instead the task of the Christian, whether minister of the Word or plumber, involves a commitment to the Great Commission as well as to the Cultural Mandate. As Armstrong writes, "Every-member ministry is not just a 1970s fad, it is the biblical model lost throughout much of the church's history." The water of Christian baptism is thicker than the blood of natural flesh: "Therefore, as we have opportunity, let us do good to all people, especially to those who belong to the family of believers" (Gal 6:10).

MORAL FORMATION

It's one thing to recognize that the institutional church has been given the authority and responsibility to minister to each individual person in support of their unique callings. It's quite another to actualize that authority in a meaningful way. How many churches take the ongoing moral formation of Christians to be one of their key responsibilities? Much attention is often focused on evangelization, and rightly so. But the Great Commission involves not only preaching to the lost, but also teaching those who have faith in Jesus Christ to be followers, disciples who grow more and more into maturity. And this means integrating the insights of the mission of God, the *missio Dei*, as expressed in the Cultural Mandate and the responsibilities to exercise productive cultural stewardship over the created order.

In terms of exposing the lack of moral formation in the evangelical church, Ron Sider's book, *The Scandal of the Evangelical Conscience*, is a noteworthy achievement. On the one hand, it represents an almost complete shift in emphasis away from left-leaning government-oriented solutions to social and economic problems that characterize the first edition of his popular *Rich Christians in an Age of Hunger*. This movement had already become apparent by the time Sider released the twentieth

24. See Cornelius Plantinga Jr., *Engaging God's World: A Christian Vision of Faith, Learning, and Living* (Grand Rapids: Eerdmans, 2002), 37.

anniversary edition of *Rich Christians*, in which, as we have seen in the context of micro-finance advocacy, he embraces increased access to markets and capital investment as necessary components of solutions to global poverty. In *The Scandal of the Evangelical Conscience*, Sider explicitly acknowledges this perspective, as he writes of "the stunning success of market economies in producing ever-greater material abundance."[25]

Sider is thus able to recognize the basic goodness of creation: "Historic Christianity has been profoundly materialistic. The created world is good. God wants us to create wealth and delight in the bounty of the material world." A key part of Sider's project is to properly and relatively value the material and temporal in light of the spiritual and eternal. Thus he rightly notes that "historic Christianity also placed firm boundaries on this materialism. Nothing, not even the whole material world, matters as much as one's relationship with God."[26]

Sider time and again emphasizes the call to Christian faithfulness that has been the hallmark of his career. Freed from the pervasive distortions of leftist economic ideology, Sider's corresponding message becomes even more clear and powerful. Thus, as I noted previously, he writes, "If American Christians simply gave a tithe rather than the current one-quarter of a tithe, there would be enough *private Christian* dollars to provide basic health care and education to all the poor of the earth. And we would still have an extra $60–70 billion left over for evangelism around the world."[27] Contrast this with the rather less optimistic view of Jim Wallis, who says, "I often point out that the church can't rebuild levees and provide health insurance for 47 million people who don't have it."[28] It's one thing to say that the church shouldn't have the responsibility for providing such things; it's quite another to say that the church is *unable* to do so.

By acknowledging the relative but real good of wealth, Sider is able to incisively point out the dangers that necessarily flow out of affluence. Sider argues that the opportunity and responsibility that come with wealth have created a corresponding temptation, and "nurtured a practical materialism that has maximized individual choice. Desiring ever-growing sales to produce ever-greater profits, businesses discovered the

25. Sider, *Scandal of the Evangelical Conscience*, 89.

26. Sider, *Scandal of the Evangelical Conscience*, 88.

27. Sider, *Scandal of the Evangelical Conscience*, 118.

28. Jim Wallis, "A Responsibility to Care," *Sojourners* (September/October 2008). Available at: http://sojo.net/magazine/2008/09/responsibility-care.

power of seductive advertising." He maintains that American Christians "must dethrone mammon and materialism in our hearts and congregations through a more faithful use of our money."[29]

Sider's main adversary in this book is the licentious antinomianism of American evangelical Christianity. He writes, "Scandalous behavior is rapidly destroying American Christianity. By their daily activity, most 'Christians' regularly commit treason. With their mouths they claim that Jesus is Lord, but with their actions they demonstrate allegiance to money, sex, and self-fulfillment." Sider's call is to a rigorously faithful and pious Christianity, consistent in both theory and practice. As he argues, "We proudly trumpet our orthodox doctrine of Christ as true God and true man and then disobey his teaching."[30]

In this project, Sider issues a prophetic lament over the behavior of American Christians:

> We divorce, though doing so is contrary to his commands. We are the richest people in human history and know that tens of millions of brothers and sisters in Christ live in grinding poverty, and we give only a pittance, and almost all of that goes to our local congregation. Only a tiny fraction of what we do give ever reaches poor Christians in other places. Christ died to create one new multicultural body of believers, yet we display more racism than liberal Christians who doubt his deity.[31]

The downside of Sider's prophetic zeal is that the book is characterized by a reactionary tone, and this leads to some conflicting emphases and propositions despite Sider's desire for consistency. Thus he can say on the one hand, in good evangelical fashion, that nothing matters as much as one's personal relationship with God, and that "forgiveness of sins is at the center of Jesus's proclamation of the gospel of the kingdom." But he can also say that "the gospel and salvation involve far more than forgiveness of sins," and, "An exclusive emphasis on personal, individualistic approaches without a parallel concern for structural causes and solutions is wrong at several points."[32] It isn't that such statements are in necessary conflict, but there is a delicate balance between the valuation of the spiritual and the material that must be maintained.

29. Sider, *Scandal of the Evangelical Conscience*, 89.

30. Sider, *Scandal of the Evangelical Conscience*, 12, 50.

31. Sider, *Scandal of the Evangelical Conscience*, 50.

32. Sider, *Scandal of the Evangelical Conscience*, 61, 58, 75.

Sider attempts to synthesize these truths by using the complementary images of Christ as both Savior and Lord. He writes, "Many contemporary Christians act as if it is possible to divide Jesus up, accepting him as Savior and neglecting him as Lord. But Jesus is one person. He cannot be torn apart that way. Either we accept the whole person, Lord and Savior, or we do not accept him at all."[33] Generally speaking, Christ as Savior refers to the personal forgiveness of sins, while Christ as Lord refers to the rule of Christ's kingdom in social structures.

The challenge for Sider and those following him will be to rightly emphasize both the individual and social aspects of the gospel message without swinging the pendulum too far the opposite way. Indeed, if evangelicals have traditionally emphasized the personal at the cost of the social, progressives have traditionally done the reverse. Sider makes an admirable attempt to mediate between these two extremes, and although he is not completely successful, he does provide us a useful model.

Dietrich Bonhoeffer once worried that for thoroughly secularized churches "the blessings of suffering and of the rebirth that might follow from it are withdrawn from the church."[34] Sider's book is an attempt to emphasize the costliness of grace and the sacrifices that we must be willing to make in faithful service to our Lord. The American church is largely a comfortable church and is not accustomed to suffering. In this way we are unlike our Lord, "a man of suffering, and familiar with pain" (Isa 53:3). For this reason, Sider's message is a timely one that ought not be ignored. We ought to take seriously the warning of Christ:

> To the angel of the church in Laodicea write:
>
> These are the words of the Amen, the faithful and true witness, the ruler of God's creation. I know your deeds, that you are neither cold nor hot. I wish you were either one or the other! So, because you are lukewarm—neither hot nor cold—I am about to spit you out of my mouth. You say, 'I am rich; I have acquired wealth and do not need a thing.' But you do not realize that you are wretched, pitiful, poor, blind and naked. I counsel you to buy from me gold refined in the fire, so you can become rich; and white clothes to wear, so you can cover your shameful nakedness; and salve to put on your eyes, so you can see. Those whom I love I rebuke and discipline. So be earnest, and repent. Here I am! I stand at the door and knock. If anyone hears my

33. Sider, *Scandal of the Evangelical Conscience*, 67.

34. Dietrich Bonhoeffer, *Ethics*, vol. 6, Dietrich Bonhoeffer Works (Minneapolis: Fortress Press, 2005), 127.

> voice and opens the door, I will come in and eat with him, and he with me. To him who overcomes, I will give the right to sit with me on my throne, just as I overcame and sat down with my Father on his throne. He who has an ear, let him hear what the Spirit says to the churches. (Rev 3:14–22)

As Sider makes clear, biblical Christian faith is a matter of words as well as deeds, beliefs as well as actions. What does this mean for the nature of Christian political action? What place ought the political to occupy in the life of the Christian believer? It's worthwhile to reflect a bit here on the notable impetus in North American evangelical Christianity to emphasize the importance of politics. Indeed, it is apparent that the term *evangelical* has, at least in much public discourse, come to have primarily political significance, rather than theological or ecclesiastical, such that *Time* magazine could include two Roman Catholics (the late Richard John Neuhaus and Rick Santorum) among its 2005 list of the 25 most influential "evangelicals" in America.[35]

Indeed, when the accusations of sexual sin came to light about Ted Haggard, a megachurch pastor who made *Time*'s list, leading to his resignation as president of the National Association of Evangelicals and eventual dismissal from New Life Church, the first instinct by many was to see this as primarily a political event. James Dobson said of the Haggard scandal, "It appears someone is trying to damage his reputation as a way of influencing the outcome of Tuesday's election."[36] Perhaps the timing of the charges did indeed have political motivations, but Haggard's admission of guilt carries with it implications that reach far beyond mere politics, into the realm of the spiritual.

It should be noted that after the truth of Haggard's actions came to light, Dobson did say that the scandal had "grave implications for the cause of Christ," and Pastor Larry Stockstill, head of the oversight board in charge of Haggard's investigation, said "that politics played 'zero' role in the haste of the process that led to Haggard's removal, and that the oversight board received no political pressure from anyone."[37] But even so, the fact

35. See "The 25 Most Influential Evangelicals in America," *Time*, February 7, 2005. Available at: http://www.time.com/time/specials/packages/article/0,28804,1993235_1993243,00.html.

36. See "Scandal Clouds Conservative Christian Vote," *Washington Wire*, November 2, 2006. Available at: http://blogs.wsj.com/washwire/2006/11/02/scandal-clouds-conservative-christian-vote/.

37. See Eric Gorski, "Disgraced Haggard: I am a 'deceiver and a liar,'" *Denver Post*,

that Haggard has been portrayed as a political heavyweight (with access to the president) and the National Association of Evangelicals has been described as "a powerful lobbying group," rather than an ecumenical and ecclesiastical organization, speaks volumes about the connection between evangelicalism and a particular brand of political engagement.

A piece from about the same time from Michael Luo in the *New York Times* is instructive on a number of levels.[38] First off, the article attempts to point out widening "fissures" among evangelicals, in which "new theological and political splits are developing." While the article does talk at the end about so-called "theological" differences, the bulk of the piece is spent discussing the political divisions.

Michael Luo writes, "Fissures between the traditionalist and centrist camps of evangelicalism have begun to emerge much more prominently in recent months in the political realm." He points specifically to the issues of global warming and immigration. These are common touchstones for the political analysis of evangelicals by the news media nowadays. From issues like immigration to global warming, the press is eager to find the fault lines of evangelical politics. And moving beyond the typical Religious Left/Religious Right dichotomy, there are real and honest disagreements among evangelicals on any number of political issues.

This stems from the fact that political policy is most often about the prudential application of principles, and thus is a matter where there can and should be a variety of informed and committed voices.

Thus, says Thomas Aquinas, human law should not seek to make illegal everything that is immoral, but only that which is necessary for the maintenance of a just society. He writes,

> Many things are permissible to men not perfect in virtue, which would be intolerable in a virtuous man. Now human law is framed for a number of human beings, the majority of whom are not perfect in virtue. Wherefore human laws do not forbid all vices, from which the virtuous abstain, but only the more grievous vices, from which it is possible for the majority to abstain; and chiefly those that are to the hurt of others, without the

November 5, 2006. Available at: http://www.denverpost.com/ci_4607865.

38. Michael Luo, "Evangelicals Debate the Meaning of 'Evangelical,'" *New York Times*, April 16, 2006. Available at: http://www.nytimes.com/2006/04/16/weekinreview/16luo.html?_r=1&.

> prohibition of which human society could not be maintained: thus human law prohibits murder, theft and such like.[39]

For Aquinas then, human law is the result of the prudent and contextual application of the natural and divine law. And it's not surprising that among a diverse group like evangelicals, different opinions will exist as to what considerations are relevant to the construction of a particular policy.

With respect to immigration reform, for example, Alan Cooperman reported that a letter signed by numerous evangelical leaders outlining four major points of emphasis was sent to members of the federal government.[40] Among the national evangelical organizations that signed on to the letter are the Christian Reformed Church in North America and the World Evangelical Alliance.

Notably absent, however, was the National Association of Evangelicals, and the lack of support for the bill was noted as the occasion for the article's headline describing a deepening "split." According to the NAE's vice president for governmental affairs, Rev. Richard Cizik, "the NAE itself did not sign the letter because its members are divided on how to deal with immigration." Since the letter makes rather specific policy proposals rather than general moral and theological guidelines, many evangelicals were not ready to endorse the statement. The same is true for the statement of the Evangelical Climate Initiative, which endorses particular policies with respect to global warming. This is another example of a statement where a number of prominent evangelical leaders signed on, but the NAE did not. This was the result of a bit of backtracking on the part of Cizik after it became clear that evangelical support for the climate initiative did not reach the level of consensus. Previously Cizik had said of his activities at the NAE, "We are currently working on a paper that is scheduled to come out this month on climate change that will get into some policy details, but for the moment we have no specific positions on any environmental legislation."[41]

Cizik's name and affiliation still appeared on the ECI ad campaign, however, despite the decision for the NAE and its representatives to abstain

39. Thomas Aquinas, *Summa Theologica* (New York: Benzinger Bros., 1947), II.1.96.ii.

40. Alan Cooperman, "Letter on Immigration Deepens Split Among Evangelicals," *Washington Post*, April 5, 2006. Available here: http://www.washingtonpost.com/wp-dyn/content/article/2006/04/04/AR2006040401606.html.

41. Amanda Little, "An interview with green evangelical leader Richard Cizik," *Grist*, October 6, 2005. Available at: http://grist.org/article/cizik/.

from signing. This is presumably because the ad copy deadline preceded the letter from the dissenting evangelical leaders. It is typical for prominent evangelical leaders on both the immigration and climate change letters clearly to include their institutional affiliation, as if to implicitly say that the institutions they represent also endorse the statements. It is one thing for this to occur with para-church and other organizations, such as is the case with Ron Sider and Evangelicals for Social Action. It is another, however, for the head of an ecclesiastical body at the denominational or higher ecumenical level to sign these kinds of statements.

This is why the NAE eventually backed off from the climate change letter and did not participate in the immigration letter. Calvin P. Van Reken, professor of moral and philosophical theology at Calvin Theological Seminary, wrote a succinct overview of this problem in an essay exploring the relationship between the church and social justice. Speaking of the church as institution (as opposed to the organic view of the church), Van Reken writes that "normally, the church should not take it upon itself to entertain the political question of how a particular society can best achieve this goal. That is, the institutional church should, in general, avoid policy statements."[42] He outlines a number of reasons for this, and the article is worth reading in its entirety so that you can appreciate his full argument. Again, he says, "the institutional church may outline the broad goals or ends of social policy but normally should not endorse specific policy proposals." That is where many church-based engagement efforts, like those discussed above, falter. They do endorse specific policy proposals, and on these matters of prudence there is great disagreement.

Van Reken does say, however, that the institutional church should speak out in favor or against specific a specific policy "when the policy is clearly immoral." One of the dangers of an institutional ecclesiastical endorsement of a specific policy is that it does not recognize the principle of prudence. Van Reken writes, "The truth is, however, that most political issues, in the Western world at any rate, are debates between two or three morally permissible policy options. Choosing among such options requires a kind of worldly wisdom to which Christians as such have no special claim." If anything, the church even tends to have a kind of naiveté when it comes to political matters.

Dietrich Bonhoeffer articulates a similar vision when he writes that there are three main ways the church can engage the state. In the words

42. Calvin P. Van Reken, "The Church's Role in Social Justice," *Calvin Theological Journal* 34 (1999): 198–202.

of Bonhoeffer, there are "three possibilities for action that the church can take vis-à-vis the state: *first* . . . questioning the state as to the legitimate state character of its actions, that is, making the state responsible for what it does."[43] This corresponds to Van Reken's argument that the institutional church can outline the broad moral goals of public policy and prophetically speak to hold the state accountable.

The second way the church can act is to offer "service to the victims of the state's actions. The church has an unconditional obligation toward the victims of any societal order, even if they do not belong to the Christian community. 'Let us work for the good of all.'" Bonhoeffer continues to say that these are ongoing responsibilities: "the church may under no circumstances neglect either of these duties."[44] The first duty refers to the extent of the policy lobbying the church may do. The second is the direct task of the church to act charitably in service of the gospel. This is actually Van Reken's primary concern, and one I share, that political lobbying will compromise the church's gospel mission.

The third and final way the church can act in Bonhoeffer's view is direct political action, "not just to bind up the wounds of the victims beneath the wheel but to seize the wheel itself."[45] This roughly corresponds with Van Reken's criteria that specific policy statements can only be made on policies that are clear moral evils, such as slavery, apartheid, and abortion.

What does this all mean? The NAE is right to avoid officially endorsing specific policies that are not morally obligatory either immediately or through its representatives. The CRC, whose executive director is a signatory of both letters and of which I am a member, should learn from the NAE's example. I happen to largely agree, for example, with the position articulated in the immigration reform letter but disagree with the proposals of the climate change letter.

If individual Christians, leaders or laypeople, want to speak out on a particular policy, they should do so. But they should do so within the framework of their own personal convictions, representing themselves or under the auspices of a voluntary association or para-church organization, such as the Evangelical Environmental Network, Evangelicals for Social Action, the Heritage Foundation, or the Acton Institute.

43. Dietrich Bonhoeffer, *Berlin: 1932–1933*, vol. 12, Dietrich Bonhoeffer Works (Minneapolis: Fortress Press, 2009), 365.

44. Bonhoeffer, *Berlin: 1932–1933*, 365.

45. Bonhoeffer, *Berlin: 1932–1933*, 365.

This is an important distinction between the nature of ecclesiastical and non-ecclesiastical institutions. The lack of a clear church polity, government, or relationship to ecumenical groups contributes to this problem, but it is not only present at the level of ecumenical associations. When denominational and supra-denominational officials sign these kinds of specific policy statements, and include their affiliation without any sort of sanction from their governing bodies, they go beyond the scope of their authority. In such a case, they cease to faithfully represent the diversity of voices within their churches.

The significance of a comprehensive vision of Christian moral formation lies, in part, in that responsible Christian action in society cannot be reduced to a particular political ideology or partisan agenda. The favorite historical targets of lampoon and derision from progressive Christians are the icons of the Religious Right: the late Jerry Falwell and D. James Kennedy, Pat Robertson, James Dobson, and the like. A standard characterization of their flaws highlights their overemphasis on political power as a means toward the alignment of society with the Christian vision. But if this critique of the politicization of the faith applies to the Religious Right, then it applies equally as well to the Religious Left.

What is shared in what we might call the "legalistic impulse" of much of both conservative and progressive political Christianity is the priority of the role of the government in determining the course of our social life. Both versions of political Christianity, to one extent or another, subsume the Church under the State as a kind of activist lobby (albeit of a special religious character). In this brand of legalism, fidelity to the Christian faith is defined in political terms.

It is in this sense that we can understand the calls of Jim Wallis for the government to coercively redistribute wealth as a means of better realizing God's kingdom here on earth as exhibiting a legalistic impulse. At the national level we see this kind progressive ideology advocated by groups like Sojourners and the National Council of Churches. But a similar progressive political agenda crystallizes on the global stage in the contemporary mainline ecumenical movement. Groups like the World Council of Churches (WCC), Lutheran World Federation (LWF), and the World Communion of Reformed Churches (WCRC), have for the last two decades and more pursued an increasingly ideological political agenda.[46] When the WCRC was formed in 2010 at a council in Grand Rapids, Michigan, the stated rationale for the merger was the commitment to "economic" and "environmental" justice.

Perhaps the most explicit (and egregious) example of this legalistic perspective appears in the Accra Confession, a document that raises a radical critique of "neoliberal" globalization and the corresponding environmental degradation to an article of the Reformed Christian's faith, a response to a *status confessionis*. In confessing against "the oppression of the global economic system," the Accra statement and the broader ecumenical movement it represents stand for a position definitive for the faithful Christian that privileges opposition to climate change, privatization, genetically-modified foods, and the neoliberal empire headed by the United States.

In this the progressive legalists have fully embraced the elevation of works over doctrine. There is here an historical irony. For at its genesis the modern ecumenical movement saw the doctrinal matters as those which were the most divisive and the most likely to foment conflict. It was with the Life and Work movement, engaged on social and political issues, rather than Faith and Order, focused on doctrine, that Christians of a variety of denominations and confessional commitments were thought to be able to work substantively together.

But nowadays the elevation of *praxis* over *doctrina* in progressive ideology means that it is not strictly teaching or doctrine that divides, but rather practical political agendas. We see this as the Accra Confession claims to be such not as "a classical doctrinal confession," but rather as a "faith commitment" and "common witness." We see it too in the statements of "communion" between denominations with as doctrinally divergent views of the Eucharist as the United Methodist Church and the Evangelical Lutheran Church in America (ELCA). "Communion" in this sense can refer only to the shared social vision and political agenda, rather than to any historically or traditionally understood doctrinal agreement. Such ecumenical unity is not on the basis of "doctrinal confession" but rather ideological and practical political platforms.

By defining unity in terms of a specific political vision, these progressive legalists have imported an alien element into the church. Progressive social activists are fond of citing the example of Dietrich Bonhoeffer, who

46. I explore recent social statements of these ecumenical groups at greater length in *Ecumenical Babel: Confusing Economic Ideology and the Church's Social Witness* (Grand Rapids: Christian's Library Press, 2010).

stood for the faith against the incursion of the Nazis into the life of the church. But Bonhoeffer himself, when he addressed the question of the church's confession, did not hesitate to characterize the imposition of a worldly ideology onto the church as a kind of "legalism." In a stunning rhetorical move, when Bonhoeffer addresses "The Church and the Jewish Question," in which he lays out the three possible actions of the church toward the state just mentioned, he accuses the German Christians who would exclude baptized Jews from the church and ministry of Pharasaical legalism.

In this essay, Bonhoeffer describes Judaism not as "a racial concept but a religious one."[47] He then goes on to describe the "Judaizers" of the German church as those German Christians who let "church membership dependent on observance of a divine law," referring to an arbitrary commandment claiming divine authorization, rather than the gospel.[48] Bonhoeffer points concretely to the claim for divine status of the legal requirement of "racial uniformity among the members of a congregation." Thus German-Christian legalism becomes in Bonhoeffer's polemic usage a Jewish-Christian type.

While progressive Christian political activists lobby government to realize God's kingdom of *shalom* here on earth, they are compelled to anathematize those within the church who disagree. As Paul Ramsey, the Princeton ethicist, similarly concluded of the ecumenical movement in 1967, "This identification of Christian social ethics with specific partisan proposals that clearly are not the only ones that may be characterized as Christian and as morally acceptable comes close to the original and New Testament meaning of *heresy*."[49] From this perspective we can say that the Accra Confession is quite literally a *heretical* confession, in that it sets up a foreign and worldly paradigm as determinative of gospel fidelity.

It is quite true that there are temptations to improperly politicize the gospel from both conservative and progressive ideologies. But traditionally there have been institutional strictures and distinctions that prevent, or at least provide obstacles to, the cooption of the institutional church by political interests, whether from the Left or the Right. And these are precisely the kinds of distinctions that must be demolished when attempting to galvanize the church politically.

47. Bonhoeffer, *Berlin: 1932–1933*, 368.

48. Bonhoeffer, *Berlin: 1932–1933*, 368.

49. Paul Ramsey, *Who Speaks for the Church? A Critique of the 1966 Geneva Conference on Church and Society* (Nashville: Abingdon Press, 1967), 56.

Fuller Theological Seminary president Richard Mouw relates his journey away from a position that sought active political engagement by the institutional church. He writes of his encounter with the evangelical figure Carl Henry in 1967, at a time when Mouw "had often felt alienated from evangelicalism because of what I saw as its failure to properly address issues raised by the civil rights struggle and the war in Southeast Asia. As a corrective, I wanted the church, *as church*, to acknowledge its obligation to speak to such matters."[50]

Mouw tells how Henry corresponded with him as an editor on suggestions to revise a piece Mouw was seeking to publish. As Mouw writes, Henry's suggestions ended up with Mouw "saying that the church can say 'no' to things that are happening in the economic and political realms, without mentioning anything about the church legitimately endorsing specific remedial policies or practices." Mouw's agreement at the time to the changes was grudging, for as he says, "There were times, I was convinced, that the church could rightly say a bold 'yes' to specific policy-like solutions. I now see that youthful conviction as misguided. Henry was right, and I was wrong." Thus, writes Mouw of Henry, "A constant theme in his writings was that the church as such has neither the competence nor the authority to address political or economic specifics."

If we are to recover from the legalistic impulse of the Religious Left and Right, it will be in no small part because we have reinvigorated principled distinctions, such as the difference between clear moral imperatives and prudential judgments. This "de-politicization" of the church would mean that we largely relegate political and economic questions to the realm of vigorous yet respectful debate and disagreement. It would also mean that when the church *does* speak institutionally to matters of social import, it does so with a clear voice, as one "crying out in the wilderness" (John 1:23).

The fact that political differences about issues on which there are a variety of defensible biblical positions is viewed as a threat to the unity of evangelicalism says something important about how the movement is more broadly perceived. That is, evangelicalism has become publicly identified as much or more with particular political views than any necessarily corresponding theological position.

Thus, while Rick Warren is identified as "theologically and socially conservative," the fact that he has generally avoided politics makes him

50. Richard Mouw, "Carl Henry Was Right," *Christianity Today*, January 27, 2010. Available at: http://www.christianitytoday.com/ct/2010/january/25.30.html.

a "centrist" rather than a "traditionalist" evangelical, according to the categories that the Pew Forum on Religion and Public Life uses. And on climate change, for example, there is "a tension that exists between the traditionalists and the centrists," according to the Rev. Richard Cizik, then-vice president for governmental affairs for the National Association of Evangelicals. (Both Warren and Cizik make *Time's* top 25 list.) Cizik now heads the New Evangelical Partnership for the Common Good.

The political aspect of evangelical identification really is a red herring, albeit one of great interest to the secular media. Aside from the few social issues on which the perspective of Scripture is rather straightforward, evangelicals should be free to express the convictions of their consciences without being perceived as outside the tent.

And the reason that such clear moral evils need to be opposed is because their affirmation would directly undermine the normativity of the Bible. If anything, this is the baseline, identifying characteristic of evangelicalism, as evidenced by the doctrinal basis for something like the Evangelical Theological Society (ETS): "The Bible alone, and the Bible in its entirety, is the Word of God written and is therefore inerrant in the autographs."[51] Likewise the "Statement of Faith" of the National Association of Evangelicals (NAE) affirms belief in "the Bible to be the inspired, the only infallible, authoritative Word of God."[52] But otherwise, where prudential judgments are concerned, evangelicals enjoy a wide freedom and diversity.

And it is with respect to the theological differences that Luo's article truly gets to the heart of real cracks in the evangelical edifice. Ultimately the unity of any group of Christian believers must be founded on doctrinal agreement. Practice is informed by belief. The eventual failure of the Life and Work and the Faith and Order movements of the global ecumenical enterprise to remain completely separate testify to this reality. This is why creeds and confessional statements have enjoyed such an important place in the history of Christianity, and why the NAE and the ETS define themselves in theological and doctrinal rather than simply political, practical, or social terms.

If the unity of evangelicalism is threatened by disagreements, however sharp, over prudential political concerns, then the so-called "unity"

51. Evangelical Theological Society, "Doctrinal Basis." Available at: http://www.etsjets.org/about.

52. National Association of Evangelicals, "Statement of Faith." Available at: http://www.nae.net/about-us/statement-of-faith.

is something more like the unity enjoyed by political parties and factions rather than that of the body of Christ. One characteristic of the spirit of sectarianism is that it makes matters of moral prudence and permissibility a litmus test of true Christianity.

This is essentially what the substitution or conflation of a political ideology with the Christian gospel and its outworking does. This is a temptation for Christians of all political persuasions, and the infatuation with political power on the part of both the Religious Left and the Religious Right is instructive.

On the Religious Left, perhaps the most egregious example of the tendency to substitute the State for the cause of Christ is in the case of the ceaseless advocacy of the welfare state, under the guise of "social justice." One of the planks in Jim Wallis' "Voting God's Politics" voting guide is titled, "Compassion and Economic Justice," and encourages voters to consider the following questions, as if these all are primary responsibilities of the government: "Does the candidate support measures that provide for family economic success and security by 'making work work,' that promote fair and decent wages, that show a serious commitment to lifting children out of poverty, and support policies on aid, debt, and trade that would bring extreme global poverty to an end?"[53] At its worst this kind of thinking replaces biblical compassion and individual charitable responsibility with impersonal government bureaucracy. It makes "compassion" something the State does as our proxy. "The Bible teaches that societies should organize so that all members have genuine access to the resources needed to live a decent life and provide for those who are unable to care for themselves," contends Wallis. It is clear that for Wallis the state is the primary means by which these societies ought to be organized.

Oftentimes the Religious Right is no better, although it usually appeals to government power on rather different issues. In an excellent column in *Christianity Today*, David P. Gushee "excoriates politicking by Christian conservatives." He writes,

> Ironically, we turn to the state to enforce the values we can't seem to advance in our own churches. We're rightly concerned about our collapsing families, internet pornography, decadent movies and music, and the weakening of sexual morality. But we often can't seem to prevent the encroachment of these problems in

53. Jim Wallis, "Voting God's Politics," *Sojourners*, November 3, 2006. Available at: http://sojo.net/sojomail/2006/11/03.

> our own Christian families and congregations. As if in response, we keep trying to change our nation's laws.[54]

There is perhaps no one better at pointing out the failings of the Religious Right than the Religious Left, and Gushee, who spent three years at Ron Sider's Evangelicals for Social Action, does an admirable job of it.

Yet oftentimes it seems as if attacking the Religious Right is all there is for the Religious Left to do; people are "looking for a deeper conversation about the role of faith and politics, rejecting the narrow political options of the Religious Right," intones Wallis. But Gushee's critique is not simply another salvo from "progressive" Christianity. It is a valid and scathing critique of all Christian political activism: "The more we find it hopeless to think that we can actually create and sustain disciplined communities of faith, the more we spend our time on political activities. We may not be able to get self-identified Christians to obey the Word of God, but we might be able to leverage our political clout to elect 'our people' to Congress."

The solution, as is so often the case, to the problem of Left vs. Right is to be found in a middle way. No, not the middle way of an "independent" or third-party political Christianity. I'm talking about the "middle way" of the Mediator, Jesus Christ. As seen above, political Christianity, of either liberal or conservative persuasion, tends to place the State as the normative institution to mediate between human relationships. Government, mediating between all persons and institutions, becomes the instrument and means by which we attempt to advance the cause of Christ.

By contrast, writes Dietrich Bonhoeffer, the only true Mediator is Jesus Christ: "*He is the mediator*, not only between God and human persons, but also between person and person, and between person and reality "[55] Here Bonhoeffer is emphasizing the scope of the curse that has been inaugurated with the life, death, and resurrection of Jesus Christ. In Genesis 3, the consequences of the fall of humanity into sin are spelled out in the form of covenant curses, and in the case of the man and woman, we find that relationships are fractured on at least three levels: between humankind and God (vertical), human interrelationships (horizontal), and between humans and the rest of creation (as in the cultural mandate).

54. David Gushee, "Children of a Lesser Hope," *Christianity Today*, November 1, 2006. Available at: http://www.christianitytoday.com/ct/2006/november/18.94.html.

55. Dietrich Bonhoeffer, *Discipleship*, vol. 4, Dietrich Bonhoeffer Works (Minneapolis: Fortress Press, 2003), 94.

But the good news of the gospel includes the proleptic (already/not yet) reversal of the curse of sin and brokenness. "Christ the mediator stands between son and father, between husband and wife, between individual and nation, whether they can recognize him or not," writes Bonhoeffer.[56]

In its activist zeal, political Christianity substitutes the State for Christ, the one who in reality stands between all human relationships. The State's proper role is therefore lost in the expansion of its purview to all social relations. "The order of creation is turned upside down; what should be last is first, the expedient, the subsidiary, has become the main thing," says Emil Brunner. "The State, which should be only the bark on the life of the community, has become the tree itself."[57] The State exists for man, and not man for the State; but man exists for God above all. Abraham Kuyper's vision of "sphere sovereignty" embodies the truth of these observations, as each social institution relied directly and immediately on God for its mandate and authority, not depending on the intercession or mediation of any other organism. He writes, "We understand hereby, that the family, the business, science, art and so forth are all social spheres, which do not owe their existence to the State, and which do not derive the law of their life from the superiority of the State, but obey a high authority within their own bosom; an authority which rules, by the grace of God, just as the sovereignty of the State does."[58]

The penultimate nature of politics only receives its appropriate valuation when viewed in relation to the ultimate reality of Christ. Thus Bonhoeffer writes,

> There is no genuine gratitude for nation, family, history, and nature without a deep repentance that honors Christ alone above all these gifts. There is no genuine tie to the given realities of the created world; there are no genuine responsibilities in the world without recognition of the break, which already separates us from the world.[59]

Christ opens the way for healing of the broken relationships, and in this new reality these relationships receive their rightful due.

56. Bonhoeffer, *Discipleship*, 95.

57. Emil Brunner, *Justice and Social Order* (Cambridge: Lutterworth, 2002 [1945]), 125.

58. Abraham Kuyper, *Lectures on Calvinism* (Edinburgh: T&T Clark, 1899), 116.

59. Bonhoeffer, *Discipleship*, 96.

In the same way, Anthony Esolen has some telling reflections on the tendency to idolize government: "It's a law of idolatry that the stark staring idol fails to deliver not only the salvation promised by the living God, but also the paltry earthly substitute for which you have carved it in the first place."[60] If evangelicals continue to place politics in place of the true Mediator, Esolen's prediction no doubt will come true.

Let us keep this perspective in place today, tomorrow, and in the future, as we strive to place our faith not in the things of this world, but in the hope of heaven, "where moth and rust do not destroy, and where thieves do not break in and steal."

PUBLIC WITNESS

Unfortunately for the health of Christian public witness and social thought, many ecclesiastical organizations have not rested content with the kind of emphasis on moral formation of individual Christians and respect for their unique vocations and conscientious convictions. There are perhaps no more egregious violators of these considerations than ecumenical groups, which tend to be less accountable as their abstraction from local congregations increases. The eleventh General Assembly of the Lutheran World Federation was held in 2010, and the theme of the conference was a petition from the Lord's Prayer, "Give us today our daily bread" (Matt 6:11). There was a good deal of reflection and self-expression from the hundreds of delegates gathered in Stuttgart, Germany, on topics related to global poverty and hunger. And while the assembly's introduction explicitly noted the contribution of the German theologian Dietrich Bonhoeffer, the LWF meeting would have been improved if there had been a more substantive integration of Bonhoeffer's views on the ecumenical movement, poverty, and work, into its proceedings.

The LWF is a global ecumenical body consisting of 140 member churches in 79 countries, representing over 70 million Christians. The LWF, founded in Lund, Sweden in 1947, has much to learn from the legacy of Dietrich Bonhoeffer, who was executed in the prime of his life by the Nazis two years earlier. LWF assembly opened on July 20, 2010, the sixty-sixth anniversary of the failed Stauffenberg plot to assassinate

60. Anthony Esolen, "Let Him Who Has Ears, Hear," *Mere Comments*, December 6, 2006. Available at: http://touchstonemag.com/merecomments/2006/12/let_him_who_has/.

Hitler, in which Bonhoeffer was implicated. This year also represents the seventy-fifth anniversary of one of Bonhoeffer's most significant essays, "The Confessing Church and the Ecumenical Movement."[61] In this essay, Bonhoeffer challenges the ecumenical movement to identify itself as either an institutional form of the Christian church, with all the attendant responsibilities and duties, or as a simple gathering of interested Christians, with no binding authority or official purview.

In the latter case, says Bonhoeffer, the actions of such a group would have "only a neutral character, not involving any confession, and this conversation might only have the informative character of a discussion, without including a judgment or even a decision on this or that doctrine, or even church."[62] In the intervening decades, Bonhoeffer's challenge continues to resonate, since the LWF, for instance, continues to waver between its self-understanding as an expression of Christian communion on the one side, and its political and social activism on the other.

A reply to my book, *Ecumenical Babel*, in which I explore Bonhoeffer's relevance for a contemporary critique of the mainline ecumenical movement at some length, challenges my use of Bonhoeffer on this very point. Christopher Dorn writes, "While acknowledging that Bonhoeffer's essay appeared more than seventy-five years ago, Ballor nevertheless insists that in the intervening decades the ecumenical movement has not been able to answer the question about its ecclesial status definitively."[63] Dorn then points to the case of the World Council of Churches (WCC) and its adoption of the Toronto Statement in 1950, which, says Dorn, "has provided the foundation for subsequent discussion of the question about the ecclesial status of the ecumenical movement, at least as it is manifested in the WCC, until now." But pointing to ecumenical statements in which groups assert that they do not function as ecclesiastical institutions of authority misses the basic thrust of my critique.

My point was not that the self-understanding of the ecumenical groups was that they are not "superchurches," to use Dorn's term. Rather, it was that they, particularly in the case of their social witness, act as if they were speaking with the institutional authority of the church or their

61. Dietrich Bonhoeffer, "The Confessing Church and the Ecumenical Movement," in *No Rusty Swords* (New York: Harper & Row, 1965), 326–44.

62. Bonhoeffer, "The Confessing Church and the Ecumenical Movement," 331–32.

63. Christopher Dorn, "The Ecumenical Movement and its Critics: A Reply to Jordan J. Ballor," *Perspectives* (April 2011). Available at: http://www.rca.org/Page.aspx?pid=7275.

churches. At one event where I discussed the Accra Confession, an ecumenical representative said that he preferred to call it "the Accra conversation." But again this characterization militates against the stated purpose of the Accra Confession itself, that is, as a binding statement of confessional conscience in response to a *status confessionis*. Dorn apparently is much more comfortable with a purported confessional document from an ecumenical organization which denounces in broad strokes the legitimacy of the vocations of millions of Christians globally than a critique of the same from an individual theologian writing out of conscientious objection to ecumenical tyrannization of Christian conscience. There is a deep category error at work here in viewing my complaint as outside the bounds of dialogue. This error is only possible if the terms of the dialogue have already been set precisely by the document that is itself supposed to be the basis of conversation rather than confessional exclusion.

There may well be a disconnect between the theoretical basis of the ecumenical movement and its activities. My criticisms were not leveled primarily against the theoretical basis of the churches as such, but rather against what I perceived to be inconsistency between the ecumenical movement's existence and stated *raison d'être*, and its functional activities. This, too, is the basic concern shared by Paul Ramsey, and thus as long as ecumenical groups *act as if* they are institutional expressions of the church in their posture towards the world, then Bonhoeffer's basic ecclesiological question remains valid. Dorn's dismissal of my criticism would apply equally, *mutatis mutandis*, to Paul Ramsey's, as another reviewer put it on this issue, my work is "Ramsey redivivus."[64]

The dubious status of various ecumenical groups in relation to their social pronouncements was on display at the Uniting General Council of the World Communion of Reformed Churches (WCRC) in 2010. Thousands of delegates, exhibitors, and volunteers gathered on the campus of Calvin College to mark the union of two Reformed ecumenical groups, the World Alliance of Reformed Churches (WARC) and the Reformed Ecumenical Council (REC). This new global ecumenical body would include 227 denominations in 108 nations worldwide, with over 80 million Christians of broadly Reformed, Congregational, and Presbyterian membership.

64. See Thomas Sieger Derr, review of *Ecumenical Babel: Confusing Economic Ideology and the Church's Social Witness*, in *Journal of Markets & Morality* 13, no. 2 (Fall 2010): 389–91.

But the proceedings over those two weeks went far beyond mere celebration and praise at the joining of these disparate groups. The future course of the newly formed WCRC was set at this first council, and all signs point to an institution defined by a narrow set of advocacy items rather than a gospel-oriented vision. The basis for the WCRC's exploration of justice is the aforementioned Accra Confession, named for the last general council of WARC, held in Accra, Ghana in 2004, which produced the text in response to a perceived crisis of the Christian faith. Again, in the words of the Accra Confession, the crisis calls for "a decision of faith commitment," specifically focused on condemning "the development of neoliberal economic globalization." At the core of this "faith commitment" is a perspective that views the developing world as victimized at the hands of a vast conspiratorial network of developed nations, multinational corporations, and global financial institutions. The primary villain in this "neoliberal empire" is the United States, cast as the leader of "the coming together of economic, cultural, political and military power that constitutes a system of domination led by powerful nations to protect and defend their own interests."

I am certainly not alone in considering the Accra Confession on its own terms as a document intended not simply as an advisory statement but rather as an ecclesiastical response to a *status confessionis*. As Averell Rust writes, "The debate on whether the 'integrity of our faith is at stake' has moved beyond an ethical discussion to a theological one. It proceeded to the call for a *status confessionis/processus confessionis*."[65] Hans-Wilfried Haase's concerns echo mine about those who would be excluded by the Accra Confession, as the document's approach "becomes a problem, however, when some possible actions take on the quality of a confession and people who, for various reasons cannot agree with those actions, are then excluded from the confession."[66] My concerns about the status of the document arise out of the inherent ambiguity of the rhetorical stance taken by ecumenical groups in claiming to in some sense represent the moral authority of hundreds of millions of Christians worldwide.

But there are problems beyond the documents standing, so to speak, which lie in its substantive treatment of economic questions. The South African economist Stan du Plessis has criticized the Accra Confession

65. Averell Rust, "The Historical Context of the Accra Confession," *Hervormde Teologiese Studies* 65, no. 1 (2009): 608.

66. Hans-Wilfred Haase, "Theological Remarks on the Accra Confession," *Hervormde Teologiese Studies* 65, no. 1 (2009): 612.

for its perspective, one that in his view "substitutes a narrow ideology for a critical understanding of modern economies."[67] The Calvin College economist Roland Hoksbergen, too, has questioned the perspective presented in the document. Hoksbergen takes the Accra Confession (AC) on its own terms, as a response to the *processus confessionis* (process of confession) and in its own words as a "decision of faith commitment." Hoksbergen's analysis is lucid and straightforward.[68] Acknowledging the negative interpretive framework of "neoliberal empire" operative in the Accra statement, Hoksbergen notes that "there are social scientists who analyze world affairs this way, but there are also many who see things very differently. For example, there are likely more books that trumpet market solutions to global poverty than there are books that find markets to be its root cause." The tone and stance of the Accra document relative to globalization and market economies in general are quite unbalanced, given this diversity of opinion. "Whereas every reference to markets in the AC is negative," writes Hoksbergen, "these scholars of the global economy are much more positive, finding that people are poor not because of what markets have done to them." The conclusion about the place of the Accra Confession for Hoksbergen is that it is "a document that powerfully identifies the concerns of the church for global economic and ecological justice, but that is suspect in its analysis of the global economy." For these reasons, concludes Hoksbergen, "the analysis in the AC should be studied and taken seriously, but it should not be confessed."

And so the problem with the Accra Confession is not just that it takes sides on questions of economic prudence and policy, although this is something that institutional churches should always be wary of. As Paul Ramsey wrote, "The specific solution of urgent problems is the work of political prudence and worldly wisdom. In this there is room for legitimate disagreement among Christians and among other people as well in the public domain—which disagreement ought to be welcomed and not led one way toward specific conclusions."[69]

67. Stan Du Plessis, "How Can You Be a Christian and an Economist? The Meaning of the Accra Declaration for Today," *Faith & Economics* 56 (Fall 2010): 66.

68. See Roland Hoksbergen, "The Global Economy, Injustice, and the Church: On Being Reformed in Today's World," in *Reformed Mission in an Age of World Christianity: Ideas for the Twenty-First Century*, ed. Shirley J. Roels (Grand Rapids: Calvin Press, 2011), 93–103. Available at: https://www.calvin.edu/admin/cccs/rcc/chapters/Hoksbergen.pdf. See also my review of *Reformed Mission* in *Journal of Markets & Morality* 14, no. 2 (Fall 2011): 580–82.

69. Ramsey, *Who Speaks for the Church?*, 19.

The compounding problem with the Accra Confession is that it takes the wrong side, the side that embraces an essentially neo-Marxist narrative of Third World alienation and victimization, and seeks "justice" in the form of retribution against First World villains. Far from promoting the kind of unity that is at the core of ecumenical efforts, this kind of rhetorical and ideological confessionalism drives apart those who ought to be joining together. It pits the rich against the poor, north against south, east against west, inserting the divisive language of economic class into the definition of the Christian church.

Wholesale rejection of globalization should not be made into an article of the Christian faith. But this is precisely what the Accra Confession does. And if the World Communion of Reformed Churches continues to treat the Accra Confession or its underlying economic worldview as a confessional litmus test, it will undermine its own stated commitment to "unite Christians for common witness and service to the world." The problem with the social witness of the LWF, the WCRC, and the broader ecumenical movement is not that it addresses problems like hunger or poverty. It is, instead, the way in which it has done so, as typified in the LWF Stuttgart meeting. Here we saw statements decrying "illegitimate debt," the privileging of "profits over people," and in the words of LWF general secretary Rev. Dr. Ishmael Noko, "the gap between those who do not have enough to eat and those who have far more than they need." But beyond this kind of activist jingoism, or pietistic bewailing, there was precious little in terms of helpful analysis of the complex realities of a globalized world.

Some may doubt whether documents like the Accra Confession really do lead to particular ideological conclusions or whether they actually do begin to elide the distinction between principle and policy. A partial affirmative response to such doubts might lie in the way in which the Accra Confession has been utilized by some of its proponents as just such a political tool. Just weeks after the closing of the WCRC synod, Allan Boesak, a leading ecumenical theologian at Stellenbosch University, called upon the moral authority of the Accra Confession as a resource for his advocacy for specific protectionist trade measures. During the World Cup soccer matches in 2010, and there were apparently a huge number of imported vuvuzelas, horns popularly used in South Africa during sporting events, coming from places like China. During the debate about potential bans and other measures to protect the domestic vuvuzela industry, Boesak wondered about the positive effects of such measures: "If the vuvuzela had been made here, how many jobs would have been saved?"[70] The immediate context for these comments was the release of a study document characterized as "an emanation of the Accra Confession." The Accra Confession is also described as "a status confessionis . . . which defined the global economic injustices leading to vast inequalities between the North and the South, or developed and developing countries, as a sin against God." The Accra Confession was also described as having been "re-endorsed last week during the launch of the new 80-million strong World Council of Reformed Churches as part of the articles of faith that every member has to adopt." So much for a conversation.

Rather than engage in the difficult work of providing a coherent and normative basis for responsible social proclamation, the LWF, for its part, preferred instead—as is so often the case in the deliberations of mainline ecumenical groups—to point to "neoliberal globalization" as the structural injustice causing extreme poverty in the world. The missing element in the LWF's poverty discussions, most recently at the General Assembly, has been a nuanced and comprehensive valuation of the role of creative work and entrepreneurship in the creation of material wealth. The social witness of ecumenical groups like the LWF have, for the better part of the past 50 years, consistently undermined work and labor as God's order of blessings to provide material sustenance for humankind.

Bonhoeffer himself identified the mandate of "work" and "culture" (in the sense of human cultivation of God's creation) as one of the four arenas (in addition to the family, church, and government) in which we fulfill our calling to serve God through our service to others. There are certainly cases in which God miraculously or specially provides material goods for our wellbeing, such as manna and quail from heaven (Exod 16) or the seemingly bottomless baskets of bread and fish (Mark 6:30–44). But the regular means that God has graciously ordered in the world for meeting our physical needs is the realm of work.

We can see this in the Apostle's injunction, "If a man will not work, he shall not eat" (2 Thess 3:10). Far too little of the LWF deliberations about the nature of food and hunger, work and poverty, have focused on the role of human labor in economic relationships. The difference

70. See Hans Pienaar, "China threat to local vuvuzela production," *Business Day*, July 1, 2010. Available at: http://www.bdlive.co.za/articles/2010/07/01/china-threat-to-local-vuvuzela-production.

between the productive worker in a modern economy and the subsistence labor in primitive societies is the extent to which the worker and the fruits of his or her labor are brought into relationship with neighbors: local, regional, national, and international.

As the Reformed author Lester DeKoster writes, "Our working puts us in the service of others; the civilization that work creates puts others in the service of ourselves. Thus, work restores the broken family of humankind."[71] This connection of work to civilization is achieved through the kind of relationships made possible in a globalized world. And the ideological opposition to globalization manifest in the ecumenical movement would relegate the labor of those in the developing world to the margins of civilization itself.

As Bonhoeffer writes of the relationship between work and our daily bread, "the bread is God's free and gracious gift. We cannot simply take it for granted that our own work provides us with bread; rather this is God's order of grace." It is precisely this "order of grace" that the developing world needs most, and the social witness of the ecumenical movement offers least.

As the forgoing has shown, and as our experience shows every day, one of the recurring problems facing the church is when it should speak, formally and institutionally, to some matter of public import. One of these issues facing the world today, taken up by the Accra Confession as well as by nonprofit advocacy groups, is the challenge of global climate change. My own denomination is one of the many Christian communities and groups within recent years to struggle with whether and how to respond.

While my church's synod, its highest deliberative body, debated and eventually passed a resolution last year, one of the delegates reflected on the process. "I'm a skeptic on much of this," he said, "But how will doing this hurt? What if we find out in 30 years that numbers (on climate change) don't pan out? We will have lost nothing, and we'll have a cleaner place to live. But if they are right, we could lose everything."

The reality is, however, that as we have seen in the case of ecumenical statements, there is a great deal to lose when the church speaks out publicly. Much is at stake, and so the church's official stances on issues must be weighed judiciously and considered carefully. Here it is worth recalling the warning of Calvin Van Reken, a professor of moral theology at Calvin Theological Seminary, about dangers facing the church as it attempts to navigate these treacherous waters. One possibility, pointing

71. Lester DeKoster, *Work: The Meaning of Your Life—A Christian Perspective* (Grand Rapids: Christian's Library Press, 2010), 2.

to the example of apartheid in South Africa, is that the church "will be silent when it should speak out." But "a second, even worse danger, is that the church will speak out and defend the wrong side of the moral issue."

So, to address the question raised by the delegate, it matters a great deal whether climate change is real, whether it is caused by human beings and whether it represents the matter of social, economic and environmental justice that many people claim that it does. Clearly the church has a great deal at stake, whether it speaks or remains silent on a particular issue.

Another thing to consider is that the church doesn't just have its own moral authority to lose if it speaks in an incorrect or untimely fashion on climate change. Some years ago noted Christian writer Andy Crouch made a similar case regarding climate change, arguing that "we have little to lose, and much technological progress, energy security and economic efficiency to gain, if we act on climate change now—even if the worst predictions fail to come to pass. But if we choose inaction and are mistaken, we will leave our descendants a blighted world."[72]

It's true: there is nothing in this world that does not involve some risk, whether action or inaction. This is in part because every choice we make, individually and institutionally, closes off some other option for action. In economics this is understood in terms of *opportunity cost*. For everything we do, there is something else we choose not to do. So again, what do we have to lose? All the other good that we might be doing instead! This raises the difficult prospect of agreeing about certain ends or goals and disagreeing about the best ways to reach those goals. As churches take action themselves and exhort others to do the same, they need to make sure to respect the prudential judgment and individual consciences of their members.

As individuals and institutions like various churches consider whether and how to react to climate change, we must take into account these multifaceted challenges and concerns. There do not seem to be any easy answers, but no matter what we do, we can't avoid the responsibility of thinking and acting as faithful Christians. That much is certain.

What might that faithful Christian public witness look like? If we turn our eyes to domestic matters, we see that religious discussions of the federal budget often generate more heat than light. The debate tends to feature sloganeering ("What Would Jesus Cut? Who Would Jesus

72. Andy Crouch, "Environmental Wager," *Christianity Today*, August 2005. Available at: http://www.culture-making.com/articles/environmental_wager.

Bomb?") and political theater ("Fasting for a Better Budget"), name calling and grandstanding ("Bully! Hypocrite!").[73] On Good Friday in 2011, the formation of a "new Christian coalition, called the Circle of Protection," was announced, intended "to resist budget cuts that undermine the lives, dignity, and rights of poor and vulnerable people." The "Circle of Protection" refers to the sacred space surrounding "programs that meet the essential needs of hungry and poor people at home and abroad."[74] A refrain from the variety of campaigns echoed throughout the Lenten season that the federal budget should not be balanced "on the backs of the poor." Most of the efforts featured predictably progressive stalwarts like the National Council of Churches, Sojourners, and Bread for the World.

However, one effort has made an explicit and valiant attempt to elevate the debate. Citizens for Public Justice (CPJ) and Evangelicals for Social Action (ESA) issued "A Call for Intergenerational Justice: A Christian Proposal for the American Debt Crisis," which in its own words was intended to "to join a trans-partisan, intergenerational movement of citizens," and, propounded by Gideon Strauss and Ron Sider, at the time heads of their respective organizations, sought to pitch a tent big enough to cover Christians from a variety of political persuasions.[75] The goal of the CPJ/ESA Call is twofold: to make clear that reducing the federal debt is a moral priority for Christians, but that doing so must not be done "at the expense of our poorest fellow citizens." There are some important merits to the CPJ/ESA Call. It introduces the fruitful concept of "intergenerational justice," which "demands that one generation must not benefit or suffer unfairly at the cost of another" and functions in this evangelical context similarly to the Roman Catholic idea of "intergenerational

73. See Shane Claiborne, "What Would Jesus Cut? Who Would Jesus Bomb?" *God's Politics*, February 28, 2011. Available at: http://sojo.net/blogs/2011/02/28/what-would-jesus-cut-who-would-jesus-bomb; Jim Wallis, "10 Reasons Why I'm Fasting for a Better Budget," *Huffington Post*, March 28, 2011. Available at: http://www.huffingtonpost.com/jim-wallis/10-reasons-why-im-fasting_b_841637.html; and Wallis, "Woe to You, Legislators!" *God's Politics*, April 14, 2011. Available at: http://sojo.net/blogs/2011/04/14/woe-you-legislators.

74. Circle of Protection, "Press Release: Christian Leaders Unite to Protect Poor People in Budget Debate," April 27, 2011. Available at: http://www.nae.net/resources/news/561-press-release-christian-leaders-unite-to-protect-poor-people-in-budget-debate.

75. Center for Public Justice and Evangelicals for Social Action, "A Call for Intergenerational Justice: A Christian Proposal for the American Debt Crisis," March 3, 2011. Available at: http://www.cpjustice.org/intergenerationaljustice.

solidarity."[76] It also makes absolutely clear the imperative to "cut federal spending" and the undeniable reality that America's "growing national debt now puts us on a path towards economic disaster."

But in the final analysis the Call must be judged to suffer from the same fatal flaw that mars its less sophisticated and more strident cousins. Christian campaigns to make particular federal programs immune from funding reductions sends the wrong basic message both to politicians and to Christian citizens. The reality of our debt crisis is that the federal government has been trying to do too much for too many for too long. Instead of focusing on ways to empower other institutions and levels of government and galvanize them to relieve the burden of the federal government, these efforts simply feed into the fundamentally false dilemma of federal action or no action at all. This dichotomy is reinforced by both major political parties. We have only two solutions at our disposal, we are told: cut spending or raise taxes. We are faced with the basic choice: pay for the federal government to do it (raise taxes) or it won't get done (cut spending).

What we don't have in any of these efforts is a framework for determining which programs and types of spending the government should prioritize. All we are provided with is the directive that "effective" federal welfare programs cannot be cut, as if some absolute level of spending on a particular program, like Pell Grants or Head Start, is a clear moral, even scriptural, imperative. A truly constructive approach to the public debt crisis would outline the various responsibilities of government at various levels, with relative priority for each responsibility. This would help us address the question of whether spending on national defense is more germane to the role of the federal government than providing bed nets to fight malaria in Africa, or whether and to what extent the federal government has a role to play in providing things like medical insurance, infant formula, and public education to its citizens. Only on the basis of these first principles of government can we start to judge how current, as well as past and future, levels of expenditure line up against what government is supposed to do. We can then begin to determine what government *has* been doing versus what it *ought* to be doing.

Things that are not properly the task of the federal government might then begin to be privatized with appropriate institutions of civil society or localized to other levels of government. Privatization might be

76. See Jordan J. Ballor, "Editorial: Intergenerational Ethics and Economics," *Journal of Markets & Morality* 14, no. 1 (Spring 2011): 1–4.

done over time and in an orderly fashion, as federal funding is phased out and private partners are formed, incentivized, or empowered to relieve the government of its responsibilities. Localization would have the advantage of compelling lower levels of government to raise funds for their own programs, rather than routing them through the federal level, and therefore keep the cost of government more transparent and accountable to its constituencies.

While privatization and localization will not always be the appropriate solution, such efforts can often advance the Christian social principle of subsidiarity, which emphasizes the sovereignty and legitimacy of the responsibilities of lower and decentralized forms of organization and social life. There are at least two basic threats that undermine the viability of such an approach, however, and they come from the government and the church, respectively. From the government there is an increasingly disturbing trend that locates the solution to social problems simply either in business or in government. The logic of this either/or mentality places us between market and state, restricting the vitality and independence of mediating institutions, particularly private charities. We see this mentality manifest itself in attacks on charities on a number of fronts, including the rhetorical conflation of "non-profit" with government, the threat of decertification of more than a 300,000 charities by the IRS, and proposed limits to charitable deductions.

Even more troubling is the mounting evidence that Christians have adopted this mentality, too. We see this in giving patterns among American Christians. The majority of evangelical church leaders, for instance, seem not to think that tithing is a biblical imperative (estimates for levels of evangelical giving typically range from 2 to 4 percent of income). The problem with the CPJ/ESA Call and the host of other Christian responses to the budget crisis is that they do not embody the urgency or the significance of this charitable responsibility. Douglas LeBlanc recently described the importance of tithing as "the beginning of breaking out of that self-indulgent life, primarily because it says to you that your money is not your own. And it's a small sacramental way of saying that your money in your life is coming to you through the grace of God, through the gifts that He's given you."[77] C. S. Lewis once said, "If you are on the wrong road, progress means doing an about turn and walking back to

77. Jeremy Lott, "Douglas LeBlanc: The RealClearReligion Interview," April 15, 2011. Available at: http://www.realclearreligion.org/articles/2011/04/15/douglas_leblanc_the_realclearreligion_interview_106236.html.

the right road; and in that case, the man who turns back soonest is the most progressive man."[78] The federal government has been on the wrong road for decades, and the answer to the public debt crisis in America lies in turning back to basic questions about the role of government in its various forms and its relationship to other aspects of social life. A truly Christian response to the challenge of intergenerational justice and the public debt crisis demands no less.

We face in America similar dynamics related to public debt and the expansion of the welfare state and its inner logic as experienced in Europe over the last century. A description of the current situation in the Netherlands by Herman Noordegraaf of the Protestant Theological University in Leiden captures the latest development in this transition quite well.[79] There are significant changes from the First Social Congress in 1891 to the Third Social Conference in 1952 up to the present day. Rolf van der Woude, senior researcher at the Historical Documentation Centre for Dutch Protestantism at the VU University Amsterdam, examines the move from 1891 to 1952, and concludes that in the post war era, "A new generation believed that the beast of the state, caged for so long, had now been tamed. At the end of the 1950s, [the older] generation retreated, the Netherlands entered a period of economic boom, and a generous welfare state was rapidly erected from the ground up wherein welfare was no longer a matter of charity but a matter of justice guaranteed by the government. The beast of the state had become an ally."[80]

Noordegraaf picks up the transition over the last half-century, in which the situation has largely remained the same, in that the church's primary responsibility is understood not merely to have to provide material assistance to the poor, but rather advocate for reliance on the welfare state for such provision. As Noordegraaf writes, a declaration on the problem of poverty in 1987 codified the approach of "aid under protest," in which the churches provide aid to the poor but only under protest that the government was not meeting welfare needs appropriately. The statement reads:

78. C. S. Lewis, *Mere Christianity* (New York: HarperCollins, 2009), 28.

79. Herman Noordegraaf, "Aid Under Protest? Churches in the Netherlands and Material Aid to the Poor," *Diakonia* 1, vol. 1 (2010): 47–61.

80. Rolf van der Woude, "Taming the Beast: The Long and Hard Road to the Christian Social Conference of 1952," *Journal of Markets & Morality* 14, no. 2 (Fall 2011): 439.

> We reject the way people are once again made dependent on charity. We plead for social security that is not charity but a right that is fully guaranteed by government. For this reason, financial aid given by churches in situations of need should be combined with protest against the causes of this need to government and society.

Noordegraaf's observation is that the churches, both locally and denominationally, have been too concerned with meeting the momentary concrete needs of the poor and need to pay more attention to the mandate to lobby the government for more expansive social welfare programs. The point is that the need for Christian or church-based charity indicts the lack of justice under a modern constitutional state, where freedom from need and want ought to be simply guaranteed.

As Nordegraaf concludes concerning recent trends, "More and more, as the above mentioned reports show, churches have been involved in material aid: when people are in need and ask for help, you give it. It is a kind of safety net under the increasingly porous safety net of the state." He continues, "The fact that the churches found this problematic reflects their belief that the principles of the welfare state are worth fighting for. This has to do with a vision of the task of the state to promote the general welfare and to secure the basic needs of people in society." Noordegraaf concludes that "it is in harmony with the calvinist approach of the responsibility of the state that churches try to make clear to government and to society at large that they have helped with material aid. This signalizing can take many forms: in letters, reports, talks, discussions, programmes in the media, articles in newspapers and so on. In this way, individual aid is combined with advocacy in the public domain."

The transition explored by van der Woude and Noordegraaf show just how much things have changed over the last 120 years in the Netherlands, when Abraham Kuyper emphasized the priority of Christian giving in 1891, arguing that "the holy art of 'giving for Jesus' sake' ought to be much more strongly developed among us Christians. Never forget that all state relief for the poor is a blot on the honor of your savior."[81] Such emphasis on private Christian charity is now understood in many places to be retrograde and obsolete.

This kind of conflation of charity and government aid is not restricted to domestic affairs. On the international development stage,

81. Abraham Kuyper, *The Problem of Poverty* (Sioux Falls: Dordt College Press, 2011), 69.

the ONE Campaign has been the most prominent example, supported by pop icons like Bono and George Clooney and Christian leaders like evangelical pastor Rick Warren. But the ONE Campaign is just the headliner of a group of like-minded initiatives, most often identifying themselves with one biblical prophet or another (like the Micah Challenge and the Isaiah Platform). What is similar in all these movements is an emphasis on the role of government in providing assistance to the poor. But it is precisely this aspect of the initiatives that is most problematic from a Christian perspective.

One of the most common refrains from Christian leaders calling various governments to action—whether those of Canada, the U.S., or other member states of the United Nations—is that governments are the only entities capable of providing the level of material assistance that is needed. In the words of a speaker to a denominational assembly I once observed, "Civil society is never enough." The message is that churches can never hope to match sums like the $40 billion the G8 has proposed to cut debt among some African nations.

This attitude simply does not give Christians enough credit, both for what they have done and what they might do if challenged. In the U.S. alone in 2004, private individuals and corporations gave a record $249 billion to charity, with religious organizations as the single largest recipient group at $88 billion.

This is more than double the debt-relief offered by the G8, and this is reached even though Christians as a group do not give nearly at a level in accord with the biblical principle of the tithe. The Barna Group reports that only 6% of American Christians gave 10 percent of their income to churches or parachurch organizations in 2004. Imagine the possibilities if Christian leaders spent more time admonishing the members of their flock to meet their biblical responsibilties! Sadly, many seem more concerned with politicking than with calling the church to its higher standard.

There's nothing inherently wrong with Christians attempting to hold governments accountable for the promises that they have made. And even with the huge levels of generosity shown among Christians, it is true that governments like the U.S. do have much more in the way of material wealth to spread around. But the irony is that the entities with perhaps the most assets to spend on poverty relief (governments) are the ones that are least able to do so effectively. The secular nature of democracies, which vigorously separate "proselytizing" and faith elements out of charity work, is a serious hindrance to the efficacy of compassion.

This restriction prevents governments from addressing anything but the material needs of the poor. While Christianity has always recognized the rich and complex body and soul anthropology of the human person, secular governments only have the tools to enact part of the solution. So why are Christians so eager to endorse what is at best a half-measure? Jesus showed us the relative priority of the spiritual over the physical when he asked, "What good is it for a man to gain the whole world, yet forfeit his soul?" (Mark 6:36).

Some kinds of Christian charity have been making this error for decades. The National Council of Churches (NCC) ignores the fact that acts of Christian mercy must always be done with a view toward the spiritual welfare of the recipient, as it continually engages in relief efforts while explicitly condemning "proselytizing." But what the NCC calls proselytizing, other Christians call evangelism. Is not the "cup of water" to be given in Jesus' name? (Mark 9:41).

Richard Baxter, the famed sixteenth-century Puritan theologian once wrote, "Do as much good as you are able to men's bodies in order to the greater good of Souls. If nature be not supported, men are not capable of other good." This accords well with both the biblical injunctions against neglecting the body in favor of the soul, or the soul in favor of the body. The book of James challenges us in the same way, "Suppose a brother or sister is without clothes and daily food. If one of you says to him, 'Go, I wish you well; keep warm and well fed,' but does nothing about his physical needs, what good is it?" (Jas 2:15–16).

A true vision of Christian charity is one that embraces the whole human person, physical and spiritual. In the same way that we cannot ignore material concerns in ministering to a person's spiritual needs, the service of the body must be done in view of the greater purpose of Christian missions: the salvation of souls. And this is something the government simply cannot do.

4

Faithful Presence, Power, and Politics

"However great the overlap in particular instances, there are nonetheless vital distinctions to be made between Christian moral judgments on the one hand and particular political, legal, and military judgments on the other; or between what is morally permitted or prohibited and what is tactically or prudentially advisable and practicable."

—Paul Ramsey

For American Christians, the freedoms we enjoy by virtue of citizenship must be recognized as the blessings they are and be properly oriented to our ultimate identity as citizens of heaven. The aspirational and foundational ideals recognized in the Declaration of Independence, the recognition of God-given rights to life, liberty, and the pursuit of happiness, represent a deeply profound insight into the nature of human social life. The Founders embedded these ideals into a larger framework of the created order that emphasizes the delicate balance of rights as well as responsibilities, spiritual as well as material goods.

President Calvin Coolidge, in a remarkable speech, observed that the Declaration was

> the product of the spiritual insight of the people. We live in an age of science and of abounding accumulation of material things. These did not create our Declaration. Our Declaration

> created them. The things of the spirit come first. Unless we cling to that, all our material prosperity, overwhelming though it may appear, will turn to a barren scepter in our grasp. If we are to maintain the great heritage which has been bequeathed to us, we must be like-minded as the fathers who created it. We must not sink into a pagan materialism. We must cultivate the reverence which they had for the things that are holy. We must follow the spiritual and moral leadership which they showed.[1]

This emphasis on the proper relationship between material and spiritual goods echoes a fundamental biblical teaching. As Jesus put it, "life does not consist in an abundance of possessions" (Luke 12:15). Indeed, when the framers of the Declaration substituted "the pursuit of happiness" for "property" in the enumeration of rights endowed by our Creator God, they enshrined a vision of social flourishing and human life that transcends the bounds of the merely material and temporal. Human beings live as creatures designed to enjoy both material and spiritual goods, and when our priorities are right then we value the things of earth in proper perspective.

Jesus commands us to seek first God's kingdom and righteousness (Matt 6:33), and promises that all our temporal and worldly goods will be provided for as well. America's long tradition of respecting religious freedom and freedom of conscience stands as a testimony to the priority of the spiritual over the material, and how the eternal in turn infuses meaning and significance into the temporal. This is a legacy to which we must always return, as the threats to liberty are ever-present, coming from within and without. Our own fallenness leads us into the idolatry of material comforts, whether in the form of individual consumerism or collectivist promises of the welfare state.

Jesus came that we might be "free indeed" (John 8:36) and to give us life so that we might "have it to the full" (John 10:10). This vision of the liberated life includes freedom from sin as well as freedom for loving worship of God and service of others. To the extent that America continues to return to and be shaped by its ideals of life, liberty, and the pursuit of happiness, it remains a blessing to be celebrated by Christians, even as we recognize that the American experiment in ordered liberty is the historical exception rather than the norm. It ought to be valued as such.

1. Calvin Coolidge, "The Inspiration of the Declaration of Independence (1925)," in *The Essential American: A Patriot's Resource*, ed. Jackie Gingrich Cushman (Washington, DC: Regnery, 2010), 232.

FAITHFUL PRESENCE

In a recent essay, Bryan Fischer, a radio host for the American Family Association, made the controversial claim that the president of the United States should be seen as a "minister of God."[2] Citing Romans 13:6, which reads that "the authorities are God's servants" (NIV), or that "the authorities are ministers of God" (ESV), Fischer concludes that "if we allow the Scriptures to speak for themselves, we are in fact choosing a minister when we select a president."

Opposition to Fischer's contention came from both ends of the American political spectrum. Candace Chellew-Hodge speaks for progressive Christians when she criticizes Fischer for his lack of regard for context: "Romans 13 cannot properly be understood without reading Romans 12—and the rest of the book, for that matter." Curiously devoid of contextual support, however, Chellew-Hodge concludes that the identification of the authorities in Romans 13 as "ministers" is more about the Roman rulers' self-understanding as having been divinely-ordained, and was "most likely put in there to ingratiate Paul to those same-said authorities."[3]

Darryl G. Hart, currently a visiting professor of history at Hillsdale College, represents a more conservative strain of opposition to a view like Fischer's, as Hart contends that ministry "invariably goes with 'the word' as in minister the word of God." Hart points to "the neo-Calvinist/evangelical clutter of 'every member ministry'" as a misunderstanding of the scriptural conception of ministry.[4]

Now it is true that we can find Fischer's assertion that public officials serve the common good of society, and are "ministers" in this sense, to be valid without following him in arguing that the qualifications for ordained ministries elsewhere in the New Testament must apply to such public ministers. On this point, Hart's criticism certainly rings true: There is a critical difference between the ordained ministries of "special

2. Bryan Fischer, "When we pick a president, we are in fact choosing a minister of God," *Rightly Concerned*, December 27, 2011. Available at: http://www.afa.net/Blogs/BlogPost.aspx?id=2147515275.

3. Candace Chellew-Hodge, "Electing 'Ministers of God,'" *Religion Dispatches*, December 29, 2011. Available at: http://www.religiondispatches.org/dispatches/candacechellew-hodge/5537/electing_%E2%80%9Cministers_of_god%E2%80%9D.

4. Darryl G. Hart, "Why Does Mahaney Get More Slack Than Nevin?" *Old Life*, July 14, 2011. Available at: http://oldlife.org/2011/07/why-does-mahaney-get-more-slack-than-nevin/.

grace," or ministries of the Word and Sacrament, and what might be called "common grace ministries," including political service.

But the understanding of political power as a form of God-ordained ministry or service is longstanding within the Reformed tradition. As the Italian reformer Peter Martyr Vermigli writes of Romans 13:6, the Greek terms translated as *ministers* "pertain not (as some think) to holy services only," but indeed, "those words properly signify public offices and functions." Likewise in a prefatory letter to the king of France to his *Institutes* in 1536, John Calvin contends, "The characteristic of a true sovereign is to acknowledge that, in the administration of his kingdom, he is a minister of God."[5]

Although these reformers would include some element of responsibility for religious expression as legitimately within the scope of the ruler's mandate, it is also clear from Paul's original context that even in times and places where the ruling authorities are not Christian (as in Rome) or there is a structural division between church and state (as in America), such magistrates still act as means of God's common grace, preserving and maintaining civil order. And as Richard Mouw, president of Fuller Theological Seminary, has written eloquently, the implications for such common grace ministries are manifold. Indeed, writes Mouw, "common grace ministries are not restricted to the political realm."[6]

The ministries of common grace are in fact as numerous as the forms that grace takes in human life, and the implication for the Christian life is clear. "We should also think about the ways in which we ourselves, in performing righteous acts that affect the lives of unbelievers, can promote the gifts of common grace," says Mouw. Another scriptural term, that of *stewardship*, can helpfully describe the pluriformity of God's grace, both special and common: "Each of you should use whatever gift you have received to serve others, as faithful stewards of God's grace in its various forms" (1 Pet 4:10).

Better attention to the overlap and varieties of these biblical terms would help us avoid a couple of errors. On the one hand, recognizing that ministry can have both a narrower and a broader meaning would help us avoid conflating or equating the kinds of service performed by

5. John Calvin, *Institutes of the Christian Religion*, trans. Henry Beveridge, 2 vols. (Edinburgh: Calvin Translation Society, 1846). Available at: http://www.ccel.org/ccel/calvin/institutes.ii.viii.html.

6. Richard Mouw, *He Shines in All That's Fair: Culture and Common Grace* (Grand Rapids: Eerdmans, 2002), 81.

ordained pastors and elected politicians. On the other hand, recognizing the validity of callings to all areas of life, including politics and business, would help us see how service in such realms can be truly other-directed and God-glorifying.

What I have primarily in mind is the way in which Scripture seems to use concepts like *ministry*, *service*, and *stewardship* somewhat interchangeably. This is undoubtedly true in the case of translations into English. The NIV and the ESV, as noted above, read Romans 14:6 alternatively as "servants" or "ministers."

And in sixteenth century editions of the Bible, the ministerial terminology was often preferred to that of stewardship, as in the NIV of today. For instance, in the Bishops' Bible, 1 Peter 4:10 reads, ". . . minister the same one to another, as good ministers of the manifold grace of God." Likewise the Geneva Bible renders the verse this way: ". . . minister the same one to another, as good disposers of the manifolde grace of God." It's in Coverdale's translation and the Catholic Douay-Rheims bibles, the latter which reads, "As every man hath received grace, ministering the same one to another: as good stewards of the manifold grace of God," that we find stewardship and ministry connected explicitly, and this follows through in the KJV text tradition.

It's interesting to note that one of the updates to the NIV since the 1984 edition has been the integration of this stewardship terminology. The 1984 edition emphasizes the idea of service, "Each one should use whatever gift he has received to serve others, faithfully administering God's grace in its various forms," while the latest update reads, "Each of you should use whatever gift you have received to serve others, as faithful stewards of God's grace in its various forms."

The relevant terms at play in the Greek here are words based on the roots διακονέω ("to serve") and οἰκονόμος ("a manager of a household"; a steward). As Martin Luther reflects on the impact of this dynamic of ministry, service, and stewardship, he writes:

> The Gospel wants everyone to be the other person's servant and, in addition, to see that he remains in the gift which he has received, which God has given him, that is, in the position to which he has been called. God does not want a master to serve his servant, the maid to be a lady, a prince to serve the beggar. For He does not want to destroy the government. But the apostle means that one person should serve the other person spiritually from the heart. Even if you are in a high position and a great

> lord, yet you should employ your power for the purpose of serving your neighbor with it. Thus everyone should regard himself as a servant. Then the master can surely remain a master and yet not consider himself better than the servant. Thus he would also be glad to be a servant if this were God's will. The same thing applies to other stations in life . . .
>
> God did not give us all equal grace. Therefore everyone should pay attention to his qualifications, to the kind of gift given to him.[7]

The Puritan William Ames draws out three reasons and two uses of the doctrine gathered from 1 Peter 4:10: "It is an office of charity to minister unto others the gifts which we have received, of what kinde soever they be."

Reasons:

1. Because the gifts of God do in their nature tend unto the glory of God in promoting the good of men.
2. Because to this end are all the gifts of God committed unto us, as stewards of the grace of God, as it is in the text.
3. Because this very thing doth the communion of Saints require, to the believing and exercising whereof all are Christians called.

Uses:

1. This may serve to comfort us, in that there is no faithfull Christian, but hath some gift, whereby he may minister something unto others.
2. To exhort us, every one to use that gift which he hath, to the good of others.[8]

It is a challenge, however, to understand what faithful Christian presence in the political realm looks like in our largely secular world. The most recent presidential nomination featured two Roman Catholics as vice-presidential nominees, Paul Ryan for the GOP and Joe Biden for the Democratic Party. John F. Kennedy, campaigning in 1960 to become the nation's first Catholic president, famously promised the Greater Houston Ministerial Alliance that he would follow his own conscience, not

7. Martin Luther, *The Catholic Epistles*, vol. 30, Luther's Works (Saint Louis: Concordia Publishing House, 1999), 124.

8. William Ames, *An Analytical Exposition of both the Epistles of the Apostle Peter* (London: Iohn Rothwell, 1641), 98–99.

the Vatican's. "I do not speak for my church on public matters—and the church does not speak for me," Kennedy said.[9]

But to what extent must faith remain a private matter for elected officials? How, if at all, should political leaders of faith inform their decision-making while doing justice to the plurality of religious beliefs among their constituencies? In a representative democracy like the United States, some feel that their religious convictions should not inform or determine their policy decisions, out of deference for differing views among the electorate. But the claim that conscience can or should be ignored in specific policy areas is disingenuous, however. Moral considerations of some sort come into play in every policy decision. Political leaders tend to distance their moral convictions from the debate in favor of public opinion only when it is politically expedient.

True statesmen are not merely mouthpieces for opinion polls. British historian Lord Acton recognized that the will of the majority could be and often is just as tyrannical as the will of a monarch, and in some cases more dangerous because the error has the support of the masses. Thus he observes, "It is bad to be oppressed by a minority, but it is worse to be oppressed by a majority," and, "The will of the people cannot make just that which is unjust." These statements speak to the biblical reality confessed by the apostles, "We must obey God rather than human beings!" (Acts 5:29).

In the United States we have compelling historical and contemporary examples of the majority siding with what were, in retrospect, clear-cut cases of injustice. The legalization and promotion of slavery by governments are a prime example, and stand as a sharp rebuke to elected officials who think they ought simply to represent the people without regard to their own conscience. Today, there are a number of hotly contentious issues—such as abortion, stem cell research and, now, marriage—whose partisans often make appeals based on poll data. Our elected officials follow the shifting temper of the electorate with rapt attention. But is this how we ask our elected officials to lead?

Pope John Paul II articulated the necessary link between faith and public policy. Politicians have a duty to bring their faith to bear in their public life.[10] "I consider it opportune to recall that the legislator, and the

9. See "John F. Kennedy in Houston, Texas," in Randall Balmer, *God in the White House: A History* (New York: HarperCollins, 2008), 180.

10. See "Pope Insists Catholic Legislators Must Never Vote Against Life or Family," *LifeSiteNews.com*, March 1, 2004. Available at: http://www.lifesitenews.com/news/archive/ldn/2004/mar/04030101.

Catholic legislator in particular, cannot contribute to the formulation or approval of laws contrary to 'the primary and essential norms that regulate moral life,' the expressions of the highest values of the human person and proceeding in the last analysis from God, the Supreme Legislator," the Pope said. Politicians do themselves and those they represent no justice by rigidly separating out their religious convictions from their policy decisions. Neither is the electorate advantaged by the omission of authentic religious discussion and engagement of political issues.

Of course simply invoking faith superficially for any issue does not constitute a valid way of meeting these obligations. A heartfelt desire to help the poor, for example, is not enough. Policymaking also requires sound economic thinking and a discernment of the moral underpinnings of competing economic systems. The Bible can and has been claimed for any number of hateful and destructive programs, both political and social. It is in the particular engagement of faith and public duty that prayer and discernment play key roles.

Political leaders of all faiths must bring their respective traditions to bear on their decisions. This is an honest exercise of conscience, and one best managed in a spirit of tolerance and respect. To do otherwise is to commit an act of moral cowardice. In an age when so many are echoing Pontius Pilate's confused question, "What is truth?" (John 18:38) too many political leaders have settled on an inadequate answer: the will of the people (and the pollsters).

Each election cycle it seems that members of the mainstream media and political pundits discover anew that conservative Christians, conservative evangelicals in particular, are deeply engaged in American politics. And each time commentators find a way to construe that engagement as problematic rather than as an obedient expression of religious conviction.

This should not be any real surprise. The experiment in American liberty has always been characteristically suspicious of deeply-held convictions, particularly religious convictions, which might represent competition for a citizen's loyalty. No less a figure than John Locke, for instance, declared that the Roman Catholic Church could not be tolerated in a modern free society because members of that church place themselves under the "protection and service of another prince."[11] Locke had in mind the pope in Rome, who was then and to this day remains the head of a sovereign state. And it was just a half century ago, as I've noted,

11. John Locke, *A Letter Concerning Toleration* (Huddersfield: J. Brook, 1796 [1689]), 55.

that John F. Kennedy had to publicly affirm his faith in "an America where the separation of church and state is absolute, where no Catholic prelate would tell the president (should he be Catholic) how to act, and no Protestant minister would tell his parishioners for whom to vote."[12]

Modern democratic societies largely follow Locke's lead and care not a whit for loyalty to "another prince," so long as that prince makes no material or political demands from his subjects. A purely spiritual loyalty is entirely acceptable, as long as that loyalty remains expressed only in the spiritual realm and makes claims on the citizenry on Sunday mornings. If the rest of the week and the concerns of person and property can be left to the political state then this other prince can be tolerated.

In the case of Christianity, then, a Jesus Christ whose kingdom is "not of this world" is welcome. A Jesus Christ to whom "every knee shall bow" is rather less so. This dynamic is the paradox of Christianity in modern life, and it has been essentially the same for the last two millennia. As Christians we understand ourselves to live in the tension between the "already" and the "not yet," the time between the first and second comings of our Lord and Savior Jesus Christ.

The basic implications of this for a modern secular state are rather easy to discern. So long as the exhortations from the pulpits and the practices of those in the pews adhere broadly to the dominant societal norms, then religious participation is in the worst case a harmless institution, and in the best case (from the point of view of the state, at least) a positive ally. But where a church proclaims a counter-cultural gospel, intellectuals and the cultural intelligentsia cast a suspicious eye, and if the proclamation becomes too troublesome, raise cry and hue of "theocracy" or "dominionism."

Rather than this alternative loyalty making Christians worse citizens, however, the opposite is actually the case. The Christian commitment to Jesus Christ as another prince, the "prince of Peace," makes us better, not worse, citizens. Because our loyalties and destiny are ultimately beyond this fallen world order and the confines of this mortal coil, Christians are free to be radically engaged in the civilizational grind for daily bread. Lester DeKoster argues persuasively that the Christian commandment to "love your neighbor as yourself" finds expression in the Christian's daily work of service to others. "Civilization," he writes, "is sharing in the work

12. See Balmer, *God in the White House*, 176.

of others."[13] Each of the threads of an individual's work are providentially woven together to form the fabric of civilization. Christians truly and deeply committed to serving others in love become the building blocks of a stable society.

In many ways, today's post-modern world mirrors the days of the early church. Towards the end of the pagan Roman Empire there was widespread cynicism, doubt, and skepticism about civilization's ability to endure. Today, in the context of global instability, financial insecurity, and pessimism about the existence of or the ability to know objective truth, we face similar civilizational challenges.

In the days of the pagan emperors of Rome it was common to blame Christians for the ills of the empire. Those who decry faithful Christian participation in politics and culture today faintly echo these persecutors of the early church. Against these accusations the apologist Tertullian defended the Christian church, showing that Christians were indispensable members contributing to the Roman commonwealth. Likewise today Christians participate at every level of government and society and in so doing contribute toward the common good.

The most important way that Christians engage the world, in all realms of culture, politics, and social life more broadly, is through their individual callings in these various spheres. In this way Christians are called to live out their faith in the world as "salt and light," or what James Davison Hunter has called "faithful presence."[14] With all this in mind, we should rather understand with Tertullian that "they deserve the name of faction who conspire to bring odium on good men and virtuous, who cry out against innocent blood, offering as the justification of their enmity the baseless plea, that they think the Christians the cause of every public disaster, of every affliction with which the people are visited."[15] Those in our day who level the baseless charges of suspicion against Christians for undermining the public good deserve to be branded as the real dissemblers and enemies of the common good.

The character of religious engagement with public life has undergone some significant shifts in recent decades, however, and suspicion

13. Lester DeKoster, *Work: The Meaning of Your Life—A Christian Perspective* (Grand Rapids: Christian's Library Press, 2010), 2.

14. James Davison Hunter, *To Change the World: The Irony, Tragedy, and Possibility of Christianity in the Late Modern World* (New York: Oxford University Press, 2010).

15. Tertullian, *Apology*, in *Ante-Nicene Fathers*, vol. 3 (Grand Rapids: Eerdmans, 1980), ch. XLII.

about religion in the public square has only intensified. Consider that the appointment of Sonia Sotomayor to the United States Supreme Court inaugurated an era for the first time in history that there is a supermajority of justices on the same court affiliated to one degree or another with the Roman Catholic Church. Indeed, half of the Catholics who have ever been on the Supreme Court are now serving simultaneously.

At the same time the number of Protestants on the court has fallen to a historic low; with the retirement of David H. Souter and John Paul Stevens, there are now no Protestants on the nation's highest court. Also noteworthy is that three justices, Ruth Bader Ginsburg, Stephen Breyer, and Elena Kagan, are Jewish. With Catholic representation on the land's highest court at its apex, and Protestant representation at its nadir, the question must be asked whether this reflects a shift in the balance of legal influence reflective of underlying deficiencies in American Protestantism.

There is nothing intrinsic to historic Protestantism that would prevent it from cultivating first-rate legal thinkers. The historical evidence in fact points to the rich matrix of social and legal thought that blossomed in the Reformation and post-Reformation periods. Luther's emphasis on the dialectic of law and gospel helped to set the stage for Philip Melanchthon's development of the so-called "third use of the law" in his debate over antinomianism with Johann Agricola of Eisleben.[16] It is well-known that John Calvin was educated as a lawyer before he became a theologian and the reformer of Geneva. But beyond these examples it is easy to point to innumerable instances of deep engagement between the reformers and the legal traditions, consisting of both civil and canon law, inherited from the medieval period. We can trace a clear line from the sixteenth to the eighteenth centuries of post-Reformation reflection on the law, including luminaries like Johannes Althusius and Hugo Grotius.

This dynamic history of Protestant legal thinking coalesced in an influential form in the heritage of British common law, associated with scholars like Richard Hooker and William Blackstone, which was so important for the American founding. However the places we might instinctively look for a Protestant vanguard, the law schools at Yale and Harvard, are those that have become increasingly secularized and disassociated from their religious roots.

In some ways this transition mirrors the broader development of Protestantism in North America and reflects the close relationship

16. See Timothy Wengert, *Law and Gospel: Philip Melanchthon's Debate with John Agricola of Eisleben over* Poenitentia (Grand Rapids: Baker Academic, 1997).

between moral, legal, and political philosophy. While there is a great deal of talk in contemporary Protestantism about "justice"—in part because of the severance between theology and law that occurred in major, historically Protestant institutions—there is precious little by way of serious pursuit after high-level legal scholarship. It is perhaps easier to pontificate about paving the path of *shalom* in the world than to set about creating and reforming the institutions necessary to realize such lofty goals. Evangelical groups like International Justice Mission stand as noteworthy exceptions to the division between word and deed.

The lack of legal influence and achievement is representative of the broader crisis in Protestant social thinking. James M. Gustafson once described the state of Protestant moral thought as "only a little short of chaos."[17] If this description was accurate three decades ago, the dysfunction has become even more pronounced in the intervening years. In an essay tracing the development of Protestantism in America from its founding to the present day, former First Things editor Joseph Bottum wrote that "somewhere around 1975, the main stream of Protestantism ran dry."[18] What had once been a unified moral witness has declined into a cacophony of competing voices, not merely on doctrinal issues like infant baptism or the Eucharist, but also on social issues like abortion and poverty.

One part of the solution to these problems in Protestantism is the embrace of the tradition in which Protestant legal thought flourished in the first two centuries following the Reformation: natural law. Natural law is not, or at least ought not to be, strictly the domain of Roman Catholic moral and legal theorists. The church historian John T. McNeill wrote presciently in 1946 that, "There is no real discontinuity between the teaching of the Reformers and that of their predecessors with respect to natural law."[19] Sadly McNeill's recognition of the continuity between the medieval traditions of natural law and those taken up by the reformers has been slow to influence the broader scholarship. It is only within the last few years that the revival or rediscovery of the natural law in Protestant thought has been heralded by significant voices, including J. Daryl Charles, Stephen J. Grabill, John Witte Jr., and David VanDrunen.

17. James M. Gustafson, *Protestant and Roman Catholic Ethics: Prospects for Rapprochement* (Chicago: University of Chicago Press, 1980), 130.

18. Joseph Bottum, "The Death of Protestant America: A Political Theory of the Protestant Mainline," *First Things* (August/September 2008).

19. John T. McNeill, "Natural Law in the Teaching of the Reformers," *Journal of Religion* 26, no. 3 (July 1946): 168.

Witte's Center for the Study of Law and Religion at Emory University is a particular example of an institutional answer to the reconnection of historic Protestantism and contemporary legal thinking.

The appointments of Sotomayor and now Kagan to the Supreme Court are not in themselves so much indictments of contemporary Protestant approaches to the law. But in the context of trends in recent decades it does represent a clear warning that even where Protestants are in the game, whether morally, legally, or politically, they are largely playing from behind. And Protestants will continue to do so until they begin again to draw from the same wells of wisdom that once nourished centuries of Protestant moral, legal, and political thought: the natural law tradition and the halls of America's elite institutions. As James Davison Hunter's study makes quite clear, it is impossible to exercise influence through "faithful presence" when you are not present at all.

One place where evangelical political presence has been positively felt is in the Tea Party phenomenon. Now years in to the movement, much continues to be written and said about the Tea Party, a movement that is still so little understood, both by its critics as well as those who are more sympathetic. The late Chuck Colson, for instance, cautioned that the Tea Parties are more dangerous than previous populist movements. "A massive wave of anti-government sentiment could shatter the political consensus, which may well leave the country virtually unmanageable," he warned.[20] Colson is certainly right to point to the dangers of political divisiveness, and indeed, the level of current political discourse on both the Left and the Right offer little in the way of constructive dialogue.

Colson criticized the Tea Parties for making "no attempt to present a governing philosophy" and instead simply embodying anti-government attitudes. Colson was correct to draw the line at anarchy; Christians are, in his words, "to be the best citizens," supportive of good government in the most fundamental and authentic ways. But by characterizing the Tea Parties as "anti-government," Colson and those of similar opinion run the risk of playing precisely the kind of divisive rhetoric that concerns him most.

Indeed, one of the clearest lessons to emerge from the reactions surrounding the Tea Parties is just how ideological and polemical political discourse has become. When liberals characterize conservatives, they typically invoke images of the extreme margins: close-minded racists,

20. Charles Colson with Catherine Larson, "Channeling the Populist Rage," *Christianity Today*, April 6, 2010. Available at: http://www.christianitytoday.com/ct/2010/april/11.60.html.

homophobes, and anti-abortionist assassins. As Cal Thomas puts it, "If you don't like President Obama's policies, you are a racist who is setting him up for assassination by a neo-Nazi who is waiting in the (right) wings for sufficient inspiration."[21] But when conservatives characterize liberals, they too tend to use those at the radical extreme to represent the entire movement: rabid pro-abortion advocates, NAMBLA members, and outright socialists.

Lost in much of the discussion is the vast, complex, and muddled middle of American politics, a middle that represents the bulk of both major parties. This middle remains politically cynical and disenchanted with the kind of polarizing language used by both parties. If political discourse is to become constructive, as Colson hoped, we all need to refine our thinking to more sympathetically and accurately represent the positions of those with whom we often disagree. Indeed, this kind of tolerance in the best sense is a critical virtue of statesmanship, a virtue in short supply nowadays.

So if we were to sympathetically describe the characteristics of the Tea Party movement, we might point to the explicit positions articulated at the center of the movement's consensus. As the "Contract from America," for instance, puts it, the Tea Parties are about "the principles of individual liberty, limited government, and economic freedom." Note here the emphasis is on "limited" government, which is not to say that the Tea Partiers are "anti-" government. This is an important distinction, and one which a broad-minded account of the Tea Party ought to take into consideration.

For Christians in particular, our public statements and private thoughts should conform to the biblical standard: "You shall not give false testimony against your neighbor" (Exod 20:16). In a classic exposition of this commandment, the Heidelberg Catechism rightly teaches that part of what God requires of the Christian is to, as far as possible, "defend and promote the honor and reputation of my neighbor." We ought to mourn that so very little of our public discourse meets this standard. The mark of the Christian is not ultimately in the love shown to those who love us, but in the love shown to our enemies and opponents.

Much angst has been expressed over the division in this country. Indeed, it's not clear that there is in fact any significant moral consensus to protect. If we are to rebuild such unity, however, it will be on the basis

21. Cal Thomas, "Protesting the protestors," *World Magazine*, April 20, 2010. Available at: http://www.worldmag.com/2010/04/protesting_the_protestors.

of principled disagreement, civil discourse, and genuine care for others, our opponents most of all.

POWER AND CORRUPTION

President Obama's State of the Union speech in 2012 focused in large part on the troubled global economy and the way forward for America. His emphasis was on the continued maintenance of the "American promise that if you worked hard, you could do well enough to raise a family, own a home, send your kids to college and put a little away for retirement."[22]

President Obama decried corporations who outsource jobs to other countries and the countries that welcome those jobs as two of the biggest threats to the continued viability of the American dream. First, the president promised to make it more costly for companies to move "jobs and profits overseas" by adjusting the tax code. Second, the president vowed to form a Trade Enforcement Unit "that will be charged with investigating unfair trade practices in countries like China." The president's faith in the American worker was clear: "Our workers are the most productive on Earth, and if the playing field is level, I promise you—America will always win."

But in casting global trade in terms of a simple win/lose proposition, the president missed a wonderful opportunity to show that Americans need not be made better off at the expense of other countries. During the speech, Laurene Powell Jobs, the widow of former Apple executive Steve Jobs, sat as a guest of the First Lady. And as it turns out, there are some important lessons for us to take to heart from Steve Jobs' success as an innovator and technology magnate. Few would argue with the fact that Apple products have made the lives of millions of Americans more productive and enjoyable. But Jobs' own insights belie the president's mandate for American business leaders, which amounts to: "Ask yourselves what you can do to bring jobs back to your country."

As the *New York Times* reported earlier that week, the previous year the president inquired of Steve Jobs why over 150 million iPads, iPhones and other products sold by Apple last year were made in other countries.[23]

22. Barack Obama, "State of the Union," January 24, 2012. Available at: http://www.realclearpolitics.com/articles/2012/01/24/transcript_of_president_obamas_2012_state_of_the_union_address_112893.html.

23. Charles Duhigg and Keith Bradsher, "How the U.S. Lost Out on iPhone Work," *New York Times*, January 21, 2012. Available at: http://www.nytimes.com/2012/01/22/

"Those jobs aren't coming back," Jobs reportedly said. The president's State of the Union speech made it seem as if the lower costs of labor and tax avoidance strategies are the only reasons that firms send jobs offshore. But according to the *Times*, "It isn't just that workers are cheaper abroad. Rather, Apple's executives believe the vast scale of overseas factories as well as the flexibility, diligence and industrial skills of foreign workers have so outpaced their American counterparts that 'Made in the U.S.A.' is no longer a viable option for most Apple products." The reality is that a complex of factors, including the cost of living in America, worker expectations, collective-bargaining realities and educational shortfalls have combined to put America, at least in some cases, at a competitive disadvantage. This is a disadvantage that has nothing to do with getting "tax breaks for moving jobs and profits overseas."

It is a disadvantage that goes to the heart of what makes companies like Apple successful. As "a current Apple executive" said in the *Times* story, "We don't have an obligation to solve America's problems. Our only obligation is making the best product possible." If American workers can help companies provide the best services and products, then companies will come here and hire them without presidential prompting. But if workers in China or India can help these companies fulfill their purpose, then those companies will create jobs in China or India. The only way to truly promote global development is to allow companies to determine what is best for their own products and customers.

This is a critical issue for Christians seeking to live justly in a global society. The president's basic message advocated forms of protectionism, seeking to favor American companies at the expense of workers in other nations. The president wants to see "millions of new customers for American goods in Panama, Colombia and South Korea." But if Americans want other nations to be free to buy their products, the basic morality of the Golden Rule (as well as economic common sense) holds that Americans should likewise be free to buy products made in other nations. And as the success of the iPhone in America shows—and as Apple executives put it—"it is a mistake to measure a company's contribution simply by tallying its employees."

This is the real lesson that Steve Jobs teaches us about jobs and our true state of the union.

---

business/apple-america-and-a-squeezed-middle-class.html?pagewanted=all&_r=0.

And it is a lesson we must urgently learn. In a speech in support of the American Jobs Act in 2011, the president made sure to communicate the significance of the crisis facing the United States. Repeatedly he exhorted Congress to "pass this bill," which the president assured would "create jobs right away."[24]

One of the important perspectives the president reminded the nation of is our dependence on the work of those who have come before us. "Where would we be right now?" asked the president, as he urged us to imagine the world without a litany of public spending projects in our nation's history, from bridges to schools to Social Security. We might just as well ask, too, where we would be right now without the promises of politicians present and past, who have run up the U.S. national debt in excess of $16.8 trillion, or where we would be without generations of innovative enterprise in the private sector.

The greatest truth President Obama spoke that night was his acknowledgment that politicians "can't solve all of our nation's woes." The one thing perhaps that the president and financial guru Dave Ramsey agree on is that, as the president put it, "our recovery will be driven not by Washington, but by our businesses and our workers." Just how much politicians can "help," however, remains the great matter of debate. The remainder of the president's speech gave the impression that he believes there is, in fact, a great deal the government should be doing. But as pastor Kevin DeYoung put it so succinctly, "profits," not politics, are "where jobs come from."[25]

The president closed his speech with a quote that illustrates perfectly the depth of the disconnect between today's Washington and a properly Christian view of work and government. President Obama invoked the words of President John F. Kennedy: "Our problems are man-made—therefore they can be solved by man. And man can be as big as he wants." *Man can be as big as he wants.* That sounds like a pretty good paraphrase of the serpent's promise, "You will be like God."

Rather than making grandiose claims about what human beings can and cannot do, whether through politics or other social spheres,

24. Barack Obama, "Obama Jobs Speech," *Huffington Post*, September 8, 2011. Available at: http://www.huffingtonpost.com/2011/09/08/obama-jobs-speech-text-video_n_954705.html.

25. Kevin DeYoung, "Daddy, Where Do Jobs Come From?" *The Gospel Coalition*, September 8, 2011. Available at: http://thegospelcoalition.org/blogs/kevindeyoung/2011/09/08/daddy-where-do-jobs-comes-from/.

the Christian acknowledges, as the Heidelberg Catechism puts it, that all things, including wealth and poverty, come by God's "fatherly hand." Our own participation in that providential order comes about through God's gracious inclusion of human beings as his instruments. Our work, in whatever form and in whatever sphere, is by definition secondary and subservient to God's greater providential purposes.

This means ultimately that even if our problems are "man-made," the solutions to them start not with man but with God. As the Psalmist puts it, "Do not put your trust in princes, / in human beings, who cannot save," but instead in "the Maker of heaven and earth," who "upholds the cause of the oppressed and gives food to the hungry" (Ps 146:3,6–7). It's time for Christian citizens to ask what trust we've been putting in princes, elected or otherwise, and what the real responsibilities of government are and are not.

The significance of understanding and articulating the responsibilities and limits of government has become paramount in view of the debate over so-called the "fiscal cliff," a series of discretionary spending cuts and tax increases that, in lieu of some action taken in the meantime, were set to kick in automatically at the end of 2012 and the beginning of 2013.

The net gains from these actions, also referred to as "sequestration," are estimated to amount to a reduction of the federal deficit by $607 billion, or 4 percent of gross domestic product (GDP) in FY 2012 and 2013. To put this in some perspective, the deficit as enacted for FY 2012 is in the neighborhood of $1.37 trillion, so fiscal restraint represented by the cliff represents a major dent in the spending patterns of the last decade and more. The last year the deficit was under $1 trillion was 2008, when it measured $642 billion, which at the time was the largest deficit in American history. As significant as the fiscal restraint imposed by the cliff is, however, it would not quite get us back to even those historically high levels of expenditure.

As Republicans continue to control the House of Representatives into President Obama's second term, the message coming from the GOP will be that the deficits of the last four years are the result of a spendthrift administration and the Democratic Party, who have overdosed on stimulus spending and continue to show disregard for the fiscal realities facing the United States. For their part, Democrats in the Senate and the White House will continue to argue that to address the unique challenges facing the country we will need to raise revenue and decrease spending. As with most things in politics, the truth lies somewhere in between these two extremes.

The reality is that deficit spending became part and parcel of federal policy long before President Obama was elected to the White House. It is true that deficits over the last four years have been historically high, but it is also true that we have endured the greatest economic downturn during this time since the Great Depression, while at the same time facing military challenges in Iraq and an ongoing war in Afghanistan.

At the same time, to argue that the challenge confronting the federal government really is a problem of revenue and not of expenditure is to ignore these same decades of political trends. For the last half century and more, there has been no significant period of time when the spending of the federal government did not exceed, often by wide margins, the amount of revenue being taken in. As Richard Vedder and Stephen Moore summarized in the *Wall Street Journal*, "over the entire post World War II era through 2009 each dollar of new tax revenue was associated with $1.17 of new spending. Politicians spend the money as fast as it comes in—and a little bit more."[26] In assessing blame for the Great Recession, much has been made of the debt leveraged by corporations. But the same sort of analysis ought to be applied to government spending, and what we find is that lawmakers historically have been unable to resist leveraging increased tax revenues with matching increases in deficit spending. As Vedder and Moore put it, even while manipulating the variables for different time periods and other factors, "higher tax collections never resulted in less spending."

This track record gives little hope that this time around things would be any different. There are simply no structures in place, such as a balanced budget amendment or limitations on increases of the debt ceiling, to prevent the same kind of leveraging of taxes into greater and greater levels of spending. Raising taxes without such assurances, even for such a critical cause as the public debt crisis, is pure folly. To really address the structural deficits at the heart of the federal budget, particularly with respect to entitlement programs like Social Security, Medicare, and Medicaid (which together accounted for 40 percent of federal spending in 2010), the government simply needs to find ways to do less with less.

The New Testament gives us a good standard for judging what responsible stewardship looks like, with respect to finances as well as other realities. As Jesus said, "Whoever can be trusted with very little can also be

26. Stephen Moore and Richard Vetter, "Higher Taxes Won't Reduce the Deficit," *Wall Street Journal*, November 21, 2010. Available at: http://online.wsj.com/article/SB10001424052748704648604575620502560925156.html.

trusted with much, and whoever is dishonest with very little will also be dishonest with much" (Luke 16:10). In the case of the federal spending, the government has proved to be untrustworthy with very much. It's time to see if the politicians in Washington can learn to be trustworthy with less.

Indeed, the origins of the debt crisis are a bi-partisan reality. If one party has been steering us towards the fiscal cliff, then the other has been pressing down firmly on the accelerator. Without some kind of structural change to the culture of Washington, there is little indication that raising taxes would result in anything different this time around.

But apart from the numbers themselves, the framing of the issue by politicians and pundits ought to give us pause. The idea that returning deficit spending to 2008 levels represents a "cliff" is not just political hyperbole. It reveals something deeply broken about not only our political system, but even more of our cultural expectations. As long as we continue to expect politicians to deliver programs and policies that are not sustainable, they will continue to promise them, and what is perhaps even worse, they will continue to try to make good on them, no matter the cost to current and future generations. It is the tendency over time for the reach of government to increase. This is why Thomas Jefferson observed, "The natural progress of things is for liberty to yield and government to gain ground."[27]

In the case of representative democracy, there are important contributing factors which exacerbate this tendency. The Founding Fathers envisioned a system of government in which the representatives served a term of duty and then returned to their vocation or profession. In the intervening centuries, however, politicking has become a profession. Hardball host Chris Matthews reminded us of this in an exchange with then-Senator Zell Miller, that it was Thomas Jefferson who also once said that the first order of the statesman is to get elected.[28] To that end, it behooves an incumbent to be as active as possible in order to have a positive record on which to run for reelection. To be "rehired," a legislator must show that he or she has "done something" during their time in office.

I have seen this firsthand. I spent time during college as a legislative intern in state government for a politician who openly attempted to make full use of the maximum number of bills that could be introduced

27. Thomas Jefferson to Edward Carrington, Paris, May 27, 1788. Available at: http://www.monticello.org/site/jefferson/natural-progress-things-quotation.

28. "'Hardball with Chris Matthews' for Sept. 1," *MSNBC*, Sept. 2, 2004. Available at: http://www.nbcnews.com/id/5892840/#.UYIObrVJM1I.

per session. For a member of the minority party of the legislature, the introduction of a bill becomes even more meaningful. It might be the only tangible action that he or she is able to control, since bills are often left languishing in committee.

"What have you done?" This is the natural and proper question for any voter to ask a candidate for a political office. And so the impetus is for the legislator who has an interest in being reelected to add new laws to our already existing web of legislation. More and more of these bills and programs address narrower and narrower slices of life. This multiplicity of legislation leads the government ever to seek new areas of life in which to insinuate itself.

And therein lies the difficulty. Where government moves beyond the scope of its legitimate interests, it tyrannizes the proper authority of other spheres of existence. These institutions of civil society possess an inherent dignity and sovereignty that should limit the extent and duration of legitimate government intervention.

Journalist John Stossel once responded to a question about what one thing he would do to fix the system by saying that he would require that, for every new law that was put into effect, two old laws would have to be taken off the books. A solution elegant in its simplicity and revolutionary in perspective, Stossel's answer exposes just how far legislators and bureaucrats are from recognizing the danger of excessive legislation.

For Stossel's solution to work, both candidates and constituents would need to be convinced that reigning in the scope and size of the state is "doing something." We should all understand that getting rid of bad or superfluous laws is just as central to the role of legislator as making new ones. And for this to occur, voters will need to pressure lawmakers. As Lord Acton reminded us: "Everybody likes to get as much power as circumstances allow, and nobody will vote for a self-denying ordinance."

But failure to put some sort of structural safeguards into effect is simply not an option. We cannot count on the culture of Washington lawmakers to provide the kind of incentive for politicians to turn into statesmen. That the United States is in the midst of a public debt crisis is indisputable. The numbers are simply staggering. One standard measure examines the total outstanding governmental debt as a share of gross domestic product (GDP). By this standard, the gross public debt in 2010 had climbed to 62.2 percent, its highest level in nearly 60 years. When the current level of debt is placed in the context of skyrocketing entitlement costs over the coming decades, the picture is gloomy indeed.

Even so, the fiscal cliff does not represent some apocalyptic moment in American history. In fact, the debate over sequestration obscured the more pressing and long-term matters facing this country, particularly the intertwined demographic and entitlement "cliffs" we face in America and more sharply across the globe. In this way, the question of debt and fiscal cliffs must be recognized as an opportunity for necessary and responsible reform. Christians, whose citizenship is ultimately not of this world and whose identity and perspective must likewise be eternal and transcendent, should not let our viewpoints be determined by the tyranny of the short-term. If we continue the current course of American politics, the fiscal cliff will end up being nothing more than a bump in the road toward the cultural, economic and political bankrupting of America. But if we take this as an opportunity to reassess our values, both temporal and eternal, then the fiscal cliff is as good an occasion as any to seek deeper and more meaningful reform of ourselves, our families, our churches, our businesses, and our governments.

The significance of what has been called a "principled pluralist" approach to the social order cannot be overstated. A healthy political realm depends on vigorous institutions of civil society. All too often we give in to the temptation to equate the government and governmental action with ushering in the kingdom of God. The text of the Call for Intergenerational Justice, for instance, claims there is a direct connection between the "biblical teaching that God has a special concern for the poor" and the obligation of the federal government to provide funding for poverty programs. But such an application of a valid biblical insight does violence to the reality that the government is not the only agent of God's work in the world.

Here it is appropriate to appeal to the example of Abraham Kuyper, whose influence is still felt in Reformed thought today. Kuyper's witness is an important—even essential—source for understanding the way forward out of the complex discussions of budgets and debt, moral obligation and social institutions. This is precisely why it is so critical to get Kuyper's views correct. Kuyper's most famous assertion comes from his speech on sphere sovereignty: "Oh, no single piece of our mental world is to be hermetically sealed off from the rest, and there is not a square inch in the whole domain of our human existence over which Christ, who is Sovereign over all, does not cry: 'Mine!'"[29]

29. Abraham Kuyper, "Sphere Sovereignty," in *Abraham Kuyper: A Centennial Reader* (Grand Rapids: Eerdmans, 1998), 488.

We must keep foremost in mind that Kuyper's famous quotation attributes the claims of lordship over "every square inch" of the world to *Christ*, not to the *government*. To miss this critical distinction is to undermine the very basis of Kuyper's comprehensive and variegated social thought. For Kuyper, there are important differences among the responsibilities of the government, the church, the family, schools and a host of other social realities.

Indeed, as I noted previously in a speech on "The Problem of Poverty," given at the First Social Congress in Amsterdam in 1891, Kuyper clearly and vigorously distinguished between the roles of the government and the church with respect to material assistance to the needy. "Never forget," he said, "that all state relief for the poor is a blot on the honor of your Savior."

Only after uttering such strong words did he add that only when all other institutions fail in their responsibilities would the state have a role as a refuge of last (and temporary) resort. With this he rightly placed the primary responsibility for caring for the poor with Christians and churches, working both individually and institutionally, organically as well as systemically. Only secondarily, and in light of that primary responsibility, does he admit that government might have some temporary role in providing material assistance to the needy. In a footnote to his contention, Kuyper admits, "It is perfectly true that if no help is forthcoming from elsewhere the state must help." He goes on to say, however, that it must do so "quickly and sufficiently," such that state aid remains transitional and temporary.

In arguing for the fundamental place of social welfare programs, both domestic and international, in the federal budget, campaigns like the Circle of Protection, "What Would Jesus Cut?" and "A Call for Intergenerational Justice" present a view of the federal government as having a primary role in the provision of direct assistance to poor. In this, they do not do justice to the rich witness of Scripture, the vision of Abraham Kuyper, or to the truly dire nature of our federal debt crisis, which threatens our very livelihood for generations to come.

A great source of confusion in debates surrounding budgets, debt, and social programs is a lack of clarity about the purpose of government. Many public statements are largely devoid of serious and principled analysis of the basic role of government. When faced with a spending crisis as pressing as America currently confronts, the priority must be to articulate the fundamental responsibilities of government and examine all spending in light of that standard. The "What Would Jesus Cut?" and "A Call for Intergenerational Justice" campaigns want to make particular social programs immune from these calculations. But the government's fiscal straits are so dire that no program or area of spending can be privileged thus. All government spending, including entitlements, defense, and other programs, must be subjected to rigorous and principled analysis.

This means that the fundamental role of government in the provision of various services must likewise be explored. This requires a return to basics, the first principles of good governance, that does justice to the varieties of governmental entities (local, regional, state, federal) and institutions of civil society (including families, churches, charities, and businesses). We must ask ourselves: What is government for? What is the *federal* government for? Is the government primarily and essentially a means of upholding civil order by the application of retributive justice? Are civil magistrates "God's servants, agents of wrath to bring punishment on the wrongdoer" (Ro 13:4)? Or are they primarily to be agents of the redistribution of wealth, to take from the rich and give to the poor?

The United States does have a standard by which to judge the various responsibilities of the federal government: the Constitution. This is the first place that we must look in attempting to do the often difficult moral and economic calculus of governing. But just as the borders of any healthy social order must pass well beyond the limits of governmental influence, the responsibilities for addressing various social problems must be rightly distributed between levels of government, on the one side, and various other private social institutions, on the other.

The basic problem with recent Christian campaigns on the federal budget crisis is that they do not recognize sufficiently that the primary responsibilities of the federal government do not consist in permanently and perpetually providing direct aid to the poor. These campaigns do not adequately hold the two halves of Kuyper's contention in proper relation. If we do not properly respect the division of responsibility for social problems amongst a host of social institutions, we are left with no principled line to limit the responsibilities of the government. And that lack of principled limit is precisely what has led us to our current budgetary crisis. It's time to get back to the basics of government budgets.

One thing you hear from many is that we need a "both/and" solution: we need to both cut spending and raise revenue in order to close the annual deficits. I'm not really convinced of this, in part because as we've seen the federal government has historically shown that increased revenue always results in increased spending. The government spends what it takes in, with a little bit more to boot. There has to be something structural and meaningful to stop this from continuing to happen, especially since we can't count on the political culture to do so itself. Whether that structural obstacle is a balanced budget amendment or some other kind of binding agreement, something like that has to be put in place.

I don't think it's fair on the other side, though, to say that closing some tax loopholes, making tax avoidance more difficult, and simplifying the tax code is tantamount to "raising taxes" either. So in that sense there might be a case for raising revenues in this limited sense if it gets the tax system focused on what it is supposed to do (raise revenues) rather than using it as a tool for rent-seeking, social engineering, and pandering to special interests.

What's more important than the question of revenues vs. cuts, however, is recognizing that the size of the federal government has stayed about roughly constant when you look at it in terms of tax receipts relative to GDP. The economist Anthony Davies does a nice job illustrating this.[30] He points out that the government basically takes in amounts roughly equal to 18% of GDP (+/- 2%). So that's essentially what the government needs to learn to live on. By contrast, we spent about 24% of GDP in 2011, and that number only goes higher as entitlement promises come due.

So how about this for a both/and solution: we cut spending to get within a couple of percentage points of 18% of GDP, *and* we focus on tax policies that will grow GDP in a sustainable way in the longer term.

There's a big problem with this proposed solution, and that's the scarlet letter "A" that's been affixed firmly in the minds of many with respect to the idea of austerity. The fiscal realities of the global economic downturn are forcing many European nations to make hard choices about what governments can and cannot do. These choices are on one level merely pragmatic: given particular levels of tax income, there are limits to what the government can actually fund. But on a deeper level these pragmatic decisions reflect a more thoroughgoing view of the role of government in human social life. It is this deeper conversation that holds the hope for a more thoroughgoing and comprehensive reform of government, and it remains to be seen whether and how America might learn from some of the difficult decisions being made in Europe.

30. Antony Davies, "Tax Rats vs. Tax Revenues," *Mercatus Center*, July 12, 2011. Available at: http://mercatus.org/publication/tax-rates-vs-tax-revenues.

In Great Britain, for instance, Prime Minister David Cameron instituted a Comprehensive Spending Review that involves substantive budget cuts. These austerity measures are, in the words of George Osborne, the Chancellor of the Exchequer, intended to "confront the bills from a decade of debt." While in some cases these "cuts" amount to paring the growth of budgets rather than net reduction in spending, the announcement of budgets that some estimate would result in the loss of half a million government jobs by 2014–15 is a remarkable act of political courage, especially in a climate of relatively high unemployment.[31] Unemployment ticked up in the UK in the meantime, from a recent low of 7.6 percent in August of 2010 to 8.4 percent in October of 2011. Perhaps even more noteworthy than Cameron's internal austerity fight is that Cameron also made the case for austerity measures for the broader EU coalition.[32]

The political and economic climate in America is such that those attempting to make similar arguments run the risk of being vilified as anti-government ideologues. Columnist Paul Krugman, for example, has been leading the rhetorical charge against austerity measures in the United States, arguing that such austerity calls are faddish, mythical, and merely trendy.[33] What this kind of analysis ignores, however, is the inherently *unpopular* nature of austerity measures.

Whether or not one agrees with the particular cuts and concrete choices made by the Cameron government, it's easy to see that the popular thing to do in such economically and politically contentious times is to simply tell people what they want to hear: the government can go on spending and running up deficits indefinitely, and everything will be fine in the end. It is remarkably difficult to stand up and tell voters and citizens what they don't really want to hear: that times are tough and that difficult decisions have to be made, that governmental largesse has its limits.

The only way that such arguments can be made and sustained in the long-terms is if they arise not simply out of pragmatism but out of a deeper, principled commitment to keeping the reach of government

31. See "Spending Review 2010: George Osborne wields the axe," *BBC News*, October 20, 2010. Available at: http://www.bbc.co.uk/news/uk-politics-11579979.

32. See Leo Cendrowicz, "Cameron's E.U. Austerity Drive: Mixed Results," October 29, 2010. Available at: http://www.time.com/time/world/article/0,8599,2028300,00.html.

33. Paul Krugman, "British Fashion Victims," *New York Times*, October 21, 2010. Available at: http://www.nytimes.com/2010/10/22/opinion/22krugman.html?src=twrhp&_r=0.

within the limits of its own nature. What this means is that the global austerity discussion has two things to teach us as we reflect on yesterday's mid-term elections in the United States.

First, it teaches us that it takes courage to stand up and tell the unpopular truth and then to follow through and act on that reality. This is something that those who have been newly-elected to the House and Senate need to keep in the forefront of their minds as they begin their legislative careers. True statesmen (rather than calculating politicians) are willing to do what is unpopular or difficult if they are really convinced that it is in the best interests of the nation.

And second, we see that such political courage only arises out of a broader and principled vision of a society that is characterized by both freedom and virtue. This is a vision that recognizes that government has a critically important role in human flourishing, but a role that is limited and must leave room for vigorous endeavors in other spheres of human life. If the 2010 Tea Party "tsunami," as it has been called, is to have any lasting effect, it will be because of a commitment to the limits of government rooted in a rich and variegated civil society.

If such politicians are to become statesmen, then they must run the risk of being branded with the scarlet letter "A" by critics like Krugman, and bring the audacity of austerity to out-of-control government spending. They must make the hard choices in the short-term and stick to them in the long-term. That's what the virtue of political courage looks like today, and we ought consider it no vice.

To say that our public discourse today stands in need of some improvement is undoubtedly an understatement, but perhaps no area of our common life requires more careful consideration than our political speech. The state of affairs on talk radio and cable news is simply shocking. And all too often we find public discussions of political economy cast in stark terms, such as "socialism" versus "capitalism." Very often these characterizations fall out along party lines, with Democrats branded as socialists by conservatives, and Republicans branded as free-market fundamentalists by progressives. But this basic paradigm is badly flawed, and helps obscure the true nature of the relationship between government and economics in America today.

Edmund Phelps and Saifedean Ammous explore the need for increasingly nuanced and careful accounts of the social order by exposing the fallacies behind describing our contemporary order as "capitalism."[34] We are dealing instead today with a capitalist system that "has been corrupted." Describing this system as "corporatism" rather than "capitalism," Phelps and Ammous write, "The managerial state has assumed responsibility for looking after everything from the incomes of the middle class to the profitability of large corporations to industrial advancement." To help understand some of the differences between corporatism and capitalism, we might point to some of the systems' respective features.

Capitalism is (or was) an "economic system in which capital was privately owned and traded; owners of capital got to judge how best to use it, and could draw on the foresight and creative ideas of entrepreneurs and innovative thinkers." The main dynamic of the market system is the relationship between the producer and the consumer. Corporatism, by contrast, brings to the fore the role of the "managerial state," in which the government takes on an increasingly larger task in telling producers what they should produce and consumers what they should consume. This can be done in many ways, some more implicit and others more aggressive. Corporatism is distinct from socialism, because under corporatism the means of production (capital) remain in private hands. But the private firms are not simply free to respond to market signals. Instead, under a corporatist structure, the government directs firms in the ways in which they should employ their resources, sometimes through moral suasion, but more often through regulation, tax policy, and legal directives. Fascism, which uses coercion, bullying, and demagoguery to control private firms, is an extreme form of corporatism.

The consequences of contemporary corporatism can be seen most strikingly in the recent growth and collapse of the housing market bubble. It would be hard to overstate the role of the government in fostering the conditions leading up to the collapse. For decades politicians have been extolling the ideal of home ownership as constitutive of the "American dream," in speeches and in concrete policy. George W. Bush made his vision of the "ownership society" a critical component of his domestic agenda, and in his 2012 State of the Union address, President Barack Obama echoed this emphasis, calling its survival part of "the defining issue of our time."

34. Saifedean Ammous and Edmund S. Phelps, "Blaming Capitalism for Corporatism," *Project Syndicate*, Jan. 31, 2012. Available at: http://www.project-syndicate.org/commentary/blaming-capitalism-for-corporatism.

But beyond presidential rhetoric, various administrations and legislative sessions have pursued domestic policies that intend to make good on the American promise of homeownership for all. Whether or not homeownership is something that is good for everyone was never seriously questioned; the only question was the way in which the government could persuade, incentivize, and even coerce individuals and institutions to become home mortgage borrowers and lenders. The phrase "ownership society" takes on a much more tragic connotation when uttered on this side of the millions of foreclosures that occurred during this crisis.

The role of the government in promoting home ownership is indicative of a corporatist system, a system whose assumptions need to undergo close scrutiny. As finance and economics professor Robert Bridges wrote, "we have put excessive emphasis on owner-occupied housing for social objectives, mistakenly relied on homebuilding for economic stimulus, and fostered misconceptions about homeownership and financial independence. We've diverted capital from more productive investments and misallocated scarce public resources."[35] This misallocation laid the foundations for the housing crisis.

Politicians, and perhaps current and would-be presidents most especially, need to abandon the dominant logic of corporatism and the crises that inevitably result. The Declaration of Independence wisely left the "pursuit of happiness" indeterminate, linking it instead with the attendant rights of "life" and "liberty." These rights involve the freedom of self-determination in defining happiness and the means to achieving it. As Lord Acton put it, "liberty is not a means to a higher political end. It is itself the highest political end." This political protection of liberty stands diametrically opposed to corporatism, and is instead instrumental to, not determinative of, "the pursuit of the highest objects of civil society, and of private life." The American people do not need politicians to tell them what happiness is and how it should be pursued. These are functions that our families, churches, and friendships fulfill.

Perhaps one of the greatest instances of injustice and the corruption of government's good purposes is the state promotion of gambling in the form of lotteries. The injustice of these schemes becomes clear when we

35. Robert Bridges, "A Home Is a Lousy Investment," *Wall Street Journal*, July 11, 2011. Available from: http://online.wsj.com/article/SB10001424052702304259304576375323652341888.html.

realize that the poorest among us are contributing much more to lottery revenues than those with higher incomes. A 2004 Gallup poll found that people who played the lottery with an income of less than $20,000 annually spent an average of $46 per month on lottery tickets. That comes out to more than $550 per year and it is nearly double the amount spent in any other income bracket.

The significance of this is magnified when we look deeper into the figures. Those with annual incomes ranging from $30,000 to $50,000 had the second-highest average—$24 per month, or $288 per year. A person making $20,000 spends three times (by percentage of annual income) as much on lottery tickets on average than does someone making $30,000. And keep in mind that these numbers represent average spending. For every one or two people who spend just a few bucks a year on lotteries, others spend thousands.

All of this is taking place in a system of legalized gambling that is monopolized and promoted by those in political power. Where state governments are supposed to be looking after the welfare of their citizenry, the commonwealth of all the people, the establishment of a lottery has in fact betrayed the citizenry. The legality of gambling itself is somewhat less problematic. The Catechism of the Roman Catholic Church gets this right when it states, "Games of chance (card games, etc.) or wagers are not in themselves contrary to justice. They become morally unacceptable when they deprive someone of what is necessary to provide for his needs and those of others. The passion for gambling risks becoming an enslavement."

The insidiousness of state lotteries comes with government involvement in the industry. What begins as a well-intentioned plan to provide for the needs of the people—education funding for example—very often becomes just another source of revenue for a voracious state treasury. Lotto revenue is often diverted for new purposes through legislative and bureaucratic chicanery.

The highly promotional nature of state lotteries becomes clear as they bombard us with advertising in every available medium. When jackpots get particularly large, the media blitz becomes a frenzy, as the government-run lotteries attempt to dazzle us into a modern-day form of "gold fever." For one multi-state Mega Millions lottery promotion, Michigan officials tempted players with the promise of "$24,300 per day!" in a press release that described winning the jackpot as "a pretty nice payday." This is standard fare, and in this way, state lottery boards and commissions "come to you in sheep's clothing, but inwardly they are ferocious wolves" (Matt 7:15).

The effectiveness of such media campaigns is apparent from the Gallup poll on lotto spending. Among the lowest-income bracket, 62 percent of those who purchased lottery tickets in the past year denied having participated in legal gambling. In other words, the government has managed to convince many of us that lotteries are not indeed gambling but rather a form of civic duty, a valid and even commendable form of public service. This is evident in such rhetorically benign mottos as, "Benefiting All Rhode Islanders Since 1974," "It's Only a Game" (Montana), and "Odds Are, You'll Have Fun" (Ohio).

Certainly when Jesus said, "The poor you will always have with you," (Mark 14:7) he meant it as a description of the inevitable result of human sin and social evil. Such evil is exemplified well in the case of state lotteries, which have effectively codified Jesus' statement into an institutional goal. There is dignity in contributing to the common good. But it should be done through straightforward means rather than disguised as gambling for the public good.

The 2012 presidential campaign between Barack Obama and Mitt Romney codified some other numbers that for each side would end up being winning formulas. On the one side, the hapless 99 percent was set against the predatory 1 percent. On the other, the 47 percent who "pay no income tax" was set against the rest who do. This latter framing illustrates a deep tension at the heart of democracy that is worth examining more closely.

"No taxation without representation" was a slogan taken up and popularized by this nation's Founders, and this idea became an important animating principle of the American Revolution. But that was also an era when landowners had the primary responsibilities in civic life; theirs was the land that was taxed and so theirs too were the rights to vote and be represented. Thus went the logic. But the question that faces us now, nearly two and a half centuries later, is the flip side of the Revolutionary slogan: To what extent should there be representation without taxation?

In the intervening centuries, driven by a wide variety of social, economic, political, and other cultural factors, the franchise was gradually extended to non-landowners, women, ethnic minorities, and the poor. One of the consistent worries from classical liberal thinkers at each stage had to do with the dynamics of class conflict and responsibility. Some of the concern was no doubt rooted in traditional ideas about the limited abilities of the lower classes to contribute to and take responsibility for public life. There are some decidedly anti-democratic, anti-populist, and anti-modern motivations that appear in these discussions.

But another motivating factor for concern about universal suffrage has to do with the realities of political economy and concerns about the protection of minorities against the tyranny of majorities, even wealthy minorities against poor majorities. One of the great pillars of the classical Western tradition is its deep concern for formal equality before the law, its insistence that no one class or group receive systematic favor from the political power. This is one outworking of the biblical warning against partiality for either the poor or (more often) for the rich as it is expressed in the Torah: "Do not pervert justice; do not show partiality to the poor or favoritism to the great, but judge your neighbor fairly" (Lev 19:15).

The nineteenth-century French political economist and journalist Frédéric Bastiat captured the essence of such threats to the rule of law in his unfinished reflections on what he called "legal plunder." He once memorably defined government as "the great fiction through which everybody endeavors to live at the expense of everybody else." This fiction is based on the idea that many, and perhaps even most, people can live and flourish while the rest (the super-rich, perhaps) pick up the tab.

Bastiat gave a rule for determining when legal plunder occurs: "See if the law benefits one citizen at the expense of another by doing what the citizen himself cannot do without committing a crime."[36] So let us look at an example from private relations: Should the richest person at a dinner party always pick up the tab for everyone else? Or is there instead some inherent dignity in each person deciding what to eat and paying for his or her own meal? In the same way, there is a dignity inherent in each citizen having the privilege to contribute materially to what has been characterized as the "cost of civilization."

Those whose rights to vote and to be represented have been recognized should also be acknowledged as having the responsibility to be invested in, to have some stake in, the unique political experiment that is the United States. This does not mean that progressive taxation is inherently unjust, or that a flat tax is the only permissible system, or even that every single citizen must be a net contributor to the federal coffers. But we do need to acknowledge the variety of ways that people do contribute directly and indirectly to the cost of governing, through

36. Frédéric Bastiat, *The Law* (Irvington-on-Hudson: Foundation for Economic Education, 1998), I.3.

sales and property taxes, through activities that grow the economy and the tax base, and through charitable service and contribution that lessens the need for government expenditures. In this way we can recognize the responsibility involved in the maintenance of our commonwealth and the inherent dignity of our shared responsibility, from the wealthiest to the poorest, to contribute, in one way or another, to its upkeep.

"People are beginning to realize that the apparatus of government is costly," Bastiat wrote, "But what they do not know is that the burden falls inevitably on them." If we do not begin to recognize the dignity of paying taxes, what is more likely given the nature of our entitlements, our national debts, and the conceptual narrowness of the tax base today, is that the burden will fall inevitably on our children and our children's children.

This lesson in shared responsibility resonates equally against a casting of the rapacious 1 percent against the 99 percent. A more nuanced view of the relationship between elites and the populace is portrayed the finale to Christopher Nolan's Batman trilogy, "The Dark Knight Rises." In Nolan's retelling of the Batman saga, the superhero becomes a remarkably apt vehicle for reflection on the dynamics of contemporary society and an image for sacrificial love. All superheroes are by definition exceptional, whether in terms of strength, intelligence, ability, or some combination of these and other gifts. But in a universe filled with the superstrong (such as Superman and Wonder Woman), superfast (the Flash), and superpowered (the Green Lantern), Batman is remarkable in part because of his lack of super abilities. He is very intelligent, incredibly dedicated, and highly skilled, to be sure. But like Tony Stark (a.k.a. Iron Man) of the Marvel universe, one of Batman's greatest tools is his wealth. His superpower is essentially that he is superrich.

Batman and his alter ego, the billionaire playboy orphan Bruce Wayne, thus personify the idea of the privileged 1 percent on multiple levels. Batman is one of the few with the gifts and abilities to fight injustice apart from the regular structures of law enforcement. Bruce Wayne is gifted with wealth and resources inherited from his parents, particularly in the form of Wayne Enterprises. Both of these factors are at play in "The Dark Knight Rises," which depicts the responsibilities shouldered by those with power, and the broader social consequences that result when the (super) wealthy and (super) powerful shirk these responsibilities.

When "The Dark Knight Rises" opens, eight years have passed since the conclusion of the second film, "The Dark Knight." At the close of that film, Batman voluntarily takes on the blame for various crimes actually committed by district attorney Harvey Dent (a.k.a. Twoface), and Batman and Commissioner Gordon conspire to use Dent's death as a symbol to rally the city of Gotham to eliminate organized crime. By many measures the intervening years have been successful. More than 1,000 criminals have been locked up and Batman has disappeared, leaving the city in relatively stable peace and ongoing prosperity.

The villain in the trilogy's finale is Bane, a mercenary with incredible strength of will and body. Bane uses the rhetoric of class conflict to turn the city's inhabitants against the Gotham elite: the authorities, the privileged, and the decadent. Bane becomes, in some ways, a kind of Che Guevara on steroids, and proves to be Batman's equal, if not his better, in his understanding of and ability to manipulate and deceive the masses. It is in this basic conflict between Bane, the representation of unrighteous indignation at the corruption and decadence of Gotham's elite, and Batman, the apotheosis of wealth and privilege, that the film's most striking implications for our world today take shape.

By perpetrating the fraud of Harvey Dent's legacy, Batman has essentially abdicated his responsibility to the people of Gotham. Likewise Bruce Wayne has become a recluse, and his anti-social disposition has reached a critical nadir in this film. This is illustrated most poignantly in an exchange concerning the funding of a home, run by a priest, for the city's orphans. The home no longer has the resources to care for boys over the age of sixteen because the Wayne Foundation has stopped providing funds. Why? As Lucious Fox explains it to Bruce, Wayne Enterprises has to turn a profit in order to have something to donate, and amid Bruce's withdrawal the company has been adrift and profitless. These kinds of moral and social failings give people like Bane the entryway into turning the poor against the rich, the many against the few.

In this way, "The Dark Knight Rises" is in fundamental ways about the profoundly destructive consequences of individuals, whether of the 1 percent or the 99 percent, thinking that they do not have positive social obligations toward their neighbors. These obligations might take the form of comforting a small child in the midst of suffering, as Gordon did to a newly orphaned Bruce Wayne. They might take the form of putting on a uniform and standing up against injustice, as thousands of police officers do in a dramatic way in the film. They might also take the form of allocating significant resources to worthy causes, as Bruce Wayne does in the case of the orphanage or his industrial research.

Solomon exhorts us: "Do not withhold good from those to whom it is due, when it is in your power to act" (Prov 3:27). Some of us have greater power than others, and more occasions to do greater good to greater numbers of people. But each one of us has the power (and the corresponding responsibility) to help someone and to do something. This reality is a staple of superhero literature, and is represented perhaps no more memorably than in Uncle Ben's words to Peter Parker: "With great power comes great responsibility." Even better, in the words of Jesus, "From everyone who has been given much, much will be demanded; and from the one who has been entrusted with much, much more will be asked" (Luke 12:48).

This moral responsibility is something that Batman must be reminded of in "The Dark Knight Rises," and once he again realizes his calling to serve the people of Gotham the sides are finally set in sharper contrast. Batman recognizes the corruption and moral filth of a city like Gotham, and yet is compelled to do what he can to help those who are suffering and in need. Bane sees the decadence of Gotham, yes, even Western civilization, and desires to watch it burn.

It may seem strange, but on this matter we see the billionaire Bruce Wayne and Mother Teresa to be in accord. As she said, "For our part, what we desire is not a class struggle but a class encounter, in which the rich save the poor and the poor save the rich." Bane becomes the demon haunting a society that has forgotten this fundamental lesson, and Batman becomes the only one who can exorcise this scourge on Gotham City. But he can only do so by recognizing and responding to the social solidarity required by love, and by being willing to lay down his life for others, imitating the greatest act of love ever recorded, the humiliation of Jesus Christ: "Becoming obedient to death—even death on a cross!" (Phil 2:8)

POLITICS AND PROTECTION

The tagline for the British television series *Luther* asks, "What if you were on the devil's side without knowing it?" But a closer examination of what drives Luther in the series shows that a more appropriate question might be, "What if Luther is on God's side without knowing it?"

The case for John Luther as a moral hero is perhaps best illustrated by examining the dynamics of one of the plots developed throughout the second season, namely his interaction with a young girl, Jenny. There are other themes and scenes, perhaps more visually evocative, that also warrant reflection. In the second series finale, for example, Luther douses himself in gasoline, risking the very real possibility of a horrific baptism by fire, in an attempt to minimize the damage posed by a suicide bomber. And one of the few instances of noteworthy religiosity in the series comes as an estranged mother and daughter meet in a church, a confrontation that has little to do with spiritual reconciliation and everything to do with the concrete brokenness caused by human sin.

But in John Luther's dealings with Jenny, we find out that what drives Luther is an overriding need to protect other people from injustice and harm, and even sometimes the consequences of their own sin and guilt. Just how "Lutheran" this impulse is becomes apparent when we examine the Lutheran doctrine of vocation.

The reformer Martin Luther is justly famous for his doctrine of vocation, or calling, and its implications for the Christian life. Luther understood vocation as a Christian's place of responsibility before God and for others in the world. One of the critical aspects of Luther's view of vocation was that we represent God to others in our service to them. He said that Christians act as masks or "coverings" of God (*larvae Dei*), the visual and physical representations of God's action on earth. In some real and deep sense, the hands of Christians serving others are the hands of God. Even non-Christians, in their roles in the social order, can be said to represent God's preserving action in the world.

Luther also understood the ambiguity inherent in any action undertaken in a fallen world. His doctrine of justification made it clear that on no account might humans presume to stand before God with a presumption of innocence or merit based on their own works. No matter how faithfully a Christian might work, or what good things a Christian might seek to do, none of this can justify us before God's righteous judgment. Our justification in this sense depends solely on the righteousness imputed to us on the basis of the redemptive work of Jesus Christ.

One of Luther's famous sayings in this regard is the curious imperative: "Sin boldly!" As I have previously noted, he quickly follows it up with a second command: "Be a sinner and sin boldly, but believe and rejoice in Christ even more boldly. For he is victorious over sin, death, and the world." Luther then concludes with a clear statement about the moral ambiguity inherent in this world: "As long as we are here we have to sin. This life is not the dwelling place of righteousness, but, as Peter says, we look for new heavens and a new earth in which righteousness dwells."[37] This is another way of saying that we cannot avoid getting our hands dirty in our daily work, and indeed in some sense we are called to do so, but that we are not to rest in the merits of that work but rather look forward in hope to the day when every hand will be clean.

The Lutheran theologian and pastor Dietrich Bonhoeffer takes this Lutheran understanding of vocation and radicalizes it in his doctrine of "vicarious representative action" (*Stellvertretung*). In Bonoheffer's view, we act as representatives of God to one another precisely in our ability to take on, in a limited and provisional way, the guilt of others. For Bonhoeffer this action means that we live "for others," just as Christ lived, died, and was raised "for us." As Robin Lovin puts it, "Responsible action is a true imitation of Christ, a willingness to be despised and abused for the sake of those who have themselves been despised."[38] This idea of vicarious representative action, of living for others in a deeply sacrificial way, is what animates the life and work of DCI John Luther.

John Luther's willingness to suffer, to be despised, and even to be killed for the sake of others is manifest throughout the series. In a line of work that is characterized by the daily risk of life and limb, the risks Luther takes on a regular basis are foolhardy, at best. When Jenny Jones's mother, with whom Luther has a complicated history, comes calling, Luther finds himself unable to follow his safer judgment and remain uninvolved. He feels responsible in some way for the plight of Jenny, who after her father's death has become addicted to drugs and a victim ("actress" seems like the wrong word) in the pornography business.

Luther ventures onto the set just as filming is about to begin and (to put it delicately) "removes" Jenny from the situation. He follows through and delivers Jenny to her mother, and the task he had been asked to complete has been finished. But everything is not well. Jenny knows that living with her mother will not be healthy. She knows she needs help and she pleads with John to help her. Again, despite his "better" judgment, Luther cannot resist helping. He cannot bring himself to simply tell her, "Go and sin no more," and leave it at that. John Luther is thus in a very real way, like Seth Bullock of *Deadwood*, a *natural* lawman. His innate sense of justice and of obligation is so deep that he simply cannot stand by and leave broken things alone. He has to try to help, even if it means risking his reputation, his livelihood, and indeed his life.

37. Martin Luther, *Letters I*, vol. 48, Luther's Works (Philadelphia: Fortress Press, 1999), 282.

38. Robin Lovin, "Ethics for This World," *Christian Century*, April 19, 2005.

He ends up risking all three in Jenny's case. Those who run the porn ring have orchestrated the whole arrangement in order to get Luther into a position where he is exposed and compromised. At one point the gangsters nail Luther's hand to a table: Luther is literally pierced for Jenny's transgressions. He has put himself in this position willingly, knowing what it might cost. In the process, the gangsters do end up getting some leverage on Luther so that he has to appear to do their bidding, at least for a time.

To Luther's colleagues, Luther seems to have been compromised. When DS Erin Gray asks Luther's friend and protégé Justin Ripley about Luther's suspicious actions, Justin expresses full, even perhaps credulous, faith in Luther's fidelity. "There's loyalty, and there's naivety," says Gray. Justin responds, "There's a difference between getting your hands dirty and being dirty." Justin knows Luther, and he knows that Luther will risk getting his hands dirty in order to do what he feels morally obligated to do. Likewise Justin doesn't hesitate to get his own hands dirty to protect Luther. Luther's brand of responsible action is contagious, it seems.

In this difference between "getting your hands dirty and being dirty," we have a seminal expression of Bonhoeffer's idea of vicarious representative action and Luther's idea of moral ambiguity. We don't always know when the line is crossed and we become dirty. But getting dirty, and even being dirty, is a risk we are bound to take, a risk we are bound to take in trust that it is not on the basis of our clean hands but rather on the redemptive work of Jesus that we might be justified. Jesus, in fact, is the exemplar of this vicarious representative action, the scapegoat of the Old Testament, who takes on the sins of others. As the Apostle Paul writes, "God made him who had no sin to be sin for us, so that in him we might become the righteousness of God" (2 Cor 5:21). Because of Christ's atoning work, we are free to risk getting our hands dirty.

John Luther is a deeply troubled man. We get no real insight into his spiritual life, and he begins the second series of episodes on the verge of suicide. There is likewise little overt religiosity in *Luther*. But in the vicarious representative action of the natural lawman DCI John Luther on behalf of others, we see a broken and fragmentary expression of common grace, God's preserving work in the world.

As Bonhoeffer writes, in a creative modification of one of Luther's dictums, "God would rather hear the curses of the godless than the hallelujahs of the pious."[39] And in the case of John Luther, it might just turn out that as a servant of justice in the world, amidst heartbreak and brokenness, this godless man is on God's side, even without knowing it.

Perhaps the most pressing problem of our times in relation to politics is keeping the political in its proper place. There are three basic questions that we can explore to address this problem: First, "What are politics supposed to do?" Second, "What do politics do today?" And finally, "What should we do as Christians?"

So the first thing we have to do is to define politics by answering the question, "What are politics supposed to do?" Other ways of getting at this same concern would be to ask, "What is the purpose of politics?" Or we might wonder, "What is the end or *telos* of politics?" R. R. Reno of *First Things* helps us understand why this question, this point of departure, is so important: as he writes, there are really two different questions.

One way of framing the question is, "Who is going to win?" That is the Marxist and Machiavellian question, the pragmatic question, the question that only sees things in terms of the power of political economy. This is usually the question we start with:

> Today as we shift toward a seemingly ever-increasing interest in the machinery of partisan politics, we're becoming Marxists by default. Marx held that economic realities are fundamental, and questions of culture are epiphenomenal.
>
> To use the technical terms of Marxist theory, the struggle for economic power functions as the base of social reality, while literature and poetry, music, and the arts are part of the "superstructure" that is determined by the base. Thus the primacy of politics, for whoever controls the levers of state power can influence and guide economic affairs, and thus control everything.[40]

So that's one way of framing the place of politics, and it isn't the one I'll be endorsing, for what should be obvious reasons.

The second way of framing the question is to ask the classical question: What are politics for? And here I'll take the formulation of Lord

39. Dietrich Bonhoeffer, *Ethics*, vol. 6, Dietrich Bonhoeffer Works (Minneapolis: Fortress Press, 2005), 124.

40. R. R. Reno, "Culture Matters More Than Politics," *On the Square*, October 28, 2010. Available at: http://www.firstthings.com/onthesquare/2010/10/culture-matters-more-than-politics.

Acton, who said, "Now liberty and good government do not exclude each other; and there are excellent reasons why they should go together. Liberty is not a means to a higher political end. It is itself the highest political end." Notice the modifier "political" in that quotation. It makes all the difference in the world. So the purpose of politics, in this view, is for "liberty," and this answer begs the question of how political liberty relates to other institutions and spheres of human life, such as families, churches, charities, clubs, sports teams, businesses, and so on.

Indeed, Lord Acton goes on to say of liberty that "it is not for the sake of a good public administration that it is required, but for security in the pursuit of the highest objects of civil society, and of private life." So how do politics and civil society and private life relate? Michael Novak makes a compelling case for the interdependence of the political, economic, and civil societal spheres. "The moral-cultural institutions of the system, including churches and neighborhoods, are vital to the threefold system. The system is far from heartless; the family is far more than a haven. The family is a dynamic, progressive force. If it is ignored or penalized, its weakening weakens the whole."[41] So instead of having political economy as the bedrock of reality, as in the Marxist question, here we have something else, namely the family and morality. Similarly, Alexis de Tocqueville observed the reciprocal nature of moral virtue and political laws when he wondered, "How is it possible that society should escape destruction if the moral tie is not strengthened in proportion as the political tie is relaxed?" And Edmund Burke concurred: "Society cannot exist unless a controlling power upon will and appetite be placed somewhere, and the less of it there is within, the more there must be without."[42] So that, in brief, is what government and political life is supposed to do: preserve, protect, and promote liberty for human flourishing in other spheres of life.

But our second question brings us to the present day when we compare what politics is supposed to do with what it actually does. The question is, "What does politics do today?" Or, "What are the problems in our world today and what role do politics play in relating to those problems?" And while politics does a great deal, I'm going to focus on three things that I think it does in our lives today that are particularly problematic.

41. Michael Novak, *The Spirit of Democratic Capitalism* (New York: Touchstone, 1982), 156–57.

42. Edmund Burke, *The Works and Correspondence of the Right Honourable Edmund Burke*, vol. 4 (London: Francis & John Rivington, 1852), 389.

The first thing politics does is *divide* us. We've all heard the partisanship and sniping that goes on in the media and inside the Beltway. We've all experienced the level of political discourse, the basic lack of civility in our public life together (at least in vast swaths of the mainstream conversation as well as new and social media). In this vein I'll point to the need for the book by Richard Mouw, president of Fuller Theological Seminary, on Christian civility, *Uncommon Decency*.[43] But beyond the lack of civility or the rudeness of our political discourse in general, I'm going to highlight the political divisions between Christians. For many of us, our political affiliations and identifications trump those of our shared faith, often in practice if not in profession.

Here I'll point to another book, by Carl Trueman of Westminster Theological Seminary in Philadelphia.[44] His book *Republocrat* takes a point of departure in the close linkage in his experience between conservative politics and orthodox Christian theology. Trueman helpfully criticizes the facile identification of the gospel with political conservatism in the context of confessional Presbyterianism in North America. As he puts it, Trueman's work is an outgrowth of his "belief that the evangelical church in America is in danger of alienating a significant section of its people, particularly younger people, through too tight a connection between conservative party politics and Christian fidelity."

Depending on one's own context, of course, this claim may have more or less merit and existential pull. That is, a mainline Protestant churchgoer is far less likely than an evangelical to be faced with the identification of conservative politics and the Christian faith. Trueman is sensitive to this, though, and defends his choice of focus on conservative politics, since "the USA is my adopted context and the Religious Right is where I see the most immediate problem. But hard-and-fast identification of gospel faithfulness with the Left, or even with the center, can be just as problematic. The gospel cannot and must not be identified with partisan political posturing."

Underscoring this commitment to unraveling *any* easy identification of particular political views with the Christian faith, Trueman proceeds, in six brisk chapters, to excoriate the New Left, secularism and American civil religion, Fox News and political reportage in general, free-market

43. Richard Mouw, *Uncommon Decency: Christian Civility in an Uncivil World* (Downers Grove: InterVarsity Press, 2010).

44. Carl Trueman, *Republocrat: Confessions of a Liberal Conservative* (Phillipsburg: P&R Publishing, 2010).

capitalism and Christianity, contemporary democracy in America, and the simplification of politics. Trueman is at his best when smashing these various idols, the many different ways that Christians all too easily accommodate the dominant worldly culture. His analysis of the transition from concerns of the Old Left (primarily economic and objective) to the New Left (primarily psychological and subjective) is particularly penetrating. Trueman's project is not about demonizing capitalism, wealth, or profits on the one hand, or political power on the other. It is about putting the pursuit of profit and power in its proper place. Thus what he writes about the market applies equally well to the government: "no economic system, least of all perhaps capitalism, can long survive without some kind of larger moral underpinning that stands prior to and independent of the kinds of values the market itself generates." It is in this larger and prior system of belief and action, the Christian faith, that we are to seek our primary identity and unity, and in pursuit of this, Trueman's book is a bracing and worthwhile effort.

A final example that brings these two claims together (politics dividing us as a commonwealth and as Christians) is a piece from *Christianity Today* by David Gushee of Mercer University titled, "Christians Belong Outside the Tea Party."[45] There are a number of problems with this piece, but here I just want to point to the juxtaposition between *the* Christian political position on the one hand and the Tea Party on the other. The clear implication is that a Christian can't in good conscience or faithfulness belong to the Tea Party movement. That's simply wrongheaded and misguided. I want Christians to be involved in all areas of life, culture, politics, and would be very, very loathe to say that a particular party alignment is forbidden as such. We ought to celebrate political diversity amongst Christians in this sense and not let these disagreements be what ultimately divides us. For the political to divide us it would have to be over something as clear as the Nazi idolatry or some other clear moral absolute, and certainly not something like what Gushee points to, the prudential judgments about government's role in helping the poor.

So politics today divides us, both as a nation as well as a church. What else does it do? It *feeds and serves* itself. Here you can think of all the problems of bureaucracy that you've heard about and experienced. You can think of the idea of government as the Leviathan, as well as the

45. David P. Gushee, "Christians Belong Outside the Tea Party," *Christianity Today*, October 27, 2010. Available at: http://www.christianitytoday.com/ct/2010/october/30.54.html?paging=off.

insights about government self-interest that we've gained from the public choice theorists. People don't simply check self-interest, even selfishness, at the door when they get elected (just as they don't when they open a business). These problems with government are underscored by the sense that elections don't really matter all that much because they don't change the fundamental nature of government in its contemporary expression. As one writer at the *Economist* observed, "Our minds have been warped by relentless marketing designed to engender false consciousness of stark political brand contrasts. It's as if Crest is telling us that Colgate leads to socialism and Colgate is telling us that Crest leads to plutocracy and all of us believe half of it."[46] Part of this has to do with our "Marxist" (to use Reno's term) conception of what politicians are supposed to be doing. The *Economist* writer describes things thusly:

> Think of government as a huge pool of money. Control of government means control over that pool of money. Parties gain control by putting together winning coalitions of interest groups. When a party has control, its coalition's interest groups get more from the pool and the losing coalition's interest groups get less.

In the end elections don't really matter, because everything comes down to the question of money and power, and we hear the Marxist questions echoing again, "Who is going to win?" We could say a great deal more about our ideas about what we want our politicians doing. Don't we expect them to bring home as much lucre to their district as they can? Often we think politicians are there to make laws and to dole out power, and there are structural incentives to this (e.g. limits on bills to be introduced each session, term limits). But all too often today, politics simply feeds itself. Politics today is deeply self-referential.

One way it feeds or serves itself is in what I'll point to as the third characteristic of what politics does today: it *deceives* us. It makes us think that it can solve everything. It makes promises it cannot deliver. Here I want to make the claim that turning in the first place to the government to solve problems, whether from the Left or the Right, is a form of Statism. Again, this is a complete reversal of the proper view. Politicians, by and large today and generally speaking in a democratic form of government, are actually followers, not leaders. Politicians make a living on making promises that no government could possibly deliver (or if it

46. See "It doesn't matter much," *Democracy in America*, October 27, 2010. Available at: http://www.economist.com/blogs/democracyinamerica/2010/10/stakes_november.

could be delivered by the government it would not be something anyone would really want).

So, if politics is for the preservation, protection, and promotion of liberty in civil society and private life, and in actuality today it tends to divide us, serve itself, and deceive us, it remains to answer, "What should we do as Christians?" Here I'll just point tentatively and briefly to three further points.

The first is that we need to put politics and political life in its proper place. That is, we need to properly relate the political to everything else (culture, business, family, charity, church). One thing we learn from John Calvin (and here he's following Augustine quite closely) is that the human heart is an idol factory. We make idols of everything, particularly those things that promise us worldly success and power. So, we must recognize that politics in the fallen world does not *save*, it *preserves*. This will help prevent the political from becoming an idol.

The second thing we can do is to make sure that we are not simply seeking political solutions to problems that are deeper than the merely political. If the problems are spiritual and moral, we should be starting there. In this way, the best limits on government come from *outside* government, from other healthy, vital, and robust spheres and institutions that simply won't allow themselves to be subsumed and tyrannized. If and when these institutions do fail in their responsibilities, be sure that government will step in to fill the void. But if we allow no moral vacuity, then there are no cracks for governmental intervention to gain a foothold. Another way of saying this is that we need to read both Romans 12 and Romans 13 together.

And thirdly, on an individual level, we are to be faithful in our vocations in all of its implications: the political as well as the economic, familial, charitable, and ecclesial. Don't let the political tyrannize everything else. And here's a simple concrete suggestion: As a spiritual exercise, be friends and worship with people who disagree with you about political matters. That will help us to put and keep politics in its place.

Epilogue

The Dirtiest Job

"He was despised and rejected by mankind, a man of suffering, and familiar with pain. Like one from whom people hide their faces he was despised, and we held him in low esteem."

—Isaiah 53:3

The greatest comfort and the greatest encouragement in the call to get our hands dirty is that the dirtiest job has already been accomplished. "It is finished," cried Jesus as he died on the cross. Jesus came to earth to save sinners, and through his work in life and in death that purpose has been achieved. The Apostle Paul draws on the church's early liturgical piety in describing the process of Christ's humiliation. "Christ Jesus," writes Paul in Philippians 2, "did not consider equality with God something to be grasped, but made himself nothing, taking the very nature of a servant." Christ took on this human nature, "being made in human likeness," and in this Christ "humbled himself and became obedient to death—even death on a cross!"

Think about that for a moment: The one who made the heavens and the earth humbled himself to become embodied out of the same dirt that he had made. And not only was he incarnated, enfleshed, embodied as we are, but he willingly suffered the humiliation of a criminal's death, the curse of one hanged on a tree (Gal 3:13). Jesus came and suffered all this so that his people "may have life and have it to the full" (John 10:10). As the church father Irenaeus put it, "For the glory of God is a living man; and the life of man consists in beholding God. For if the manifestation of God which is made by means of the creation, affords life to all living in the earth, much more does that revelation of the Father which comes through the Word, give life to those who see God."[1] The glory of God is man fully alive, and the firstborn of the new creation, Jesus Christ, is this "living man" and "living Word."

Just like we are sometimes tempted to derogate the physicality of labor, the embodiment of our work, we are sometimes tempted to view Jesus Christ as somehow above the muck and the mud of our world. But he wasn't. He was (and is), in fact, "fully human in every way" (Heb 2:17). As Johnnie Moore put it in a recent commentary, "In Jesus we meet a Savior who understood the desire to sleep just a few more hours, and who had to control his temper sometimes. In Jesus we find a God we can relate to because he chose to relate to us." Indeed, says Moore, "He was the God who became dirty so that the world's souls might be made clean."[2]

But Jesus doesn't just cleanse our souls; he promises to cleanse the work of our hands, too. That's why we have not only been freed to get them dirty in his service, but rather we have been mandated to do so. Dietrich Bonhoeffer recognizes this weighty responsibility and the paradoxical lightness of the burden. "It is out of the question for a Christian to ask someone else to do the dirty work so that he can keep his own hands clean," said Bonhoeffer. "If one sees that something needs to be done, then one must be prepared to do it whether one is a Christian or not. If one sees the task as necessary according to one's own conscience. If I see that a madman is driving a car into a group of innocent bystanders, then I can't as a Christian simply wait for the catastrophe and comfort the wounded and bury the dead. I must try to wrest the steering wheel out of the hands of the madman."[3] But elsewhere, as Bonhoeffer observes, the call is "costly, because it forces

1. Irenaeus, *Against Heresies*, in Ante-Nicene Fathers, vol. 1 (Grand Rapids: Eerdmans, 2001), IV.20. Available at: http://www.ccel.org/ccel/schaff/anf01.ix.vi.xxi.html.

2. Johnnie Moore, "My take: Jesus was a dirty, dirty God," *CNN Belief Blog*, January 5, 2013. Available at: http://religion.blogs.cnn.com/2013/01/05/my-take-jesus-was-a-dirty-dirty-god/.

3. As recounted by Emmi Bonhoeffer and quoted in the Trinity Forum, *Heroes of Character* (1999), 5–24. Available at: http://archive.org/details/whennooneseeso6trin.

people under the yoke of following Jesus Christ; it is grace when Jesus says, 'My yoke is easy, and my burden is light.'"[4]

The Pharisees were worried about keeping their hands clean, and in doing so they turned into hypocrites whom Jesus described as those who "clean the outside of the cup and dish," but who on the inside "are full of greed and wickedness" (Luke 11:39). We can be so concerned about keeping our hands clean that we neglect to see that doing so can leave our souls unclean.

Sometimes Paul's description of Christ's humiliation is abstracted for use in doctrinal discussions about Christology or Trinitarian relations. It is certainly relevant for that, but concentrating too much on the systematic theological import of the passage obscures Paul's basic point: Paul is encouraging us to emulate Christ in his humiliation. Paul opens his description of Christ's dirty work by exhorting us to "have the same mindset as Christ Jesus" (Phil 2:5).

In this way, Paul says, "continue to work out your salvation with fear and trembling," not hesitating to get your hands dirty when you must, comforted in the fact that the dirtiest job has already been done, once and for all, in the words of the Nicene Creed, "for us and for our salvation."

4. Dietrich Bonhoeffer, *Discipleship*, vol. 4, Dietrich Bonhoeffer Works (Minneapolis: Fortress Press, 2003), 45.

Selected Bibliography

Ames, William. *An Analytical Exposition of both the Epistles of the Apostle Peter*. London: Iohn Rothwell, 1641.

Aquinas, Thomas. *Summa Theologica*. New York: Benzinger Bros., 1947.

Augustine. *The Works of Saint Augustine: A Translation for the 21st Century*. New York: New City Press, 1990–.

Baker, Hunter. "Reflections on Social Justice, Government, and Society." *Journal of Markets & Morality* 15, no. 1 (Spring 2012): 143–59.

Baker, Robert C., ed. *Natural Law: A Lutheran Reappraisal*. St. Louis: Concordia Publishing House, 2011.

Ballor, Jordan J. *Covenant, Causality, and Law: A Study in the Theology of Wolfgang Musculus*. Göttingen: Vandenhoeck & Ruprecht, 2012.

———. *Ecumenical Babel: Confusing Economic Ideology and the Church's Social Witness*. Grand Rapids: Christian's Library Press, 2010.

Bastiat, Frédéric. *The Law*. Irvington-on-Hudson: Foundation for Economic Education, 1998.

Bavinck, Herman. *The Christian Family*. Translated by Nelson D. Kloosterman. Edited by Stephen J. Grabill. Grand Rapids: Christian's Library Press, 2012.

Baxter, Richard. "How to Do Good to Many." In *The Practical Works of Richard Baxter*, vol. 4, 936–50. London: George Virtue, 1838.

Berghoef, Gerard and Lester DeKoster. *Faithful in All God's House: Stewardship and the Christian Life*. Grand Rapids: Christian's Library Press, 2013.

———. *The Deacons Handbook: A Manual of Stewardship*. Grand Rapids: Christian's Library Press, 1980.

Blomberg, Craig. "Neither Capitalism nor Socialism: A Biblical Theology of Economics." *Journal of Markets & Morality* 15, no. 1 (Spring 2012): 207–25.

Bonhoeffer, Dietrich. *Dietrich Bonhoeffer Works*. 16 vols. Minneapolis: Fortress Press, 1996–.

Brunner, Emil. *Justice and Social Order*. Cambridge: Lutterworth, 2002 [1945].

Burke, Edmund. *The Works and Correspondence of the Right Honourable Edmund Burke*. Vol. 4. London: Francis & John Rivington, 1852.

Calvin, John. *Institutes of the Christian Religion*. Translated by Henry Beveridge. 2 vols. Edinburgh: Calvin Translation Society, 1846.

Charles, J. Daryl. *Retrieving the Natural Law: A Return to Moral First Things*. Grand Rapids: Eerdmans, 2008.

Claar, Victor V. *Fair Trade? Its Prospects as a Poverty Solution*. Grand Rapids: PovertyCure, 2012.

Clement of Alexandria. "Who Is The Rich Man That Shall Be Saved?" In *Ante-Nicene Fathers*, vol. 2. Buffalo, NY: Christian Literature, 1885.

Corbett, Steve and Brian Fikkert. *When Helping Hurts: Alleviating Poverty Without Hurting the Poor . . . And Yourself*. Chicago: Moody, 2009.

DeKoster, Lester. *Work: The Meaning of Your Life—A Christian Perspective*. Grand Rapids: Christian's Library Press, 2010.

Dorn, Christopher. "The Ecumenical Movement and its Critics: A Reply to Jordan J. Ballor." *Perspectives* (April 2011).

Dreher, Rod. *Crunchy Cons*. New York: Crown Forum, 2006.

Du Plessis, Stan. "How Can You Be a Christian and an Economist? The Meaning of the Accra Declaration for Today." *Faith & Economics* 56 (Fall 2010): 65–80.

Glendon, Mary Ann. *Rights Talk: The Impoverishment of Political Discourse*. New York: Free Press, 1991.

Greer, Peter and Phil Smith. *The Poor Will Be Glad: Joining the Revolution to Lift the World out of Poverty*. Grand Rapids: Zondervan, 2009.

Grenz, Stanley J. *A Primer on Postmodernism*. Grand Rapids: Eerdmans, 1996.

Gustafson, James M. *Protestant and Roman Catholic Ethics: Prospects for Rapprochement*. Chicago: University of Chicago Press, 1980.

Heyne, Paul. *"Are Economists Basically Immoral?" and Other Essays on Economics, Ethics, and Religion*. Edited by Geoffrey Brennan and A.M.C. Waterman. Indianapolis: Liberty Fund, 2008.

Himmelfarb, Gertrude. *The De-Moralization of Society: From Victorian Virtues to Modern Values*. New York: Vintage, 1996.

Hoksbergen, Roland. "The Global Economy, Injustice, and the Church: On Being Reformed in Today's World." In *Reformed Mission in an Age of World Christianity: Ideas for the Twenty-First Century*. Edited by Shirley J. Roels, 93–103. Grand Rapids: Calvin Press, 2011.

Hopper, David. *Divine Transcendence and the Culture of Change*. Grand Rapids: Eerdmans, 2010.

Hunter, James Davison. *To Change the World: The Irony, Tragedy, and Possibility of Christianity in the Late Modern World*. New York: Oxford University Press, 2010.

Irenaeus. *Against Heresies*. In *Ante-Nicene Fathers*, vol. 1. Grand Rapids: Eerdmans, 2001.

John Paul II. Encyclical Letter *Centesimus Annus*. May 1, 1991.

Kuyper, Abraham. *The Problem of Poverty*. Sioux Falls: Dordt College Press, 2011.

———. *Wisdom & Wonder: Common Grace in Science & Art*. Edited by Jordan J. Ballor and Stephen J. Grabill. Translated by Nelson D. Kloosterman. Grand Rapids: Christian's Library Press, 2011.

———. "Sphere Sovereignty." In *Abraham Kuyper: A Centennial Reader*. Grand Rapids: Eerdmans, 1998.

———. "Sphere Sovereignty." In *Political Order and the Structure of Society*, ed. James W. Skillen and Rockne M. McCarthy. Atlanta: Scholars Press, 1991.

———. *Lectures on Calvinism*. Edinburgh: T&T Clark, 1899.

Lewis, C. S. *Mere Christianity*. New York: HarperCollins, 2001.

———. "The Weight of Glory." In *The Weight of Glory and Other Addresses*. New York: Touchstone, 1996.

———. "Work and Prayer." In *God in the Dock*. Grand Rapids: Eerdmans, 1970.

Lomborg, Bjørn, ed. *Global Crises, Global Solutions*. New York: Cambridge University Press, 2004.

Luther, Martin. *Luther's Works*. 55 vols. Minneapolis and Saint Louis: Fortress Press and Concordia Publishing House, 1957–1986.

———. *The Large Catechism*. In *The Book of Concord: The Confessions of the Evangelical Lutheran Church*. Edited by T. G. Tappert. Philadelphia: Fortress Press, 1959.

Mariana, Juan de. *A Treatise on the Alteration of Money*. Translated by Patrick J. Brannan. Grand Rapids: CLP Academic, 2011.

McDaniel, Charles A. "Reviving Old Debates: Austrian, Post-Keynesian, and Distributist Views of Financial Crisis." *Journal of Markets & Morality* 15, no. 1 (Spring 2012): 37–63.

McNeill, John T. "Natural Law in the Teaching of the Reformers." *Journal of Religion* 26, no. 3 (July 1946): 168–82.

Mouw, Richard. *Uncommon Decency: Christian Civility in an Uncivil World*. Downers Grove: InterVarsity Press, 2010.

———. *He Shines in All That's Fair: Culture and Common Grace*. Grand Rapids: Eerdmans, 2002.

Moyo, Dambisa. *How the West Was Lost: Fifty Years of Economic Folly—And the Stark Choices Ahead*. New York: Farrar, Straus, and Giroux, 2011.

Niebuhr, H. Richard. *The Social Sources of Denominationalism*. New York: H. Holt, 1929.

NIV Stewardship Study Bible. Grand Rapids: Zondervan, 2009.

Noordegraaf, Herman. "Aid Under Protest? Churches in the Netherlands and Material Aid to the Poor." *Diakonia* 1, vol. 1 (2010): 47–61

Novak, Michael. *The Spirit of Democratic Capitalism*. New York: Touchstone, 1982.

Read, Leonard. *I, Pencil*. Irvington-on-Hudson: Foundation for Economic Education, 1999.

Plantinga, Cornelius, Jr. *Engaging God's World: A Christian Vision of Faith, Learning, and Living*. Grand Rapids: Eerdmans, 2002.

———. *Not the Way It's Supposed to Be: A Breviary of Sin*. Grand Rapids: Eerdmans, 1995.

Ramsey, Paul. *Who Speaks for the Church? A Critique of the 1966 Geneva Conference on Church and Society*. Nashville: Abingdon Press, 1967.

Rauschenbusch, Walter. *Christianizing the Social Order*. New York: Macmillan, 1914.

Schmidtz, David. *The Elements of Justice*. New York: Cambridge University Press, 2006.

Sider, Ron. *The Scandal of the Evangelical Conscience: Why Are Christians Living Just Like the Rest of the World?* Grand Rapids: Baker, 2005.

Stossel, John. *Give Me a Break*. New York: HarperCollins, 2009.

Tertullian. *Apology*. In *Ante-Nicene Fathers*, vol. 3. Grand Rapids: Eerdmans, 1980.

Trueman, Carl. *Republocrat: Confessions of a Liberal Conservative*. Phillipsburg: P&R Publishing, 2010.

Van Duzer, Jeff. *Why Business Matters to God (And What Still Needs to be Fixed)*. Downers Grove: IVP Academic, 2010.

Van Reken, Calvin P. "The Church's Role in Social Justice." *Calvin Theological Journal* 34 (1999): 198–202.

Wesley, John. "The Use of Money." In *The Works of the Reverend John Wesley*, vol. 1, 440–48. New York: Emory and Waugh, 1831.

Woude, Rolf van der. "Taming the Beast: The Long and Hard Road to the Christian Social Conference of 1952." *Journal of Markets & Morality* 14, no. 2 (Fall 2011): 419–44.

Scripture Index

OLD TESTAMENT

NEW TESTAMENT

2 Thessalonians

1 Timothy

2 Timothy

Hebrews

James

1 Peter

Revelation

Names Index